The rise of global Islamophobia in the War on Terror

MANCHESTER
1824
Manchester University Press

Postcolonial International Studies

Series Editors: Mustapha K. Pasha, Meera Sabaratnam and Robbie Shilliam

Postcolonial International Studies marks out a dedicated space for advanced critical inquiry into colonial questions across International Relations and beyond. The series embraces a multitude of methods and approaches, theoretical and empirical scholarship, as well as historical and contemporary concerns. It enquires into the shifting principles of colonial rule that inform global governance and investigates the contestation of these principles by diverse peoples across the globe. Critically re-interpreting popular concepts, narratives and approaches by reference to the 'colonial question', *Postcolonial International Studies* opens up new vistas from which to address the key political questions of our time.

Originally presented as *Kilombo*, this series retains the ethos reflected by the bricolage constituency of Kilombos – settlements of African slaves, rebels and indigenous peoples in South America who became self-determining political communities that retrieved and renovated the social practices of its diverse constituencies while being confronted by colonial forces.

Forthcoming from Manchester University Press

Imperial Inequalities: The politics of economic governance across European empires

Edited by Gurminder K. Bhambra and Julia McClure

Previously published by Rowman & Littlefield:

Meanings of Bandung
Edited by Quỳnh N. Phạm and
Robbie Shilliam

Politics of African Anticolonial Archive
Edited by Shiera S. el-Malik and
Isaac A. Kamola

Asylum after Empire
Lucy Mayblin

Decolonising Intervention
Meera Sabaratnam

*Global Development and Colonial
Power*
Daniel Bendix

*The Postcolonial African State in
Transition*
Amy Niang

*South Africa, Race and the Making of
International Relations*
Vineet Thakur and Peter Vale

Postcolonial Governmentalities
Edited by Terri-Anne Teo and
Elisa Wynne-Hughes

Beyond the Master's Tools?
Edited by Daniel Bendix;
Franziska Müller and Aram Ziai

Creative Presence
Emily Merson

Domination Through Law
Mohamed Sesay

Diplomatic Para-citations
Sam Okoth Opondo

*Selective Responsibility in the United
Nations*
Katy Harsant

The rise of global Islamophobia in the War on Terror

Coloniality, race, and Islam

Edited by Naved Bakali and Farid Hafez

MANCHESTER UNIVERSITY PRESS

Published by Manchester University Press
Oxford Road, Manchester M13 9PL

www.manchesteruniversitypress.co.uk

British Library Cataloguing-in-Publication Data
A catalogue record for this book is available from the
British Library

ISBN   978 1 5261 6175 8   hardback

First published 2022

Typeset
by New Best-set Typesetters Ltd

This work is dedicated to all peoples suffering under the yoke of oppression. We hope that this work will contribute towards a brighter future for Yusuf, Maryam, Zaynab, and all the children of future generations.

Contents

Contributors

Tahir Abbas FRSA, FAcSS, is Chair in Radicalization Studies at the Institute of Security and Global Affairs at Leiden University in The Hague. He holds a PhD in Ethnic Relations from the University of Warwick (2001). His current research interests are the intersections of Islamophobia and radicalisation, gender and violence, inter-generational transmission of Islamism, and ethnic relations. He is the author, editor, and co-editor of fifteen books (eighteen volumes), including *Islamophobia and Radicalisation: A Vicious Cycle* (Oxford University Press 2019), *Countering Violent Extremism: The International Deradicalisation Agenda* (I.B. Tauris 2021), and over seventy peer-reviewed articles, book chapters, and encyclopaedia entries.

Naved Bakali is an Assistant Professor of anti-Racism Education at the University of Windsor, Ontario. Prior to this, he served as an Assistant Professor at the American University in Dubai. He completed his PhD from McGill University, Montreal, in Cultural and International Studies in Education. Drawing from critical race theory, cultural and media studies, and postcolonial theory, Naved's research focuses on the study of anti-Muslim racism in North America, Europe, and Asia. He has been the recipient of major national and departmental grants and awards in recognition of his work. He is an innovative and dynamic scholar who believes in socially oriented action-research that challenges prejudice and inequality by combining his research with grassroots activism. He is the author of *Islamophobia: Understanding anti-Muslim Racism through the Lived Experiences of Muslim Youth* (Brill/Sense 2016), as well as the co-editor of the edited volume *Teacher Training and Education in the GCC* (Lexington Books 2021).

François Burgat is Emeritus Senior Research Fellow at the French National Centre for Scientific Research. He has lectured across the world for a wide range of academic institutions and think-tanks such as the World Economic Forum, NATO, and the European Union. A permanent resident in the Middle East for over twenty-three years, he has taught and researched at the University of Constantine, Algeria (1973–80), at the French CEDEJ in Cairo (1989–93), served as a director of the French Centre for Archaeology and Social Sciences in Sana'a, Yemen (1997–2003), researched at the IREMAM (Institut de Recherches et d'Etudes sur le Monde Arabe et Musulman) in Aix-en-Provence (2003–8), and directed the Institut Français du Proche Orient (Syria, Jordan, Lebanon, Palestine, Iraq) based in Damascus (2008–12) and then in Beirut (2012–13).

Farhan Mujahid Chak is an Associate Professor of Political Science at Qatar University. He has worked at the United Nations, the Canadian Parliament, and the Prince Al-Waleed bin Talal Center for Muslim–Christian Understanding at Georgetown University. His research interests include: Islam and politics, leadership, secularism, epistemology, and fundamentalism. He is the author of *Islam and Pakistan's Political Culture* (Routledge 2014).

Todd H. Green is Executive Director of America Indivisible in Washington, DC. A nationally recognised expert on Islamophobia, he formally served as a professor of religion at Luther College, where he taught courses on Islam, Islamophobia, and interfaith dialogue. He also served as a Franklin Fellow in the US State Department in 2016–17, where he analysed and assessed the impact of anti-Muslim prejudice in Europe on countering violent extremism initiatives, refugee and migrant policies, and human rights. He has been interviewed by a variety of media outlets on Islamophobia, including CNN, National Public Radio, the *Washington Post*, Al Jazeera, Reuters, and The Intercept. He is the author of *The Fear of Islam: An Introduction to Islamophobia in the West* (Fortress Press, 2nd edition 2019) and *Presumed Guilty: Why We Shouldn't Ask Muslims to Condemn Terrorism* (Fortress Press 2018).

Farid Hafez is a Class of 1955 Visiting Professor of International Studies at Williams College. He is also a Senior Researcher at Georgetown University's 'The Bridge Initiative' at the School of Foreign Service. In 2017 he was a Fulbright visiting professor at University of California Berkeley. He received the Bruno Kreisky Award for political book of the year for his anthology *Islamophobia in Austria* (co-edited with John Bunzi). He has published over 120 books, chapters for edited volumes, and peer-reviewed journal articles covering topics relating to Muslims in the West. He is the editor of the annually published *Islamophobia Studies Yearbook* and co-editor of the annually published *European Islamophobia Report*.

Mohamed Natheem Hendricks is a Senior Lecturer at the Institute of Post School Studies, at the University of the Western Cape. He received his doctoral degree in the field of International Studies, focusing on Human Security. His publication, *Manufacturing Terrorism in Africa: The Securitisation of South African Muslims* (Palgrave Macmillan 2020), explores how Muslims have been constructed as a security threat in Africa and challenges the media and policy experts' assertions, which associate terrorism with Islam and Muslims. In particular, the publication shows that claims of a growing 'Islamic' terrorism threat in South Africa are often motivated by Islamophobia.

Derya Iner is Senior Lecturer and Research Coordinator at the Centre for Islamic Studies (CISAC), Charles Sturt University, Australia. Iner completed her PhD in Cultural Studies and Gender Studies in Wisconsin-Madison (USA). Her research focuses particularly on Islamophobia, especially women and children's experience with Islamophobia, Western Muslim youth and their religious identity, and women in Islam and Islamic cultures. Iner is the chief investigator and editor of the Islamophobia in Australia Reports I, II, and III (2017, 2019, and forthcoming). Iner co-edited *Islamophobia and Radicalisation: Breeding Intolerance and Violence* (Palgrave Macmillan 2019) with John Esposito. She is also an executive board member of the Islamophobia Register Australia and co-founder of International Islamophobia and Children Network. She currently conducts research on mosque attacks in Australia, children of Islamophobia, and Islamophobia in Australia Report III.

Uzma Jamil is Senior Research Equity Advisor at McGill University in Montreal, Canada. Her research is in Critical Muslim Studies, with a focus on Muslims as racialised and religious minorities in Quebec and Canada. She has published on the construction of knowledge about Muslims and their securitisation in the War on Terror, Islamophobia, racialisation and Muslim minorities in Quebec. Dr Jamil previously taught Critical Muslim Studies at the Chicago Theological Seminary and was also a Visiting Scholar in the Islamic Studies Institute at McGill University. She is Associate Editor and founding member of the editorial board of *ReOrient: The Journal of Critical Muslim Studies* as well as a contributor to the podcast Network ReOrient.

Sean McManus is a New Zealand Police officer of thirty-nine years' service. He has a Master of Education degree and a passion for training and development of others, being privileged to have led several significant training development programmes for New Zealand Police. His interest in Islam was piqued through work he completed while on secondment to the Australian Institute of Police Management (Sydney) in 2017. He recognised his lack of knowledge of Islam, identifying that the limited perspective he possessed was largely driven by Western media reporting. Seeking to rectify this imbalance, he began exploring Islam further and as part of this journey is currently enrolled in a Master of Contemporary Islamic Studies degree course at Charles Sturt University.

Silvia Montenegro is a researcher at the National Scientific and Technical Research Council, Argentina and a professor in the Department of Socio-cultural Anthropology at the Universidad Nacional de Rosario, Argentina. She has published books, book chapters, and articles in peer-reviewed journals in multiple languages examining the experiences of Arab and Muslim communities in Latin America.

Sean R. Roberts is Professor of International Affairs at George Washington University. He is a renowned expert in and has been studying Uyghur history, culture, and politics for almost thirty years. He has done extensive research on the Uyghur people in the People's Republic of China's Xinjiang Uyghur Autonomous Region as well as in Central Asia and Turkey. He has authored numerous academic articles, popular commentary, and policy-related essays about the Uyghurs. He is the author of *The War on the Uyghurs: China's Internal Campaign against a Muslim Minority* (Princeton University Press 2020).

Leyla Yıldırım completed her BA in World Religions, with a major in the Social Scientific Study of Islam, at Leiden University, Netherlands, where she also received her Master of Arts from the programme 'Islam in the contemporary West'. In the Netherlands, she worked at the Islamic University of Applied Sciences Europe as an education coordinator and programme developer of BA and Master's degrees in Islamic Spiritual Care and Islamic Theology. In Turkey, she worked at Istanbul Sabahattin Zaim University as a research assistant for the project 'The human rights report of the Netherlands'. She has authored the reports of the years 2017 and 2018 on Netherlands for the *European Islamophobia Report*. Currently, she is working on her PhD. Yıldirim's research interests are Muslims in Europe, Islamophobia, race, gender, racism, and cultural secularism. Besides her native languages, Turkish and Kurdish, she also speaks Dutch and English and reads German.

Acknowledgements

This work would not have been possible without the help and support of many individuals, whom we would like to acknowledge. Firstly, we would like to extend sincere thanks to a late friend and mentor of Naved Bakali, Aziz Choudry. He provided us with support and advice in developing the proposal for this project before his sudden passing. May he rest in peace and power. A big thank you to Jasmin Zine, Shirley Steinberg, Christopher D. Stonebanks, Tarek Younis, and Shaheen Shariff: they have been wonderful and supportive mentors and colleagues over the years. We would also like to extend our gratitude to our friends and colleagues at the International Islamophobia Studies and Research Association. Their diligence, commitment, and strenuous efforts have paved the way for works of this nature. Many thanks to Robert Byron, our commissioning editor, Lucy Burns, Alun Richards, and the team at Manchester University Press who helped to bring this work to fruition. Their professionalism, hard work, and dedication are greatly appreciated. We would also like to extend our thanks to all the people enabling the subaltern to share their works, thoughts, and insights, at a time when their voices are increasingly being silenced. Naved Bakali would like to extend his thanks to his dear colleagues: Ken Montgomery, Andrew Allen, Clinton Beckford, Aamer Shujah, Catherine Vanner, Lana Parker, James Oolo, Lindsey Jaber, Bonnie Stewart, Kara Smith, Clayton Smith, Christine Vaderkooy, George Zhou, and all the faculty and staff at the Faculty of Education at the University of Windsor for their relentless help and support.

Abbreviations

AIPAC American Israel Public Affairs Committee
ATN All Together Now
BVT Federal Office for the Protection of the Constitution
FPÖ Freedom Party of Austria
IGGÖ Islamic Religious Community
ISIL Islamic State of Iraq the Levant
ISIS Islamic State of Iraq and Syria
MENA Middle East and North Africa
ÖIF Austrian Integration Fund
ÖVP Austrian People's Party
ON   One Nation
SPÖ Social Democratic Party of Austria

Introduction

Understanding Islamophobia across the global North and South in the context of the War on Terror

Naved Bakali and Farid Hafez

Living through the consequences of Islamophobia in the global North and South

It was the early hours of the morning in Vienna, Austria. As my (Farid's) wife awoke, she noticed some strange movements outside the bedroom window of our second-floor apartment. We peered out into the street and noticed heavily armed men in tactical gear standing below. To us, they appeared as soldiers ready for battle in a war zone. It was then that we began to notice the infrared dots speckled over our upper bodies. The terrifying glow of these red beams was accompanied by violent screaming, commanding us to put up our hands. All of a sudden, armed men burst into our bedroom, pointing large artillery weapons at us. My mind could not fully grasp what was happening. For a moment, I began to believe we had somehow been transported to some faraway war-torn nation in our sleep. Still unable to grasp the severity of the situation, I began to plead with these armed state henchmen to not disturb our children, as they were still soundly sleeping in their rooms, seemingly a world away from the chaos ensuing on the other side of their door. The men had callously burst into the next rooms pointing their guns and flashlights at our children, whose only crime was to have a father who was an outspoken scholar and critic of draconian state measures that have targeted minority communities in Europe, particularly Muslims.

Since that horrific night, my children have trouble sleeping. Not a single evening passes where my children are able to go to bed independently. Being alone and in the dark now fills them with fear and anxiety. When our children are able to catch moments of sleep, they often have vivid and horrifying dreams of their mother being beaten and their father being shot by the police. These nightmares are only interrupted by their wakeful screams for their parents, fearing that the police are coming to get them.

*   *   *

We (Naved) boarded a jam-packed plane in the middle of the night to begin our journey to Bangladesh. Settling into our cramped spaces, with knees pressed up against the seats in front of us, it was clear that this would be the first of many inconveniences on our journey to the Kutupalong Rohingya refugee camp, in Cox's Bazar, Bangladesh. Reading the numerous accounts of the Rohingya genocide, which drove nearly three-quarters of a million people from their homes in Rakhine State, Myanmar, to what became the world's fastest-growing refugee camp in Cox's Bazar, there would be much for us to learn and digest from this experience. When visiting Kutupalong, we were fortunate to speak directly to Rohingya refugees and hear first-hand accounts of their escape from genocide. We met children who had witnessed the most brutal acts of violence imaginable perpetrated against their families. We spoke with men and women who had to flee from their homes after their loved ones were killed in front of them. One of the most tormenting of these stories was of a woman named Zubaida. Zubaida was unable to speak; her mental and physical scars prevented her from doing so. An aid worker familiar with her escape shared her story with us. Shot by the Myanmar military in the head and left for dead, when she miraculously awoke, Zubaida found her family was no more. Despite the wounds to her body and soul, she somehow found the strength and wherewithal to make her way to the Myanmar–Bangladesh border to join the swathes of Rohingya refugees making their way to the camps. She remains now only as a shell of the person who used to once inhabit her body. She continues to exist, but ceases to live.

*   *   *

The manifestations of anti-Muslim racism, or Islamophobia,[1] are many and have had tragic consequences for people globally. From the victims of senseless hate crimes in North America, to the securitisation and criminalisation of outspoken scholars and political activists in Europe, to the ethnic cleansing of Muslims in China, to the genocide of Muslims in Myanmar, we see the dire realities wrought by Islamophobia in the War on Terror. Much of the literature on Islamophobia focuses on specific country contexts. The few volumes which examine Islamophobia across multiple nations overwhelmingly focus on the global North. However, in the context of the

War on Terror, more and more nations from the global South are taking up Islamophobic rhetoric, conceptually mirroring the anti-Muslim racism manifesting in Western nations, while organising their Islamophobic policies and campaigns through localised politics and relations of power. The growth of Hindutva nationalist policies in India – aiming to make segments of Indian Muslims stateless; the ongoing ethnic cleansing of Uyghur Muslims in Xinjiang, China; and the Rohingya genocide in Rakhine State, Myanmar, all represent an Islamophobia 'breaking point' and demonstrate the need to examine Islamophobic structures beyond Western contexts. Islamophobia is a global phenomenon. This simple, yet substantial claim is the basis for this edited volume.

The new frontiers of Islamophobia

The so-called 'War on Terror' ushered in a new era of anti-Muslim bias and racism globally. Islamophobia is textured and influenced by local economies, power structures, and histories. However, the War on Terror, a conflict undefined by time and place, with a homogenised Muslim 'Other' framed as a perpetual enemy, has reinforced Islamophobia on a global scale, creating transnational sites of struggle.

Several academics and commentators have examined Islamophobia as a historical phenomenon. Their works view anti-Muslim racism as a continuum through historical moments including the Crusades, European colonialism, the 1973 oil crisis, the Iranian Revolution, the Gulf War, as well as other instances in which there were conflicts and tensions between Muslim majority nations and the West (Gottschalk and Greenberg 2008). These works provide a historical grounding to understand Islamophobia, but are predominantly expressed through the constructed dichotomist relationship between the West and Islam.[2] In the War on Terror, a broader meta-narrative of Islamophobia has emerged, transcending global North and South barriers. This meta-narrative has been greatly influenced and structured around racialised Muslim subjects (Bayoumi 2006; Aziz 2021), who are framed as a security threat (Kundnani 2014). Drawing on Frantz Fanon, Junaid Rana has adopted the concept of the 'Muslim racial becoming' to make sense of the violence of anti-Muslim racism in the War on Terror. For him, this racial logic refers to a constantly racialising formation:

> The process of racialization is imagined as constant becoming in a temporal and spatial context. [...] this idea of racialization as a process is not exactly complete, but in the figure of the Muslim is always a state of becoming. [...] Identifying who is a Muslim, and such suspicions, is part of the apparatus of racialization and racial becoming. This notion of the Muslim is not only one

of religious affiliation and practice but also one that draws on notions of threats that are related to terror in a commonplace logic of the counterterror state based in preemption and potentials. This is a distinct formation related to the racialization of the figure of the Muslim that may be found in other racialized groups but specifically emerges from an anti-Muslim racial formation. (Rana 2016: 119)

Hence, the notion of Muslim racial becoming expands the idea of Muslims as a constructed security risk articulated as a distant foreign 'Other' requiring military interventions. Through this framework, Muslims are reconstituted and framed as a threat in various localised state policies in different contexts beyond the global North. Therefore, deradicalisation policies which have targeted the Muslim subject become relevant in various contexts. For example, in Denmark, social daycare is used to assimilate Muslims in order to prevent 'radicalisation' (Salem 2018). Islamophobic counter-terrorism programmes also draw on social and health services to identify suspected 'terrorists' in various European states (Qurashi 2018). In China over a million Uyghur Muslims have been imprisoned in forced re-education camps under the pretext of deterring extremist views and militancy (Roberts 2018). The making of the Muslim enemy functions and at the same time reflects the power relations within society.

Through the War on Terror, the first 'de-radicalisation' programmes were introduced in Britain and the Netherlands. Thereafter, a number of European Union members implemented similar protocols. The United Nations followed suit by adopting resolutions aimed at countering violent extremism (CVE). UN Resolutions 2178, 2354, and 2396 were introduced to implement CVE projects across member states from the global North and South. These programmes and resolutions were articulated in neutral terms, not explicitly mentioning the threat of terrorism, political violence, or extremism of any specific ethnic or religious groups. However, they flourished in the aftermath of the War on Terror and have disproportionately targeted Muslim communities globally (Kundnani and Hayes 2018). Hence, the War on Terror has literally become a global undertaking. While the notion of 'radicalisation' had not existed prior to 2004, today it has become normalised and has found its way into everyday parlance (Kundnani and Hayes 2018).

This edited international volume examines the differing manifestations of Islamophobia, as well as resistance confronting it from various global contexts. The purpose of the volume is to map out Islamophobia across the global North and South. These are the localised histories, politics, conflicts, and present-day geopolitical realities in the context of the War on Terror which have influenced and textured the ways that Islamophobia has materialised. Interpersonal forms of Islamophobia such as racial violence, vandalism of religious structures, and satirical and racist portrayals in media have been well documented both prior to and since 9/11. However, Islamophobia is also an institutional form of racism that has become endemic in political rhetoric, in legislation, and in state security apparatuses, as demonstrated in numerous scholarly works and case studies (Kundnani, 2014). Both forms of Islamophobia in the War on Terror are intimately connected and have contributed to the growth and emboldening of nativist and populist protest movements in the United States of America (USA) (Elsheikh and Sisemore 2019), Europe (Bayraklı and Hafez 2015–2020), Australia (Iner et al. 2019), India (Thompson, Itaoui, Bazian 2019), China (Shibli 2021), Myanmar (Bakali 2021), and other spaces across the global North and South.

The main argument of this book is that Islamophobia exists interpersonally and institutionally across numerous international settings. The cohesion between individual actors of racism and targeted state policies and actions, within localised histories of cultural supremacy, coloniality, race, and current-day geopolitics, provides insights into manifestations of Islamophobia across the global North and South. This has resulted in a typology ranging from Islamophobia which is openly contested through political activism and grassroots mobilisation, to a 'breaking point' – years of relatively unchallenged Islamophobia that has culminated in genocide and massive state violence.

Theorising and historicising Islamophobia

Arguably the most influential work from which the term 'Islamophobia' acquired the greatest currency and usage that relates to current understandings arose from a report entitled *Islamophobia: a challenge for us all* by the Runnymede Trust in 1997. The report described Islamophobia as the 'shorthand way of referring to dread or hatred of Islam – and therefore, to fear or dislike all or most Muslims' (Runnymede Trust 1997: 1). Twenty years on from this report, the Runnymede Trust published an updated version where it reassessed the academic debate on Islamophobia over the intervening two decades (Runnymede Trust 2016). They concluded that Islamophobia should best be theorised as anti-Muslim racism. Despite critiques of the first report,[3] its model of Islamophobia laid the foundations for some of the most common and widespread definitions and conceptualisations of Islamophobia. Though the term 'Islamophobia' became popularised through the Runnymede Trust, Islamophobia as an idea traces its origins to over a millennium ago. As Paul Weller has observed, 'Islamophobia is undeniably rooted in the historical inheritance of a conflictual relationship that has developed over many centuries involving the overlap of religion, politics and warfare' (Weller, Feldman, Purdum 2001: 8).

'Otherised' perceptions of Muslims and Islam date back as early as the seventh century, when Muslim armies began to make inroads into the Eastern Roman/Byzantine Empire. These perceptions were fomented through other major historical interactions and conflicts with Muslim and non-Muslim dynasties, including the Crusades and, more prominently, European colonialism. An important factor in the intellectual argument of this volume is that Islamophobia exists as an extension of a global colonial expansion rooted in a colonial heritage of classifying people, placing them into hierarchies, and differentiating between them. Furthermore, Islamophobia in recent decades, with the end of the Cold War era (Mamdani 2005) and the subsequent racialisation of Islam, through CVE projects in the War on Terror, represents a postcolonial order with which came an anti-Islamic modernity and secularity that placed Muslim agency at the periphery of society (Sayyid 2018: 8; Hafez 2020a).

Scholarly discussions and debates around Islamophobia demonstrate three different theoretical approaches in conceptualising Islamophobia in academic literature today: prejudice studies, racism and critical race studies, and postcolonial and decolonial studies (Hafez 2018a). A central assumption of these understandings – drawing from various thinkers and scholars of racism from Jean-Paul Sartre to James Baldwin (Hafez 2019) – asserts that Islamophobia tells us more about the Islamophobes than it tells us about Islam/Muslims. Rather, it represents, as Edward Said argued in his famous magnum opus about Orientalism, a domineering projection onto and imposing will to govern over a forever distant 'Other' (Said 1979). The views put forward by Said stem from a body of scholarship and literature which has greatly influenced the study of race, racism, and 'Othering', referred to as postcolonial theory.

A postcolonial reading of Islamophobia has become prominent in the examination of Islamophobia (Hafez 2018a), focusing 'on the ways particular groups of people because of notions of race or ethnicity have been excluded, marginalized, and represented in ways that devalued or even dehumanized them' (Marx 2008: 650). Postcolonial theorists have examined the impacts of colonialism on both the colonised and colonisers (Memmi 2013 [1957]; Fanon 2008 [1952]; Césaire 2001). One of the foundational works in postcolonial theory, which has examined anti-Muslim bias, was Said's *Orientalism* (1979). This work was a critique of Orientalist thought and action – the study and depiction of the Orient through an imperialist gaze to govern territories of 'Otherised' peoples – and has informed many of the current-day analyses of anti-Muslim racism. According to Said, Orientalism is 'a style of thought based upon an ontological and epistemological distinction made between the "Orient" and (most of the time) "the Occident"' (Said 1979: 2). Said noted the presence of Orientalist thought in the works of European scholars, artists, and academics throughout the nineteenth and twentieth centuries. Through examining canonical European literary works from this era, he noted the existence of misrepresentations, over-simplifications, and binaries which constructed the West as being diametrically opposed to the East. Said contended that Orientalism was a tool that was used by Western academics, scholars, and artists to assert dominance over the East. As he stated,

> Orientalism can be discussed and analyzed as the corporate institution for dealing with the Orient – dealing with it by making statements about it, authorizing views of it, describing it, by teaching it, settling it, ruling over it: in short, Orientalism [is] a Western style for dominating, restructuring, and having authority over the Orient. (Said 1979: 3)

The ideas of control and domination discussed by Said in *Orientalism* originated from the history that European nations have had in dominating Arab and Muslim-majority nations throughout the period of imperialism in the eighteenth century. In another one of his works, *Culture and Imperialism* (1993), Said discussed how the practices of imperialism persisted throughout the postcolonial era. He noted, 'In our time, direct colonialism has largely ended; imperialism ... lingers where it has always been in a kind of general cultural sphere as well as in specific political, ideological, economic, and social practices' (Said 1993: 12). This mindset of superiority is believed by Said to have laid the foundations for Orientalist thought throughout the nineteenth and twentieth centuries, which in turn constructed the 'Orient' as inferior and subordinate to Europe.[4]

Said's work, though predating a number of other studies examining anti-Muslim racism, continues to be indispensable, as lingering Orientalist myths continue to endure in dominant Western discourse about Islam. These include the notion that Islam is a monolithic religion that perpetuates gender-based discrimination, that Muslims are incapable of reason and rationality or democracy and self-rule, and that Islam is an inherently violent religion (Kumar 2012). Undeniably, Orientalist thinking has profoundly shaped contemporary Islamophobic discourse. The vast majority of scholars and theorists who describe and explore Islamophobia from postcolonial scholarship largely draw from the ideas developed by Said. As such, Islamophobia is understood as a form of racism that is constructed through Western discourse, actions, and perceptions about imagined 'Muslims' and 'Islam'. This is also true for westernised political elites in the postcolonial order (Bayraklı and Hafez 2019). However, the geopolitical realities produced by the War on Terror require a nuanced shift in our thinking about Islamophobia. If critiques of Orientalism focused thinking around Islamophobia as an antagonistic relationship between imagined 'Islam' and 'Muslims' and the West in the twentieth century, the War on Terror has operationalised Islamophobia as anti-Muslim bias and racism in a new framework that has been introduced in a globalised world by the USA and that has expanded far beyond this single country, intersecting across global sites in the twenty-first century.

Islamophobia as a form of racism needs to be understood in its differing global contexts. However, despite the different contextual manifestations of Islamophobia there are important similarities that should not be overlooked. In Farid Hafez's examination of Islamophobia in China/Xinjiang, Egypt, and the USA, he argues that although the contexts are quite different, all the forms of Islamophobia

> if understood as a global phenomenon rooted in the concurrent development of a global world system that is based on the prevailing capitalist system and white privilege on a global scale, [extend] an old formation in a new context. The 'religion line' is again central as a marker of difference for racist exclusion (Muslim ban) and oppression (re-education Camps in Xinjiang). A decolonial reading of Islamophobia allows us to understand Islamophobia as deeply rooted in epistemic racism and further kept alive in the coloniality of power. (Hafez 2020a: 17)

This and other decolonial interventions have taken the project of postcolonial critique of anti-Muslim racism a step further. For example, Ramón Grosfoguel, argues that Islamophobia takes root in Western imperialism at the global scale, leading to 'self-valorisation' of Western epistemological tradition and raising it up to the rank of 'universality', 'neutrality', 'rationality', and 'philosophy'. This claimed intellectual superiority over other civilisations, which went hand in hand with the growing political domination of Western empires as manifested in slavery, colonisation, or intellectual and cultural westernisation, resulted also in the creation of the 'world-system', which is yet again designed and dominated by the Western framework and worldview. For Grosfoguel, we all live in a world-system characterised as a contemporary 'colonial Western Christian-centric capitalist patriarchal world system' (Grosfoguel 2012: 10). In this definition, globalisation involves an international division of labour and a global system. It is constitutive of a capitalist accumulation at a world scale, a global ethnic, racial, patriarchal, religious, linguistic, and epistemic hierarchy (Grosfoguel 2006). This epistemic racism/ sexism is the underlying discourse of the world we live in. In this context, the Islamic civilisation's knowledge, values, and way of life are dismissed as 'particularistic', 'provincialist', 'subjective', 'undemocratic', 'irrational', and 'non-universal'. This is what another key decolonial theorist, Walter Mignolo, calls the 'coloniality of power', which 'presupposes the colonial difference as its condition of possibility and as the legitimacy for the sub-alternisation of knowledges and the subjugation of people' (Mignolo 2012: 16). This global pattern reflecting the power structures of the contemporary world makes Islamophobia everywhere; particularly, following 9/11 and the War on Terror, where the last remaining global superpower put the world on notice with the ultimatum: 'you're either with us or against us'. As such, Islamophobia became a globally relevant phenomenon and was only perpetuated by the War on Terror, which reiterates the centrality of coloniality and race in the making of our world today.

Understanding Islamophobia in the global War on Terror

As this volume will demonstrate that Islamophobia is relevant globally, notions of Islamophobia like those of Salman Sayyid have been useful to understand essential claims around the figure of the Muslim in the contemporary world. Sayyid believes that the problem for Muslims does not have so much to do with the essentialist concepts that are used to describe them; rather, he argues that the challenge of being Muslim today is that there is no epistemological or political space for the identity (Sayyid 2014: 8). Accordingly, the inclusion of Islam in Western epistemology as a concept would de-stabilise the colonial order. Sayyid wants to introduce a post-positivist, post-orientalist, and decolonial perspective to create this space. For him, decolonisation is the method needed to create a potential global demos. Drawing on Mignolo, he refers to decoloniality as a project of 'epistemic disobedience' (Sayyid 2014, 12). Sayyid is concerned with the attempt to give the Muslim subject a name in the world and not to leave them speechless and at the mercy of postcolonial relations, orientalist patterns of thought, and positivist epistemology. For Sayyid, Islamophobia is a process to prevent the Muslim subject from being given a place in the world as a Muslim.[5]

In the prevailing colonial order, when Muslims take agency to define their own identity and their place in the world, the state designates the Muslim subject as a threatening force that needs policing through institutional processes. Throughout the global War on Terror, this has happened principally in relation to state-sponsored programmes of countering and preventing violent extremism. The formation and promotion of these programmes creates a domino effect, where the state perpetuates fear of the Muslim subject, which prompts and stirs the suspicions of private citizens, giving them a pretext to act. In relation to this, Junaid Rana has detailed what he calls the racial infrastructure of the Terror-Industrial Complex, 'a spatial formation in which the social, political, and economic relationships of racial systems operate through dominance and discursive power' (Rana 2016: 113). He identifies it as a form of 'structural violence' (Rana 2016: 115), where 'the power of governance by the counter-terror state is based in preemption and a conditional logic of a threat of terror as excess' (Rana 2016: 121). These mechanisms of the War on Terror exist globally and have been implemented by national states throughout the global North and South.

Contemporarily, therefore, Islamophobia undergirds state policies and actions that target the Muslim subject, as well as the actions, beliefs, and speech of private individuals, groups, and organisations who construct the Muslim subject as 'Other' across global sites. These beliefs, speech, and actions at the behest of the state and private actors are interrelated. Furthermore, they are influenced by local economies, power structures, and histories, as well as contemporary domestic and international geopolitical realities. Manifestations of Islamophobia are underscored by tropes surrounding Muslims and Islam which perpetuate a mythology of Muslims being violent, backwards, oppressive, and misogynistic. In the present setting these tropes are often connected to the War on Terror. An important aspect of the above description is that Islamophobia, as an ideology and through its manifestations, exists globally and is not limited to Western contexts. Additionally, interpersonal and institutional forms of Islamophobia within this framework are expanded to describe a co-dependent relationship. This entails circumstances where there is a top-down, bottom-up, or symbiosis between institutional and interpersonal Islamophobia. In other words, when examining Islamophobia across global sites, there are instances where state actions embolden private actors, where the mass mobilisation of private actors and influencers empowers the state, as well as situations where there is a synergistic relationship between the state and private actors in promoting Islamophobia and its manifestations.

The ideas presented in this volume are timely and relevant, as the vast majority of scholarly books and edited volumes addressing Islamophobia limit its impacts to Western contexts. They seldom highlight the similarities of how Islamophobia manifests across the global North and South. The co-dependence of interpersonal and institutional Islamophobia helps to map out categorisations of Islamophobia across global sites. These delineations help to construct a more coherent and nuanced narrative of resistance and activism to challenge interpersonal and institutional Islamophobia.

Organisation of the book

This book is organised into four parts. These parts outline categorisations of Islamophobia through discussion of various countries across the global North and South. There were numerous country contexts that could have been included in this volume; however, due to length restrictions and the amount of depth of analysis in each chapter, the editors have limited the total number of nations discussed to fourteen (seven from the global North and seven from the global South). The categorisations of Islamophobia were developed by examining various global locations and grouping together nations which had similar historical legacies of race, racism, and 'Othering'; imperialist encounters with Muslim majority nations; experiences with colonisation; or extreme manifestations of interpersonal and/or institutional Islamophobia.

Part I is composed of three chapters and examines Islamophobia in settler societies. Settler societies in this volume refers to nations that were intended to be permanent European settlements through imperialist encounters. Consequently, these nations have been reimagined as states 'founded' through European colonialism. In the current climate, these states are branded as 'multicultural' nations, which helps to perpetuate the illusion that they are post-racial societies. Settler societies are underscored by racial supremacist complexes that have constructed the Muslim subject as an internal 'Other'. This projection of Muslims is often politicised to reinforce power hierarchies. The three countries discussed in this section are Canada by Uzma Jamil, Australia by Derya Iner and Sean McManus, and the United States by Todd H. Green. All three of these nation-states have a historical legacy of usurping lands from First Nations, while promoting a mythology of a white European-descent nationalist subject. This has been central to institutional and interpersonal Islamophobia both prior to and in the context of the War on Terror.

Part II discusses Islamophobia in former imperial states. Here the complexities of colonial histories ruling over the Muslim 'Other' texture the interpersonal and institutional Islamophobia manifested in these nations. Former imperial states have formulated Islamophobia through a less explicit white supremacist ideology of *Leitkultur* (dominant culture) and assimilationist political practice. A prevailing discourse in these countries is the threat of so-called Islamisation, uttered in far-right circles as the Great Replacement and institutionalised by mainstream political parties as legitimate attempts to fight what has been termed Islamist 'separatism' (see François Burgat, Chapter 7 in this volume) or 'Political Islam' (Hafez 2021), but which is in fact targeting Muslim agency (Hafez 2018b). The four chapters in this section discuss Islamophobia in the Netherlands by Leyla Yıldırım, Austria by Farid Hafez, the United Kingdom by Tahir Abbas, and France by François Burgat. All of these nations have experienced a rise in anti-Muslim protest movements, (far-right) anti-Muslim politics, as well as an intensification of national security apparatuses, which have targeted and policed the Muslim subject.

Part III discusses Islamophobia in formerly colonised states from the global South. This section comprises two chapters, focusing on four nations:

the Latin American nations of the triple frontier (Brazil, Argentina, and Paraguay) are discussed in Chapter 8 by Silvia Montenegro, and South Africa is discussed by Mohamed Natheem Hendricks in Chapter 9. Here, the focus will be on the growth of securitisation projects and infrastructure, which have manufactured an image of a threatening Muslim 'Other' through War on Terror discourse (Muhamed 2019). In the case of Latin America, this has served a dual purpose: firstly, it marginalises Muslim communities and prevents their integration; secondly, it has legitimised the rise of a securitised state that has facilitated the exploitation of natural resources to serve foreign interests. In South Africa, Islamophobia has been perpetuated by local media and think-tanks, and utilised by the state as a political tool for promoting securitisation measures to demonstrate the centrality of Africa as an arena to execute the global War on Terror. This securitisation reproduces partisan knowledge, which ultimately promotes Western nation-states' political interests. In both contexts discussed in this part, we see a perpetuation of coloniality through War on Terror politics and the securitisation of Muslims.

Part IV is comprised of three chapters focusing on Islamophobia in India, China, and Myanmar. These are global sites that have had severe manifestations of Islamophobia either through private actors, the state, or both. The chapter on India, by Farhan Mujahid Chak, describes the rise of Hindutva nationalism and its central role in political oppression, settler-colonialism, and human rights violations. The Hindutva colonial project in the War on Terror has been weaponised through acts of criminality against Muslim minorities. This involves state-endorsed violence and usurping of Muslim wealth, forced conversions, and stringent rules relating to courtship. The chapter on China, by Sean R. Roberts, examines the historical state repression of the Uyghur population and its genesis in settler colonialism. This includes the imprisoning of over a million Uyghurs in concentration camps, subjugation to forced re-education programmes, sterilisation of Uyghur women, and other forms of physical and psychological torture. Their exclusion from society is an expression of how the Uyghurs have come to symbolise an existential threat to the People's Republic of China that must be quarantined through punishment, detention, and surveillance. The final chapter in this part and the volume as a whole discusses the consequences of years of unabated interpersonal and institutional Islamophobia – a 'breaking point' of mass murder, sexual violence, and genocide, which became a reality in the case of the Rohingya Muslim population of Myanmar. This chapter by Naved Bakali outlines how the co-dependent relationship between institutional and interpersonal Islamophobia since military rule in Myanmar, in the absence of a strong and unified resistance, contributed to the genocide.

This book presents a nuanced appreciation of specific themes that critically engage with the complexity and evolution of Islamophobia. It provides up-to-date accounts and analysis of Islamophobia across the global North and South; the securitisation of the Muslim subject; the impact of Islamophobia on the political landscape of differing country contexts; and the resulting Islamophobic pathologies that have emerged. Furthermore, it discusses accounts of resistance and the need for activism that confronts interpersonal and institutional Islamophobia across the global North and South.

Notes

1 Throughout this volume the terms anti-Muslim racism and Islamophobia are used interchangeably. We draw on the working definition of Islamophobia as anti-Muslim racism, saying that 'Islamophobia is about a dominant group of people aiming at seizing, stabilising and widening their power by means of defining a scapegoat – real or invented – and excluding this scapegoat from the resources/rights/definition of a constructed "we".' (see Bayraklı and Hafez 2015: 6–7). For a further discussion of different theoretical approaches to the study of Islamophobia see Hafez (2018a).

2 One exception here is the volume edited by Enes Bayraklı and Farid Hafez on Islamophobia in Muslim-majority societies, which explicitly sets out to make sense of Islamophobia in Muslim majority contexts and frames it along decolonial lines (Bayraklı and Hafez 2019).

3 See for some foundational critique, among others, Tamdgidi (2012): 54–81.

4 There have been a number of criticisms in response to Said's ideas, most notably from the historian Bernard Lewis, whom Said had labelled as a key Orientalist scholar. One of Lewis's contentions was that Orientalism developed independently of the European imperial project, as the French and English both studied Islam prior to the period of imperialism in the sixteenth and seventeenth centuries. As such, Lewis contended that Orientalism did not advance the cause of imperialism. See Lewis (1993). However, as Said observes in *Orientalism*, '[t]o say simply that Orientalism was a rationalization of colonial rule is to ignore the extent to which colonial rule was justified in advance by Orientalism, rather than after the fact' (Said 1993: 39). In other words, Said acknowledged that there were European scholars studying Islam prior to the period of imperialism, and it was precisely the attitudes developed by these earlier scholars which created a theoretical pretext for an imperial project. Another critique of Said's work was that within his analysis of selected canonised Western texts, he reproduces the same essentialising discourse which his work sought to undermine, by portraying Western scholarship as homogeneous. In other words, some charge that Said used the same broad brush when describing those whom he was criticising by not engaging with critical and dissenting views within European scholarship. For a detailed discussion, see Ahmad (1993).

5 To name this space, the decolonial theorist Nelson Maldonado-Torres (2007: 24) proposed a way to achieve decolonial epistemic disobedience in his ten theses, which frame the decolonial project in such a way that an individual subject will

emerge as: a 'questioner, thinker, theorist, writer, and communicator'; a creator involved in an aesthetic, erotic, and spiritual decolonial turn (Maldonado-Torres 2007: 26); an agent of social change (Maldonado-Torres 2007: 28); and, lastly, an actor in a collective (Maldonado-Torres 2007: 28).

Bibliography

Ahmad, A. (1993) *In theory*, New York, NY: Verso.

Aziz, S. (2021). *The racial Muslim. When racism quashes religious freedom*, Berkeley, CA: University of California Press.

Bakali, N. (2019). Challenging terrorism as a form of 'Otherness': exploring the parallels between far-right and Muslim religious extremism, *Islamophobia Studies Journal*, 5(1): 99–115.

Bakali, N. (2019). The redefining of far-right extremist activism along Islamophobic lines, *Islamophobia Studies Yearbook*, 10(1): 82–98.

Bakali, N. (2021). Islamophobia in Myanmar: the Rohingya genocide and the 'war on terror', *Race & Class*, 62(4): 53–71.

Bayoumi, M. (2006). Racing religion, *The New Centennial Review*, 6(2): 267–93.

Bayraklı, E. and F. Hafez (eds) (2015–2020). *European Islamophobia report*, Istanbul: SETA.

Bayraklı, E. and F. Hafez (eds) (2019). *Islamophobia in Muslim majority societies*, London: Routledge.

Bayraklı, E., L. Faytre and F. Hafez (2019). Making sense of Islamophobia in Muslim societies. In: E. Bayraklı and F. Hafez (eds), *Islamophobia in Muslim majority societies*, London: Routledge, 5–20.

Beydoun, K. (2018). *American Islamophobia: understanding the roots and rise of fear*, Oakland, CA: University of California Press.

Césaire, A. (2001 [1950]). *Discourse on colonialism*, New York.

Elsheikh, E. and B. Sisemore (2019). *Legalizing xenophobia and Islamophobia in the United States*, Berkeley, CA: Haas Institute.

El Zahed, S. (2019). Internalized Islamophobia: the making of Islam in the Egyptian media. In: E. Bayraklı and F. Hafez (eds), *Islamophobia in Muslim majority societies*, London: Routledge, 137–60.

Fanon, F. (2008 [1952]). *Black skin, white masks*, New York: Grove Press.

Gottschalk, P. and Greenberg, G. (2008). *Islamophobia: making Muslims the enemy*, Lanham, MD: Rowman and Littlefield.

Grosfoguel, R. (2006). World-systems analysis in the context of transmodernity, border thinking, and global coloniality, *Review*, 29(2): 167–87.

Grosfoguel, R. (2012). The multiple faces of Islamophobia, *Islamophobia Studies Journal*, 1(1): 9–33.

Hafez, F. (2018a). Schools of thought in Islamophobia studies: prejudice, racism, and decoloniality, *Islamophobia Studies Journal*, 4(2): 210–25.

Hafez, F. (2018b). Muslim civil society under attack: the European Foundation for Democracy's role in defaming and delegitimizing Muslim civil society. In: I. Derya and J. Esposito (eds), *Islamophobia and radicalization: breeding intolerance and violence*, London: Palgrave Macmillan, 117–37.

Hafez, F. (2019). Reading Islamophobia through the lens of James Baldwin, *The Leibniz ScienceCampus: Understanding and Explaining Islamophobia in Eastern Europe*, 1: 21–26.

Hafez, F. (2020). Unwanted identities: the 'religion line' and global Islamophobia, *Development*, 63(1): 9–19.

Hafez, F. (2021). Surveilling and criminalizing Austrian Muslims: the case of 'Political Islam', *Insight Turkey*, 23(2): 11–22.

Howell, A. and Richter-Montpetit, M. (2019). Is securitization theory racist? Civilizationalism, methodological whiteness, and antiblack thought in the Copenhagen School, *Security Dialogue*, 51(1): 3–22.

Ibrahim, M. (2005). The securitization of migration: a racial discourse, *International Migration*, 43(5): 163–87.

Iner, D. et al. (2019). *Islamophobia in Australia-II (2016–2017)*, Sydney: Charles Sturt University.

Kosba, M. (2019). Paradoxical Islamophobia and post-colonial cultural nationalism in post-revolutionary Egypt. In: E. Bayraklı and F. Hafez (eds), *Islamophobia in Muslim majority societies*, London: Routledge, 107–24.

Kumar, D. (2012). *Islamophobia and the politics of empire*, Chicago, IL: Haymarket Books.

Kundnani, A. (2014). *The Muslims are coming: Islamophobia, extremism, and the domestic War on Terror*, New York, NY: Verso.

Kundnani, A. and Hayes, B. (2018). *The globalisation of Countering Violent Extremism policies: undermining human rights, instrumentalising civil society*, Amsterdam: The Transnational Institute.

Lewis, B. (2007) *Islam and the West*, New York: Oxford University Press, 1993.

Maldonado-Torres, N. (2007). On the coloniality of being, *Cultural Studies*, 21(2): 240–70.

Mamdani, Mahmood (2005). *Good Muslim, bad Muslim: America, the Cold War, and the roots of terror*, New York: Three Leaves Press Doubleday.

Marx, S. (2008). Postcolonialism. In: L. Given (ed.), *The Sage encyclopedia of qualitative research methods: Vol. 1*, Thousand Oaks, CA: Sage, 650–5.

Memmi, A. ([1957] 2013). *The colonizer and the colonized*, Abingdon: Routledge.

Mignolo, W. (2012). *Local histories/global designs: coloniality, subaltern knowledges, and border thinking*, Princeton, NJ: Princeton University Press.

Muhamed, J. (2019). Securitization of Islam in contemporary Ethiopia. In: E. Bayraklı and F. Hafez (eds). *Islamophobia in Muslim majority societies*, London: Routledge, 175–98.

Qurashi, F. (2018). The Prevent strategy and the UK 'war on terror': embedding infrastructures of surveillance in Muslim communities, *Palgrave Communications*, 4, art. 17.

Rana, J. (2016). The racial infrastructure of the terror-industrial complex, *Social Text*, 34(4 129): 111–38.

Roberts, S. (2018). The biopolitics of China's 'war on terror' and the exclusion of the Uyghurs, *Critical Asian Studies*, 50(2): 232–58.

Runnymede Trust (1997). *Islamophobia a challenge for us all*, London: Runnymede Trust.

Runnymede Trust (2016). *Islamophobia – 20 years on, still a challenge for us all*, February, www.runnymedetrust.org (accessed 31 March 2022).

Said, E. (1979). *Orientalism*, New York: Vintage Books.

Said, E. (1993). *Culture and imperialism*, New York: Alfred A. Knopf.

Salem, S. (2018). Denmark's quest to socialize the 'ghettos': the dark history of forced assimilation in Europe, *Discover Society*, July, https://discoversociety.org/2018/07/03/denmarks-quest-to-socialize-the-ghettos-the-dark-history-of-forced-assimilation-in-europe/ (accessed 26 October 2021).

Sayyid, S. (2014). *Recalling the Caliphate. Decolonization and world order*, London: C. Hurst & Co. Publishers.

Sayyid, S. (2018) Islamophobia and the Europeanness of the other Europe, *Patterns of Prejudice*, 52(5): 420–35.

Shibli, N. (2021). Political geographies of Islamophobia: Chinese ethno-religious racism and structural violence in East Turkestan, *Islamophobia Studies Journal*, 6(2): 150–66.

Tamdgidi, M.H. (2012). Beyond Islamophobia and Islamophilia as Western epistemic racisms: revisiting Runnymede Trust's definition in a world-history context, *Islamophobia Studies Journal*, 1(1): 54–81.

Thompson, P., Itaoui, R., and Bazian, H. (2019). *Islamophobia in India. Stoking bigotry*, Berkeley, CA: UCB Center for Race and Gender.

Weller, P., Feldman, A., and Purdum, K. (2001). *Religious descrimination in England and Wales*, London: Office of Justice Programmes.

Zuboff, S. (2019). Surveillance capitalism and the challenge of collective action, *New Labor Forum*, 28(1): 10–29.

Part I

Islamophobia in settler societies

Chapter 1

The racialised logics of Islamophobia in Canada

Uzma Jamil

Introduction

On 6 June 2021, in London, Ontario, four members of the Afzaal family were run down and killed by a white man, leaving their nine-year-old son as the sole survivor. Police reported that he attacked them intentionally because they were Muslim.

The London attack was a harsh reminder of a similar event a few years earlier at a mosque in Quebec City. The mosque shooting was the first incident where Muslims were killed at their place of worship in a Canadian city. On 29 January 2017, six Muslim men were shot and killed, and many others were injured, at evening prayers. That attacker, Alexandre Bissonnette, also set out to kill Muslims deliberately. He felt that Muslim immigrants in Quebec were a threat to white francophone Quebecois, expressing the combination of xenophobia and Islamophobia that is endemic to the ideology of the far-right.

Although these Islamophobic murders elicit shock and sorrow when they make news headlines, they are not isolated events. Islamophobia has been an ongoing part of everyday Muslim experiences in Canada for a number of years. Since 2016, there has been an increase in hate crimes, vandalism of mosques, and harassment and violence that Muslim women who wear the hijab face on the streets and in public spaces (Zine 2021). In Quebec, Bill 21, which became law in 2019, prohibits people who wear religious symbols from performing and receiving public services, in the name of upholding the state's commitment to secularism. In practice, the law disproportionately excludes Muslim women who wear the hijab from working in the public sector, as well as other religious minorities who wear visible religious symbols.

How do we make sense of these incidents of Islamophobia? What does it show us about the relationship between Muslims as racialised and religious minorities and white majorities in Canada? In this chapter, I explore these questions by examining the racialised logics of Islamophobia as an expression of coloniality. Far from being isolated incidents, the violence behind Islamophobia is closely tied with the violence of past and present relationships between white majorities and non-white racialised minorities in Canada as a white settler society. I trace the xenophobic attitudes towards the latter, including Muslims, in the past, before turning to the present political context to consider the impact of the War on Terror and the securitisation of Muslims as racialised threats. This securitisation has facilitated the institutionalisation of Islamophobia through laws and policies, illustrating how Islamophobia is a structural problem in society, rather than only a problem of individual negative attitudes and behaviours. Lastly, I consider Muslim politics in its assertions of political identity and agency to fight Islamophobia.

Muslims and coloniality

I begin by reflecting on the Muslim–nation relationship as the primary frame for discussing Islamophobia and Muslim minorities in Western countries. It creates a temporal boundary, assuming that the 'modern' iteration of the Western nation is the 'beginning' for understanding how Muslims have come to be excluded from it today, in all the many explicit and implicit ways that this is carried out. It also relies on the common understanding of Muslims as immigrants as a way of underlining their recent, usually post-Second World War, arrival in the Western nation and also their 'inherent' difference from it. It allows the fight for the protection of their rights and freedoms as citizens and as members of the polity to remain confined and therefore dislocated from the larger history that defines the present relationship between white majorities and racialised (non-white) minorities.

I suggest that we shift the frame to think about Muslims in relation to the racialised logics of coloniality. It means that we need to consider how Muslims are part of a much longer colonial history and relationship with the West in which they have been understood and treated as racialised and religious Others. This history includes a recognition of hundreds of thousands of enslaved Muslims in the Americas (i.e. in North America and the Caribbean and parts of South America), among the millions of enslaved Africans sent there, starting in the sixteenth century and continuing over the course of the slave trade (Diouf 1998: 70). It also includes the many who were brought to North America as part of the trans-Atlantic slave trade until the 1800s, including the United States (US) and Canada. For example, among the first

Black Muslims in Canada was Mahommah Baquaqua. He was originally from West Africa, and had been enslaved and sent to Brazil. He came to Upper Canada through the Underground Railroad in the 1850s, where he settled in southern Ontario in a community of the formerly enslaved who had fled the US (Hogben 2021: 14–15).

In the late nineteenth and early twentieth centuries, Muslims in Canada included Arabs from Greater Syria, which comprises present day Lebanon, and Ottoman Turks, primarily Albanians and Bosnians who lived in the Ottoman Empire. Though immigration data does not record the religion of these Arab and Ottoman migrants, they included Muslims and Christians. Most of these migrants worked as merchants in cities or as itinerant salesmen, or peddlers, in rural areas (Hogben 2021: 15–16). This brief history of Muslim arrivals in the Americas and in Canada illustrates how shifting the frame to include coloniality allows for a broader and more nuanced view of the presence of Muslims in Canada today. They are not simply 'immigrants', with all the connotations of foreignness that the term implies, thereby solidifying their treatment as second-class citizens. Rather, their presence in Canada, before in fact it *was* modern-day Canada, recalibrates not only their claim to belonging but also its implications in the relationship with white majorities.

I now turn to an examination of the racialised hierarchies that attend the establishment of Canada as a white settler society to illustrate how Muslims are part of a long history of racialisation and relationship between white majorities and non-white minorities. The territories that ultimately came to be known as Canada were settled by British and French settlers in the early 1500s. The racialised hierarchy that underpinned this society was created through the killing and removal of Indigenous peoples from their lands, a dispossession that continues today in its many forms. The enslavement of Black people and the participation of white British and French settlers in the slave trade consolidated Canada as a white settler society (Austin 2010).

In the late 1800s and early 1900s, 'White Canada' immigration policies were designed to keep Canada white by excluding Asians, Blacks, and other non-Europeans from entering and settling in the country. For example, the Chinese head tax, in place between 1885 and 1923, was a fee charged for each Chinese person who entered Canada. It steadily increased over the years, rising from $50 per person to eventually $500 per person, in order to discourage Chinese immigration (Chan 2016). In 1908, the Continuous Journey clause prohibited the entry of Asian immigrants if they did not travel directly (continuously) from their country to Canada. It was challenged, unsuccessfully, by the Indian passengers of the ship *Komagata Maru*, which was chartered from Hong Kong to Vancouver in 1914. The passengers were prevented from entering Canada and the ship was left in limbo at Vancouver harbour for two months. They were ultimately forced to return to India, after their legal and political challenges failed and the government refused them entry.[1] The 1910 Immigration Act made it possible to deny entry to people of African descent, including African-Americans and Black people from the Caribbean, through the discretionary designation of 'climatic unsuitability', meaning that they were unsuited to the cold climate of Canada and therefore unlikely to settle successfully (Williams 1997: 42–3). The immigration system was changed into a points-based system in 1967, removing race as a criterion for entry into Canada (Hawkins 1989).

Yet, the racialised logics that define the treatment of non-white racialised minorities in Canada remain present. The political discourse about the arrival and settlement of racialised immigrants and refugees continues to echo these themes and policies, maintaining a racialised hierarchy between immigrants and white 'founding peoples' (Thobani 2007). Muslims are situated as part of this when they are viewed as racialised immigrants and religious minorities who must be 'taught' to become citizens of the Western nation. Their essentialised difference is articulated through the binaries and hierarchies of Orientalism – the 'civilised' and 'rational' superiority of Western society vis-à-vis the 'barbaric', 'irrational', and 'uncivilized' inferiority of Islam and Muslims (Said 1978: 300). These categories of essentialised difference make it possible to not only portray Muslims as 'problems', but also place the burden on them to let go of their Muslimness in order to adequately 'integrate' into the Western nation (Sayyid 2014).

Thus, this reframing to focus on the racialised logics of coloniality places Muslims within a longer history of European settlement in the Americas, as well as in relation to the idea of the West. It allows us to see Islamophobia as the 'systematic regulation and disciplining of Muslimness by reference to a westernizing horizon' (Sayyid 2018: 423), as well as situating this specifically in the Canadian context, both past and present, in North America.

Racialised logics of coloniality and the War on Terror

The systemic securitisation of Muslims as a racialised community in the white, Western nation is not a unique phenomenon. The idea that racialised minorities within the nation need to be tracked and monitored has historical and political antecedents in Canada, beginning with its white settler roots.

The good/bad, West/non-West categories that animate the securitisation discourse today are related to the good/bad categories that defined white Western settlers vis-à-vis Indigenous peoples, the latter described as non-Western as well as non-Christian 'uncivilized savages' (Thobani 2007: 238). The settlers' response was to erase Indigenous communities, either through assimilation into white, Christian society or through death by violence

(Lawrence 2002). Various government actions, such as the establishment of residential schools, the Sixties Scoop and dispossession of ancestral lands illustrate the erasure and removal of Indigenous peoples through assimilation and death. In 2021, the discovery of more than 1,300 unmarked graves near Indigenous residential schools across the country, suspected to be of children who attended and died at those schools, illustrates both the ongoing nature and the magnitude of this erasure in the relationship between white settler society and Indigenous peoples in Canada (Gilmore 2021).

As a different kind of example, the internment of 22,000 Japanese Canadians as 'enemy aliens' in the 1940s also illustrates Canada's racialised security logic (Oikawa 2002: 73). After the bombing of Pearl Harbor in 1941, Japanese Canadians all along the west coast were rounded up and placed in internment camps. Their money, property, and possessions were confiscated and sold by the Canadian government to raise funds to run these camps. Their rights as Canadian citizens were nullified, in effect, as some were also deported to Japan (Oikawa 2002: 77–9). There was never any basis for the suspicion that they were threats to national security, only the existing prejudice of the white population that received official sanction from the government, led by Prime Minister MacKenzie King (Oikawa 2002). In 1988, Prime Minister Brian Mulroney apologised on behalf of the Canadian government and offered compensation to those affected and their descendants (Marsh 2012).

I am not suggesting that there are simple parallels or similarities between the past and present treatment of Indigenous people, Japanese Canadians, and Muslims, nor that these communities are all the same, as racialised minorities. I am arguing instead that racialised logics of coloniality shape the relationship between governing white majorities and racialised minorities in long-standing ways. The forms that these relationships take and the particular historical and political contexts that define these specific communities may differ, but the racialised logics are not new in Canada.

I make this point to situate the following discussion of the impact of the War on Terror (WOT) on Muslims in Canada within a broader historical and political context. The tendency to focus on racial profiling and Islamophobia only as outcomes of 9/11 risks making it the explanation for everything, as both the catalyst and the outcome for securitisation in the WOT (Jamil 2017: 75). It divorces the present from the past, when in fact there are continuities of coloniality and its associated and ongoing violence.

9/11 and the securitisation of Muslims

The securitisation of Muslims is made possible through the WOT discourse, which is based on Orientalist views. These views animated the West vs non-West civilisational discourse after 9/11, but they were not generated by it. Rather, they had already been present in society before 2001. While the WOT reinforced Orientalism, it also securitised Muslims through social, political, and legal processes which constructed them as racialised threats to the white, Western nation. This process of securitisation facilitated the state apparatus that institutionalised Islamophobia in its laws and policies. This process is still ongoing, twenty years after 11 September 2001.

In the immediate aftermath of the attacks in September 2001, American president George W. Bush described the conflict as between 'those who are with us' and 'those who are with the terrorists'. The 'us' included not only the US as the lead, but also its allies who considered themselves as part of the 'civilised West' vis-à-vis the equally broadly defined 'uncivilised terrorists', which included al Qaeda, Taliban, and Muslims in general. The moral and political boundaries between 'dangerous terrorist' Muslims and the 'good heroes' of the West who were fighting terrorism were grounded within Orientalist binaries, making it possible to mobilise a global discourse about 'a family of white nations, a civilisation obliged to use force and terror to defend itself' against the racialised threat posed by Muslims as the 'Others' of the West (Razack 2008: 5). Canada was part of this white, Western family of nations, as the northern neighbour that shares a long land border with the US and an ally in the US-led military intervention in Afghanistan that was launched in October 2001. The WOT became an American war, as well as a Western one.

The WOT discourse builds on Orientalist assumptions that, since Islam defines all Muslims uniformly, then all Muslims everywhere are the same – static and essentialised in their religious identities. Therefore, their potential for violence also remains uniform, something that must be either feared or mastered (Jamil 2014: 32–3). It makes terrorism an 'Islamic' problem, rather than a (geo)political one. On the domestic side of the WOT, this facilitated the implementation of national security measures based on the assumption that Muslims are a 'suspect community', including racial profiling and surveillance of Muslim communities, the use of a security certificate regime as a counter-terrorism tool, and the development of a no-fly list in Canada which disproportionately focused on Muslims. In this section, I focus on racial profiling and the no-fly list to illustrate how the WOT has securitised Muslims in Canada by implicitly institutionalising Islamophobia through laws and policies.

Racial profiling

The WOT in Canada has been driven legislatively through changes to existing legislation or the creation of new legislation since 2001. Among other laws, this includes the Anti-Terrorist Act (ATA) of 2001 (Bill C-36), Public Safety Act of 2002, Anti-Terrorist Act of 2015 (Bill C-51), and National Security Act of 2017 (Bill C-59).

There was also significant harmonisation of practices relating to border and aviation security between the US and Canada, which led eventually to Canada creating its own no-fly list in 2007. Given the shared land border, the importance of US–Canada trade and American concerns that Canada was providing a loophole to would-be terrorists who wished to enter the US through Canada after 9/11, Canada was under pressure to make legislative changes to bolster its national security and counter-terrorism capabilities (Whitaker 2003: 254–55).

The ATA of 2001 made amendments to the Criminal Code, the Official Secrets Act, the Canada Evidence Act, and the Proceeds of Crime (Money Laundering) Act (Government of Canada 2021). These and other laws, collectively, form the structural basis for the state to put in place national security and counter-terrorism measures across many different sectors, including immigration, border security, policing, taxation, finance, and banking.

Racial profiling was already part of policing strategies before 9/11, whether this was acknowledged explicitly or not. It refers to 'the use of race as a proxy for risk in the policing of criminality, and more recently, terrorism' (Bahdi, Parsons, Sandborn 2010: 32). In its overt form, an entire community is associated with criminality, and therefore individuals from that community are targeted because of this perceived higher susceptibility for criminal behaviour. It is well established in how Black men are more likely to be stopped by police, often for merely their presence as Black men (Maynard 2017: 88–92). Before 9/11, racial profiling was focused mostly on Black Canadian men, while Black and Indigenous men were the most over-represented in the criminal justice system (Bahdi, Parsons, Sandborn 2010: 34–5).

The racialised logics that were applied before 9/11 were extended to racialised Muslim communities, including those who were of Arab, South Asian, and African heritage. While the new counter-terrorism and national security laws themselves did not explicitly authorise racial profiling of these communities, neither did they expressly prohibit it. The Royal Canadian Mounted Police (RCMP), Canadian Security and Intelligence Service and other law enforcement agencies were given leeway to ensure national security objectives were achieved, implicitly allowing profiling on the basis of race, ethnicity, religion, and/or place of origin in a way that disproportionately targeted Muslim communities (Bahdi, Parsons, Sandborn 2010: 35). This also roped in all those who were deemed to 'look Muslim' and/or 'Middle Eastern' or Arab, whether or not they actually were.

Despite the fact that anti-terrorism laws do not include any reference to profiling, nor specifically target Muslim populations, in practice, the discretion offered to law enforcement and other relevant government agencies and officials to ensure national security has created the potential for racial profiling of Muslims. At the same time, this leeway has also prevented it from being adequately documented (Bahdi 2003: 297). Taken together, these laws have contributed to a climate of negative stereotyping and suspicion of Muslim communities that continues to this day.

The Maher Arar case (2002–4) is the most egregious example of this racial profiling. A Syrian-Canadian citizen, Arar was detained by the US in 2002 based on information provided by the RCMP that he and his wife were 'al Qaeda extremists'. He was sent to Syria, where he was jailed and tortured until he was released in 2004, after national pressure from activists and politicians. A public inquiry into the events in 2006 found that the Canadian government had been complicit in his wrongful detainment, leading to his subsequent imprisonment and torture in Syria, and cleared him of any associations with al Qaeda or terrorism (Jamil 2017: 80–1). The RCMP Commissioner offered a public apology to Arar and his family in the House of Commons in 2006.

A key part of the power of racial profiling in the WOT context has been in the fact that the profile itself is perceived to be legitimate by the law enforcement bodies and officials that make it. Jackman (2010) argues that the racial profiling of Arabs and Muslims is seen as legitimate because the characteristics of the profile are seen as 'objective'. It is more likely, for example, that Muslims travel to Muslim countries in the Middle East than do non-Muslims. However, Jackman argues that 'it is the character of being Arab and/or Muslim that informs the concern about travels or other such elements of a profile' (Jackman 2010: 70). In other words, it is being Muslim that makes the traveler appear 'suspicious'. The factors themselves are 'grounded in racialized characteristics' (Jackman 2010: 70). It facilitates the perception that Muslims are *already* risks to national security because of who they are, rather than potential risks where the evidence is to be ascertained. This leads us to consider the Canadian no-fly list and its impact on Muslims in Canada.

No-fly list in Canada

As the WOT has normalised the perception of all Muslims as potential threats, gathering information about who Muslims are, what they are doing, and their social networks and associations has been used as a counter-terrorism tool. It also feeds public suspicion of Muslims, such that mundane activities like speaking in Arabic (Milman 2016) or watching the news on their phones

(Wong 2015) become 'dangerous' when Muslims do them. 'Flying while Muslim' refers to the racial profiling of Muslims and those who are perceived to be Muslims as members of a 'suspect community' at airports and on airplanes. As one aspect of the 'flying while Muslim' phenomenon, the no-fly list is based on the idea that it is possible to identify and to know the characteristics that make Muslims 'dangerous' (Jamil 2017: 73–4).

Known officially as the Specified Persons List, the no-fly list was created in 2007 to prevent people from flying who may pose a security threat to the plane or its passengers. This purpose was expanded in 2015 by Bill C-51 to include preventing people from flying in order to participate in terrorist activities in other places (Jamil 2017: 73–4). There is a lack of transparency in knowing who is on the list, including how many Muslims are on it, as this information is limited to the minister and the government bodies that generate the list. However, based on publicly available information in the media, it is clear that Muslims are disproportionately affected by it.

False positives are those people who are flagged as being on the list because they share the same or a similar name as a targeted individual (Jamil 2017: 79). Although the problem has existed for a long time, since 2015 there have been a number of stories about Muslim children who have been stopped from travelling because of their names. In 2015, Suleiman and Khadija Cajee, the parents of one young boy, Syed Adam Ahmed, were surprised to find that their six-year-old son's name was a false positive on the no-fly list when the family was about to travel to the US on Air Canada (CBC News 2016a). As a result of the media reporting of this incident, other Muslim families also came forward with similar stories about their children, who were also flagged as false positives on the no-fly list. These children ranged in age from six months to seventeen years of age (CBC News 2016b). Khadija Cajee became the unofficial spokesperson for the advocacy group, known as the No-fly List Kids Coalition (noflylistkids.ca). In 2016 they were successful in lobbying then Minister of Public Safety, Ralph Goodale, to take an interest in their plight (Nasser 2016). In 2018 the federal government allocated approximately $81 million over five years to deal with false positives and others mistakenly placed on the no-fly list by creating a redress mechanism (Tunney 2018). In November 2020, the federal government moved another step forward by announcing that the new redress system would be in place by the end of the month (Tunney 2020).

While the redress mechanism is promising and important, it does not detract from the bigger picture: the no-fly list itself still exists and continues to negatively impact Muslims in Canada. Civil liberties groups have argued that there does not seem to be clear evidence for why a no-fly list is needed to prevent potentially dangerous people from flying where there are already existing tools available under the Criminal Code to prevent people from engaging in or flying to engage in terrorist activities (Vonn 2016; ICLMG 2019; Jarvis n.d.). In their submissions to the Senate for Bill C-59 (which amended Bill C-51 and the Secure Air Travel Act, both of which are relevant to the no-fly list), the International Civil Liberties Monitoring Group (ICLMG) and the National Council of Canadian Muslims (NCCM) called for better mechanisms for due process, transparency, and accountability (ICLMG 2019: 39–41; NCCM 2019).

Muslim politics

In the following sections of this chapter, I look at the emergence of a Muslim political identity and what Muslims are doing to express their political agency and resistance in the face of continuing Islamophobia from the state and society.

Muslims, as a distinct political identity, challenge the hegemonic position of the West through their agency as both racialised and religious subjects in the postcolonial/decolonial world (Sayyid 2014). Viewed in the national context, Muslims make political claims upon the state as a distinct group, exercising their agency to assert their rights and to challenge negative treatment. These assertions of both Muslim agency and Muslim political identity are central not only to challenging Islamophobia but also to decentring the West as the hegemonic frame of reference (Sayyid 2014: 13; Sayyid 2018: 423).

Islamophobia as a topic of public policy discussion is relatively new in Canada. Unfortunately, it has taken two highly visible attacks against Muslims in recent years – in Quebec in 2017 and in London, Ontario in June 2021 – to make Islamophobia prominent in national political conversation. On the other hand, these incidents have also made visible the gap between rhetorical sympathy that is offered in the moment and actual ongoing political investment and support to fight Islamophobia. Below, I discuss two examples of this and their implications for Muslim political agency.

M103 in Parliament

In December 2016, Liberal Member of Parliament Iqra Khalid tabled non-binding parliamentary motion M103 against Islamophobia. It came up for debate in February 2017, a month after the mosque shooting in Quebec City, when emotions were high. It quickly became a lightning rod and led to death threats directed against Khalid.

M103 was an attempt to give legitimacy to Muslims and their experiences of Islamophobia as a matter of national politics, and to force the government to move beyond rhetorical, 'feel good' statements. As a private member's motion, it was mostly symbolic, but it had three main points. It called for the government to: '[1] condemn Islamophobia and all forms of systemic racism and religious discrimination, [2] quell the increasing public climate of hate and fear, and [3] compel the Commons heritage committee to develop a government-wide approach for reducing or eliminating systemic racism and religious discrimination, including Islamophobia' (CBC News 2017; Parliament of Canada 2017).

Conservative MP David Anderson raised objections on the use of the term 'Islamophobia' and its lack of definition in the motion, asking for it to be removed and all religious discrimination be given equal importance. His amended motion did not pass. There were also online petitions against the motion, describing it as curtailing free speech and leading to a 'Shariah takeover in Canada' (CBC News 2017). All of these attempts were in effect efforts to minimise the emphasis and attention on Muslim experiences of discrimination as distinct.

Ultimately, M103 passed in March 2017 with support from the New Democratic Party and Liberal parties, by 209 to 91 votes. It was significant in marking the entry of Islamophobia into the national conversation as well as highlighting the political resistance to it and the articulation of a Muslim political identity.

Bill 21 in Quebec

Bill 21 stands in contrast to M103, in part because of its scope and weight; it is a provincial law. Instead of naming Islamophobia as a matter of public policy concern in Quebec, it does the opposite. It implicitly legitimises Islamophobia as a systemic issue in its outcomes, which disproportionately affect Muslim women who wear the hijab and niqab in Quebec, along with other religious minorities.

I raise it here for three reasons. First, to illustrate how it sustains Orientalist West/non-West binaries and racialised logics of coloniality in the present. Second, to illustrate how Islamophobia is institutionalised through laws that affect Muslim citizens in everyday life, distinct from the WOT impact on Muslim communities over the two decades since 2001. Third, to illustrate how the mobilisation against Bill 21 has consolidated and furthered Muslim political agency, not only in Quebec but also at a national level.

In 2019, Bill 21 became law in Quebec. Officially titled 'An Act respecting the laicity of the State', the law prohibits people who wear religious symbols from giving and receiving public services in the name of upholding Quebec's commitment to secularism (National Assembly of Quebec 2019). Laicity in Quebec takes the form of a strong state role to ensure that non-Christian religious identities, and particularly their religious symbols, are excluded from public life.[2] In practice, it discriminates against Muslim women who wear hijabs and niqabs by excluding them from working in the provincial public sector, which includes healthcare and education as well as government (civil) service. The law also excludes other religious minorities who wear visible religious symbols, such as Sikh men and women who wear turbans (Murphy 2019).

This law is grounded within the relationship between Muslims and the Western, Quebec nation. Quebec is a white settler society within Canada, distinguished by the fact that it was settled by the French originally, before becoming part of the Dominion. The basis for imagining a national identity in Quebec is politically and historically contingent. While it draws from this history, it was constructed through the events of the Quiet Revolution of the 1960s and 1970s. It was committed to centring the Quebecois as white, francophone majorities in the province and Quebec society as 'modern', secular, and committed to gender equality (Benhadjouja 2017).

As part of the racialised hierarchy of the West/non-West, this view is also grounded within Orientalist binaries of Islam as a 'patriarchal, oppressive' religion in contrast to the 'rational, modern' secularity of the West. Muslim presence as a religious minority in the nation challenges Western ideas of secular 'progress' in society, where religion ought to have disappeared altogether from public, political life (Sayyid 2014: 34–5).

This does not take into account the pervasive presence of Christian religious symbols in daily life in Quebec, but does focus attention on Muslim presence in public spaces as problematic. For example, Muslims are visible through religious practices such as their dress (hijabs and/or niqabs worn by some Muslim women), dietary requirements (halal food), and requests for accommodation for prayer spaces within public institutions, such as schools and colleges. Muslims are perceived not only as 'foreign' racialised immigrants but also as non-Christian religious minorities whose religiosity runs counter to Quebec's national ideals. Bill 21 addresses all of this through its consolidation of a state secularism that seeks to erase Muslim religiosity from public space and, by extension, from the nation. 'This legislated erasure of Muslims from every day public space normalises and legitimises Islamophobic violence, as it seeks to make their visibility and acceptance as Muslims exceptional' (Jamil 2021).

Bill 21 is part of a political project that has been ongoing in Quebec under different provincial governments for more than a decade to remove Muslims from public life and spaces. Three other bills, Bill 94 in 2010, Bill 60 in 2013 and Bill 62 in 2015, all dealt with the 'problem' of religious symbols in a 'secular' state. Even if technically the proposed laws prohibited all religious symbols, they were focused in practice on Muslim ones, i.e. hijabs and niqabs. For different reasons, none of these proposed laws was ultimately successful. The Coalition Avenir Quebec government, which came to power in 2018, succeeded in passing this most recent iteration of these 'niqab bans' in Bill 21 in 2019, amid many protests from Muslims in Quebec.

While Muslim individuals and groups had been protesting against Bill 21 since it was first proposed, after it passed in June 2019 they turned to legal challenges. Four different cases were filed to challenge its constitutionality and to address the use of the notwithstanding clause that allows Quebec to get around having to apply the relevant sections of the Canadian Charter of Rights and Freedoms. These cases involved both Muslims and non-Muslims. One of these cases was filed by the civil rights groups the NCCM and the Canadian Civil Liberties Association. Another was filed by a multi-faith group called Coalition Inclusive Quebec and three teachers who wear religious symbols. The third, led by the English Montreal School Board, focused only on the section relevant to its application for public school teachers (which include Muslim as well as Sikh women) in the English-language school system. The fourth was filed by a teachers' union, the Fédération autonome de l'enseignement, which represents 45,000 Quebec teachers, including teachers from different religious minorities. All of the cases make different arguments to challenge the use of the notwithstanding clause as unconstitutional (Montpetit 2019).

In April 2021, the Quebec Superior Court ruled that most of the law could stand because it applied the notwithstanding clause appropriately. However, English-language school boards were exempt from it because their education rights as minorities in Quebec were protected by a section of the charter that was not covered by the notwithstanding clause. Most significantly, the judge's ruling acknowledged that the law was discriminatory towards religious minorities in its outcomes and violated their rights to religious freedom and equality (Montpetit and Shingler 2021). NCCM and other groups involved in the cases have stated that they will continue to fight against Bill 21, while the Quebec government plans to appeal the Superior Court's decision. It is likely that the case will ultimately end up in the Supreme Court of Canada.

Shortly after the June 2021 attack against the Afzaal family in London, Prime Minister Trudeau was asked to explain the apparent contradiction between the federal government's commitment to fighting Islamophobia and its silence about Quebec's Bill 21. Trudeau put it back on Quebecers to address the matter, as he had stated in the past. When posed to Quebec's politicians, the same question elicited denials that there was any relationship between Islamophobia in Ontario and Islamophobia in Quebec, which is not surprising, given that the Premier believes that there is no Islamophobia in Quebec (Jamil 2021). Both of these responses illustrate the racialised contours of how Islamophobia is understood and how it is put into practice;

contours which continue to centre white majorities in the national imaginary at the expense of racialised Muslims.

Bill 21 is a significant issue of Muslim politics. Despite its obvious negative impact on the lives and careers of many Muslims who work in the public sector in Quebec, the mobilisation against the law has also created a space to make Islamophobia a public policy issue. It has facilitated the assertion of Muslim political identity and agency at both provincial and national levels. In July 2021, an online National Summit on Islamophobia was hosted by the federal government, where Muslims, as individual citizens and as representatives of many Muslim organisations across the country, presented their policy recommendations for changes to be made at federal, provincial, and municipal levels to address Islamophobia as an ongoing issue across Canada.

Conclusion

In this chapter, I have detailed how Islamophobia has been sustained in Canada through the racialised logics of coloniality in the relationship between Muslims as racialised and religious minorities and the white, Western nation and its white majorities. I have situated this analysis within the context of the whiteness of Canada and Quebec as settler societies. While Islamophobia is distinct as a set of Muslim experiences, it is also part of a long history of the state's attempts to marginalise, discipline, regulate, and at times remove, Black, Indigenous, and racialised people in and from the 'white nation' (Hage 1998), whether that be Canadian or Quebecois. The suspicion that has come to be associated with Muslim bodies as a result of the WOT is only one example of the continuation of these exclusionary practices, laws, and policies.

In conclusion, I return to a point made at the beginning, the invitation to step outside the frame of Muslim–Western nation and to look at the longer trajectory of coloniality. While I have detailed the history of it and its impact on the present, I want to consider how this analysis of Islamophobia helps to orient us towards the future. The political mobilisation against Islamophobia offers the possibility for solidarity and coalition building for Muslims transnationally, as a response to ongoing (post)colonial practices in and across the West. For example, current Islamophobic state policies and laws in France in 2021 are not too different from what is happening in Quebec. Trump's 'Muslim ban' mobilised Muslim and non-Muslim advocacy groups to fight the law in the US, but also connected them to Muslims across the different countries that were affected by it. In effect, it mobilised a transnational Muslim political identity that went beyond one national context. This is not to suggest the emergence of a united international

Muslim political identity as the solution to the problem of Islamophobia, but, rather, to open the door towards reimagining Muslimness.

Notes

1 For broader analysis and critique of how the *Komagata Maru* incident is situated in national historiography in Canada, see Bhandar and Dhanoon (2020).
2 For more on the changes in how secularism has been conceptualized and implemented in Quebec, see Béland, Lecours and Schmeiser (2021).

Bibliography

Austin, D. (2010). Narratives of power: historical mythologies in contemporary Québec and Canada, *Race & Class*, 52(1): 19–32.

Bahdi, R. (2003). No exit: racial profiling and Canada's war against terrorism, *Osgoode Hall Law Journal*, 41(2–3): 293–317.

Bahdi, R., Parsons, O., and Sandborn, T. (2010). Racial profiling: B.C. civil liberties position paper. In: R. Marcuse (ed.), *Racial profiling: a special BCCLA report on racial profiling in Canada*, Vancouver, BC: B.C. Civil Liberties Association, 31–53.

Béland, D., Lecours, A., and Schmeiser, P. (2021). Nationalism, secularism and ethno-cultural diversity in Quebec, *Journal of Canadian Studies/Revue d'études canadiennes*, 55(1): 177–202.

Bhandar, D. and Dhanoon, R.K. (2020). Introduction: unmooring the Komagata Maru. In: R.K. Dhanoon, D. Bhandar, R. Mawani and S.K. Bains (eds), *Unmooring the Komagata Maru: charting colonial trajectories*, Vancouver: University of British Columbia Press, 3–31.

Benhadjouja, L. (2017). Laïcité narrative et sécularonationalisme au Québec à l'épreuve de la race, du genre et de la sexualité, *Studies in Religion/Sciences Religieuses*, 46(2): 272–91.

CBC News (2016a). Markham boy, 6, on no-fly list, parents say, 3 January, www.cbc.ca/news/canada/toronto/markham-security-travel-watchlist-1.3387890 (accessed 20 July 2021).

CBC News (2016b). No fly list tags more Canadian toddlers as security risks, 4 January, www.cbc.ca/news/canada/toronto/no-fly-list-flags-more-canadian-toddlers-as-security-risks-1.3388927 (accessed 20 July 2021).

CBC News (2017). House of Commons passes anti-Islamophobia motion, 23 March, www.cbc.ca/news/politics/m-103-islamophobia-motion-vote-1.4038016 (accessed 2 August 2021).

Chan, A. (2016). Chinese head tax in Canada, *The Canadian Encyclopedia*, www.thecanadianencyclopedia.ca/en/article/chinese-head-tax-in-canada (accessed 18 July 2021).

Diouf, S. (1998). *Servants of Allah: African Muslims enslaved in the Americas*, New York: New York University Press.

Gilmore, R. (2021). Mapping the missing: former residential school sites in Canada and the search for unmarked graves, *Global News*, 15 September, https://globalnews.ca/

news/8074453/indigenous-residential-schools-canada-graves-map/ (accessed 5 October 2021)

Government of Canada (2021). About the Anti-Terrorism Act, www.justice.gc.ca/eng/cj-jp/ns-sn/act-loi.html (accessed 28 July 2021).

Hage, G. (1998). *White nation: fantasies of white supremacy in a multicultural society*, Sydney, Australia: Pluto Press.

Hawkins, F. (1989). *Critical years in immigration: Canada and Australia compared*, Kingston, ON: McGill-Queen's University Press.

Hogben, M. (2021). *Minarets on the horizon: Muslim pioneers in Canada*, Toronto: Mawenzi House.

International Civil Liberties Monitoring Group (ICLMG) (2019). Brief on Bill C-59, the *National Security Act, 2017*, https://iclmg.ca/wp-content/uploads/2019/05/C-59-brief-May-2019-update.pdf (accessed 21 July 2021).

Jackman, B. (2010). Sustaining investigations and security certificates through the use of profiles. In: R. Marcuse (ed.), *Racial profiling: A special BCCLA report on racial profiling in Canada*. Vancouver, BC: B.C. Civil Liberties Association, 69–79.

Jamil, U. (2014). Reading power: Muslims and the war on terror discourse, *Islamophobia Studies Journal*, 2(2): 29–42.

Jamil, U. (2017). Can Muslims fly? The no-fly list as a tool in the war on terror, *Islamophobia Studies Journal*, 4(1): 72–86.

Jamil, U. (2021). Islamophobia and epistemological ignorance, *Contending Modernities*, 29 July, https://contendingmodernities.nd.edu/theorizing-modernities/islamophobia-epistemic-ignorance/ (accessed 10 August 2021).

Jarvis, A. (n.d.). Canada's no fly list, International Civil Liberties Monitoring Group, https://iclmg.ca/issues/canadas-no-fly-list/ (accessed 21 July 2021).

Lawrence, B. (2002). Rewriting histories of the land: colonization and indigenous resistance in eastern Canada. In: S.H. Razack (ed.), *Race, space and the law: unmapping a white settler society*, Toronto: Between the Lines Books, 21–46.

Marsh, J.H. (2012). Japanese Canadian internment: prisoners in their own country, *The Canadian Encyclopedia*, 23 February, https://thecanadianencyclopedia.ca/en/article/japanese-internment-banished-and-beyond-tears-feature (accessed 18 July 2021).

Maynard, R. (2017). *Policing black lives: state violence in Canada from slavery to the present*, Halifax, NS and Winnipeg, MB: Fernwood Publishing.

Milman, O. (2016). Southwest Airlines draws outrage over man removed for speaking Arabic, *The Guardian*, 16 April, www.theguardian.com/us-news/2016/apr/16/southwest-airlines-man-removed-flight-arabic (accessed 20 July 2021).

Montpetit, J. (2019). How lawyers are trying to overturn Quebec's religious symbols ban, *CBC News*, 12 December, www.cbc.ca/news/canada/montreal/bill-21-quebec-court-challenges-1.5393074 (accessed 10 August 2021).

Montpetit, J. and Shingler, B. (2021). Quebec Superior Court upholds most of religious symbols ban, but English-language schools exempt, *CBC News*, 21 April, www.cbc.ca/news/canada/montreal/bill-21-religious-symbols-ban-quebec-court-ruling-1.5993431 (accessed 10 August 2021).

Murphy, J. (2019). Quebec Bill 21: is it OK for public servants to wear religious symbols? *BBC News*, 17 June, www.bbc.com/news/world-us-canada-48588604 (accessed 10 August 2021).

Nasser, S. (2016). Extra airport security screening for under-18s not needed, public safety minister says, *CBC News*, 7 January, www.cbc.ca/news/canada/toronto/additional-screening-under-18–1.3394628 (accessed 20 July 2021).

National Assembly of Quebec (2019). *Bill 21: an Act respecting the laicity of the State*, https://tinyurl.com/fk52hwpz (accessed 17 August 2021).

National Council of Canadian Muslims (NCCM) (2019). *Oral submissions on Bill C-59*, https://mk0nccmorganizadbkcm.kinstacdn.com/wp-content/uploads/2019/05/Bill-C-59-Oral-Submisisons-May-6-Senate_final.pdf (accessed 20 July 2021).

Oikawa, M. (2002). Cartographies of violence: women, memory and the subject(s) of the 'internment'. In: S.H. Razack (ed.), *Race, space and the law: unmapping a white settler society*, Toronto: Between the Lines Books, 71–98.

Parliament of Canada (2017). M-103 systemic racism and religious discrimination, 42nd Parliament, 1st Session, www.ourcommons.ca/members/en/88849/motions/8661986 (accessed 10 August 2021).

Razack, S. (2008). *Casting out: the eviction of Muslims from western law and politics*, Toronto: University of Toronto Press.

Said, E.W. (1978). *Orientalism*, New York: Vintage Books.

Sayyid, S. (2014). *Recalling the Caliphate: decolonization and world order*, London: Hurst & Company.

Sayyid, S. (2018). Islamophobia and the Europeanness of the other Europe, *Patterns of Prejudice*, 52(5): 420–35.

Thobani, S. (2007). *Exalted subjects: studies in the making of race and nation in Canada*, Toronto: University of Toronto Press.

Tunney, C. (2018). Families celebrating $81m in budget to fix no fly list, *CBC News*, 28 February, www.cbc.ca/news/politics/no-fly-list-families-1.4543329 (accessed 20 July 2021).

Tunney, C. (2020). Redress system for travellers caught by 'no-fly list' errors coming this month: Blair, *CBC News*, 4 November, www.cbc.ca/news/politics/no-fly-list-redress-1.5789343 (accessed 20 July 2021).

Vonn, M. (2016). The new Canadian 'no-fly' regime, British Columbia Civil Liberties Association, 20 September, https://bccla.org/2016/09/the-new-canadian-no-fly-regime-brought-in-under-the-anti-terrorism-act-2015-aka-bill-c-51/ (accessed 22 July 2021).

Whitaker, R. (2003). Keeping up with the neighbours? Canadian responses to 9/11 in historical and comparative context, *Osgoode Hall Law Journal*, 41(2–3): 241–66.

Williams, D. (1997). *The road to now: a history of blacks in Montreal*, Montreal: Vehicule Press.

Wong, G. (2015). Police: 'Suspicious activity' on Chicago-bound plane was just someone watching news on phone, *Chicago Tribune*, 18 November, www.chicagotribune.com/news/breaking/ct-4-passengers-removed-from-chicagobound-plane-in-baltimore-20151117-story.html (accessed 22 July 2021).

Zine, J. (2021). Muslim family killed in terror attack in London, Ontario: Islamophobic violence surfaces once again in Canada, *The Conversation*, 8 June, https://theconversation.com/muslim-family-killed-in-terror-attack-in-london-ontario-islamophobic-violence-surfaces-once-again-in-canada-162400 (accessed 4 August 2021).

Chapter 2

Islamophobia in Australia: racialising the Muslim subject in public, media, and political discourse in the War on Terror era

Derya Iner and Sean McManus

Introduction

According to the Australian 2016 census, there are 604,200 Muslim Australians – 2.6 per cent of a total population of approximately 23.4 million. Almost 40 per cent are Australian born, and of the 60 per cent born overseas the mix is highly diverse, originating from 183 different countries (Hassan 2015). In Australia, particularly since 11 September 2001 (9/11), the view of Islam and Muslims has been influenced by the growing discourse of Islamophobia (Poynting and Briskman 2018). It could be argued that Islamophobia is a new word for an old concept; from Said's *Orientalism* in the 1970s it has been widely accepted that the 'West' has long associated Islam with negative images, sentiments, and stereotypes (Bleich 2011). Discrimination against Muslims has increasingly become normalised and even presented as prudent precaution against violent extremism. Since the turn of the millennium, political leaders and media entities have contributed to this negativity, vilifying Muslims while defending 'Australian values' (Poynting and Briskman 2018), the Muslim 'Other' now becoming the 'folk devil' of our time (Morgan and Poynting 2012).

The first section of this chapter will discuss the changing nature of political representation since 9/11, the transition of politics to centre right and far-right, and the impact that this changing composition has had on political rhetoric in respect to Australian values and citizenship. Elements of these shifts can be linked to the 'War on Terror' and subsequent securitisation of Muslims. It will critically analyse the portrayal of Islam and Muslims in Australia's political discourse, within the context of identified high-profile incidents generating challenges for Muslim communities. The chapter will next discuss the interaction between institutionalised Islamophobia and everyday Islamophobia, which causes ordinary Australian Muslims to experience anti-Muslim hate incidents as part of their daily routines.

Portrayal of Muslims in the Australian political landscape

Prior to Australians choosing a new national government in May 2019, there were a record number of independent/minor party representatives across the national, state, and territory legislatures. Evidence shows that the Australian political cycle begins at the state level and flows through to the national level only several years later as it matures, with the public accepting greater diversity among political parties. This record reflects longer-term trends, including the rise of the Greens party, the success of moderate independents in normally safe conservative seats, and the growth of parties considered far-right such as One Nation (ON), Shooters, Fishers and Farmers Party, Rise Up Australia, and Australian Liberty Alliance. Australia has previously had periods of non-major party success: these were generally limited to the upper house of Parliament, whereas independents and minor parties are now securing seats in the lower house, where governments are formed. This means that they can exert more power to influence government policy (Earl 2019). Although competing views exist as to causes behind this shift, what is agreed is that the trend away from support for major parties is not based on their actual performance but, rather, on the life experience and motivation of voters (Roggeveen 2019). Hull (2019) opines that the most significant factors are the breakdown of life-long employment; reduced influence of family and religion; removal of bureaucratic hindrances to entrepreneurship; greater individualism; and the rise of self-centred pursuit of instant gratification, coupled with the growth of the internet. The removal of bureaucratic controls spelled doom for the major-party monopoly, widening choice. This has been aided by three long-standing elements of the Australian political system: preferential voting; proportional voting in the state; and federal upper house and public funding. The effect of these dynamics has seen the political landscape turn increasingly to the right since 9/11, especially with respect to Muslims' place in Australia. This has been spurred by the political dominance of Australia's conservative Liberal Party, which has governed for nineteen of the past twenty-five years (1996–2007, 2013–2022), as well as the ascendance of far-right parties. These far-right parties have advocated platforms strongly focused on immigration and multiculturalism, initially targeting Asians before gradually morphing into opposition to Islam and Muslims (Pauline Hanson's One Nation 2019).

This anti-Muslim/immigration stance resonates with Australia's immigration policy in earlier historical periods.

As a settler colonial project of the British Empire, Australia was constituted through the dispossession, genocide, and domination of its Indigenous population. The ideological and Christian organising frames for this colonising mission were rooted in European ideologies of race, and the global cartography of power 'hierarchies' (Abdel-Fattah 2017). On 23 December 1901 the Australian Immigration Restriction Act was enacted as law. It was among the first pieces of legislation introduced in the newly formed federal parliament. The legislation was specifically designed to limit non-British migration to Australia and represented the formal establishment of the White Australia policy. It addressed the widely held view that non-white groups were less advanced, especially morally and intellectually (National Museum of Australia n.d.). This idea focused particularly on people of Asian descent but applied to all non-whites, including Indigenous Australians, who were considered a 'dying race' (National Museum of Australia n.d.). The White Australia policy had an immediate impact, rapidly changing the country's demographics. In the early post-First World War period, migrants and refugees were expected to assimilate and blend into the population as quickly as possible. This ethnocentric approach assumed an indisputable superiority of the 'host' over the foreign cultures, which were deemed inferior (Rumbaut 1997). The government's assimilation policies were based on assumptions that new arrivals would not find this difficult (Koleth 2010). An unintended consequence of this policy was to revitalise a mindset among Australians of non-British immigrants as 'Other', particularly those of different skin colours or ethnicities. The projections of Australia as a white nation have similarly contributed to variant forms of Islamophobia (Hage 2012). At the same time, it became obvious that British migration and strict adherence to the White Australia policy was an impediment to population growth. Australia's first Department of Immigration was established in 1945 to manage the post-Second World War immigration of migrants and displaced persons. By the 1960s and 1970s, the focus on 'assimilation' had progressed to 'integration'. The concept of 'multiculturalism' was consolidated during the 1980s, in recognition of the challenges facing migrants in settling into Australian society (Koleth 2010). This was accompanied by acceptance that new arrivals might wish to retain their cultural identity. An end to the White Australia policy was announced with the introduction of policies like the Racial Discrimination Act in 1975 (National Museum of Australia n.d.).

Since its inception, multiculturalism has been a contested policy and concept. While its roots lie in responses to post-settlement issues facing migrants, through the 1980s and 1990s the policy was articulated more broadly as an element of Australia's nation-building narratives. Leading up to 2010, multiculturalism was subjected to criticism in public and political debate, with expressions of support for earlier policies of assimilation and integration. Over the same period, public and political debate about multiculturalism was significantly impacted by international events. Chief among these have been concerns regarding the threat of terrorism and the challenges of achieving social cohesion in societies characterised by ethno-cultural diversity (National Museum of Australia n.d.). The commitment from Australia to supporting the War on Terror resulted in increased concerns about the threat of terrorism. Although the term 'terrorism' has been problematised as 'a political weapon designed to protect the strong' (Said and Hitchens 2001: 13), this chapter uses this term deliberately to showcase how varying levels of anti-Muslim hate are legitimised and normalised in the War on Terror era. Existing tensions towards Islam and Muslims increased post 9/11, and were accentuated and inflamed through political rhetoric and policy, as well as media and public commentary. The focus on multiculturalism diminished and a broader and more targeted focus on 'Australian values' and what it meant to 'be Australian' grew. This commentary was in respect to 'foreigners' and asylum seekers, being heavily instigated by politicians but amplified by media (Poynting and Briskman 2010).

Prior to 9/11, evidence existed of elements of the political establishment being anti-immigration, with a particular bias toward Asian immigrants. In the 1998 Queensland state election, ON received almost 25 per cent of the votes, and almost one in ten votes in the federal election that followed shortly after. The phenomenon of ON represents the first time in post-war Australian politics that race and immigration became electoral issues (Gibson, McAllister, Swenson 2002). While public protests and political criticism followed Hanson's maiden parliamentary speech – 'we are in danger of being swamped by Asians' – it was internal issues that derailed the party rather than their policies (Baker 2019). Analysis has subsequently linked ON's performance to the consequences of global competition for regional Australia and the resultant major job losses and withdrawal of many services (Gibson, McAllister, Swenson 2002); this economic discontent saw voter defection from major parties to ON, reinforcing the earlier discussion of voters' 'wants' influencing voting patterns (Hull 2019). In August 2001, the reaction towards the arrival of the ship *MV Tampa* carrying 439 Afghan asylum seekers into Australian waters illustrated a hardening of Australian government attitudes towards asylum seekers and immigration. The proposed introduction of retrospective legislation making it lawful to 'turn-around' refugee boats prior to entering Australia waters was under debate when 9/11 occurred. The eventual 'Pacific Solution' increased the government's ability to implement harsher border protection policies (Mathew 2002).

This also witnessed the commencement of rhetoric from mainstream political parties in respect of 'Others', with Prime Minister John Howard stating repeatedly that 'we decide who comes in and under what circumstances', while at the same time reiterating Australia's generous track record of accepting refugees (Kleist 2013). Political speeches and commentary from Australian politicians in the years following 9/11 positioned Muslims as a national security threat, 'different' and separate from other, mainstream Australians. In 2006, then-Deputy Prime Minister Costello heavily singled out Muslims, proclaiming:

> Before entering a mosque, visitors are asked to take off their shoes. This is a sign of respect. If you have a strong objection to walking in your socks don't enter the mosque. Before becoming an Australian you will be asked to subscribe to certain values. If you have strong objections to those values don't come to Australia. (Costello 2006)

The same year, Prime Minister Howard asserted that elements of the Australian Islamic community held extremist views and 'it is not a problem that we have ever faced with other immigrant communities who become easily absorbed by Australia's mainstream' (Cole 2017). The self-appointed white guardians of the land simply cleared themselves from any shortcomings (including extremism) by projecting their fears arising from European supremacist white-settler colonialism onto Muslims through Islamophobia (Poynting 2020).

The introduction of Tony Abbott as Prime Minister in late 2013 generated a deliberate effort to be less critical of Islam and Muslims when addressing concerns regarding terrorism; however, this still impacted on the Australian Islamic community. Research of Abbott's rhetoric in the lead-up to Australia committing to the coalition opposing the Islamic State in Syria (ISIS) shows consistent categorisation of ISIS as a 'death cult', and discussion of the threats to Australia and the world. These threats manifested in late 2014 through several events: first, Australian and State counter-terrorism police and intelligence personnel conducted the largest ever counter-terrorism raids in Sydney and Brisbane, breaking up an alleged ring intending to behead Australians on Australian territory – on ISIS's instructions; second, a young Muslim man, Nouman Ali Haider, was shot dead after attacking two police officers outside a police station – he was to be questioned regarding his relationship with ISIS. Following these events, the majority of Australia's Muslims became objects of media and public scrutiny, a frequently occurring pattern since 9/11 (Lentini 2015). These events provide examples of overseas events impacting on Australia and its Muslim communities – how politicians respond in speeches and public discourse influences the public's perceptions of Muslims within their communities.

In demonising ISIS, Abbott deliberately made distinctions between ISIS members and the majority of Muslims, including Australian Muslims. In so doing, he affirmed Muslims' status within the framework of Australian citizenship. This seemed to be a deliberate departure from previous administrations. However, Abbott rarely mentioned Muslims outside references to terrorism, vicariously linking Islam and Muslims in Australia to terrorism (Lentini 2015). This was further accentuated in February 2015, when he attracted wide criticism for his statement suggesting that the Islamic community did not do enough to stamp out extremism (Medhora and Safi 2015). These statements received significant coverage and support from mainstream media (Sky News Australia 2016). Abbott's blaming of the Muslim community discloses the official psyche categorising Muslims as allies and enemies (i.e. the good Muslims saving the nation from the bad Muslims). Yet officials constantly expressed their disappointment with the lack of ideal Muslims by seeing the Muslim community as part of the problem with 'a supposed violent and criminogenic culture' and blaming them for not 'controlling their young men' (Poynting 2017: 23). ON leader Pauline Hanson, re-elected to the Senate in 2016, wore a burqa into Parliament and queried whether the government would work with her to 'ban the burqa in Australia considering there have been 13 foiled national threats against us with terrorism' (Murphy 2017). ON had also promoted a ban on Muslim immigration and sought a royal commission into Islam. In his maiden speech Senator Fraser Anning (Katter's Australia Party) called for a 'final solution' and implementation of a ban on Muslim immigration (Maters 2018). This terminology, describing the Nazi regime's genocidal policy of exterminating Jewish people, was widely criticised due to its association with the Holocaust.

Since 9/11, increased political and media scrutiny of Islam has seen Islamic religious practices, rituals, clothing, and customs frequently treated with suspicion and hostility. Areas targeted are sharia law, wearing of burqas and face veils, and halal certification. As in other Western countries, concerns about sharia law and compatibility with Western democracy have been raised. The predominant concern is that sharia law will infiltrate Australian domestic law and all Muslims will seek a separate legal system. Senator George Christensen warned of a 'slow spread of a Sharia-style dispensation of justice which is quietly executed in Australian mosques on a daily basis' (Cole 2017: 46). Former Senator Jacqui Lambie, from her self-founded Jacqui Lambie Network Party, claimed that people who follow sharia law are 'maniacs and depraved humans' and anyone 'supporting' sharia should leave the country (Jennet 2014). She has also been vocal about the wearing of the burqa, stating that followers of Islam would continue committing 'cold blooded butchery and rapes until every woman in Australia wears a burqa and is subservient to men' (Jennet 2014). Political debates frequently cited burqas as a symbol of radicalism, with politicians stating that, rather than demonstrating pride of religious identity, they are symbolic of an uncivilised culture and female oppression. Australian women have been targeted in relation to wearing of burqas, niqabs, and other Islamic face veils (Cole 2017). Ironically enough, while everyone is obliged to wear a face mask due to COVID in 2021, lacking a face mask increased the tensions and distrust between communities, providing further fuel for exclusivist propaganda and polarisation. Similar to linking burqas with national security concerns, some politicians have suggested that halal certification is used as an enterprise to fund terrorist groups. A Senate inquiry into third-party food certification established that fraudulent conduct in terms of potential money-scamming practices existed; however, no evidence existed to support the assertion that halal certification processes funded so-called 'terrorist organisations'.

Following 9/11, the threat of terrorism was elevated to the highest level in Australia. The budgets, resources, and legislative mechanisms that law enforcement, security, and intelligence agencies were given to work with dramatically increased. The budget for the Australian Security Intelligence Ogranisation increased by 655 per cent, while the budget for the Australian Federal Police was increased by 161 per cent (Dobell 2011). The Australian government rapidly developed and enacted a multitude of hard-line counter-terrorism policies, enabling large-scale expansion of police, security, and intelligence powers. Scholars, when critically assessing the impact of the Australian government's counter-terrorism policies, raised several prominent concerns: the proportionality of Australia's hard-line response compared to the risk of a so-called terrorist attack and the speed with which hard-line policies have been enacted into Australian law. The most-featured concern, however, has been the impact of counter-terrorism policies on Muslim Australian citizens. According to Safi and Evershed's study, close to 75 per cent of 800 surveyed Muslims believe they are unfairly targeted by anti-terror laws, of which sixty-four separate pieces were issued from 9/11 until 2015. The War on Terror has legitimised the securitisation of Muslims under the guise of prevention and countering violent extremism, and thereby triggered in the community the sense of being 'under siege' (Safi and Evershed 2015).

This section of the chapter has critically analysed the portrayal of Islam and Muslims in Australia's political discourse, focusing predominantly on rhetoric since 9/11. Islam and Muslims have in many cases been perceived as 'suspect communities' because of this discourse and fear. Government policies aimed at reducing this fear have in fact heightened it, particularly for Muslims. The chapter turns now to examine the Australian media and its promotion of Islamophobic tropes and discourses.

Media and Islamophobia in Australia

The media is quite influential in distorting images of Islam and Muslims in the West (Ogan et al. 2014; Cesari 2011; Gardner et al. 2008). This applies to Australian media, where Muslims are mostly portrayed as the enemy within and conflated with terrorism (Ewart et al. 2017; Dreher 2007; Rane and Hersi, 2012). The media also introduce Islam and Muslims to the public as different, strange, threatening, and inferior (Poynting and Noble 2003). Furthermore, the media plays an important role in amplifying anti-Muslim sentiments which are publicly articulated and endorsed by political figures ranging from Australian prime ministers to small, far-right parties.

The Australian media provides a fertile ground for anti-Muslim racism in Australia. The industry is dominated by News Corp and Nine (65 per cent of circulation). The right-wing content produced by News Corp is often endorsed by white nationalist Facebook groups, some of which were visited by the Christchurch mass murderer (Bridge Initiative Team 2019). The biased representation of Islam and Muslims cannot be effectively altered, since the differing voices and views in the media are continually shrinking with the closure of small and middle-scale alternative media outlets, due to the economic recession, especially after COVID-19 (ATN 2021).

The Australian media's marginalising of Muslims can be explained through *categorisation, decontextualisation,* and the *process of Othering* (Poole, 2016). Firstly, Islam and Muslims are categorised in relation to 'terrorism', 'extremism', militancy, Islamism, and jihadism. Secondly, Islamic belief and Muslimness are decontextualised by linking them to acts of terrorism without providing any historical, political, and/or theological context. This has caused perception of Islam as a motivating element to commit violence. Thirdly, the *process of Othering* is fulfilled by stereotyping Islam and Muslims as dangerous entities who deserve eviction from the collective national entity (Ghauri and Umber 2019; Colic-Peisker et al. 2016).

The *categorisation* phase has a long history in Australian media. Since 9/11, media representations can be distinctively divided into two phases: pre- and post-9/11 portrayal of Muslims. While Muslims were previously illustrated as asylum seekers and youth gangs who were incompatible with 'Australian values', since 9/11 Muslims have been portrayed as terrorists or supporters of terrorism who deserve suspicion and scrutiny (Poynting and Briskman 2018).

The topic of terrorism by nature served the priorities of the sensational media. While the media sought shocking news for wider readership and always headlined terrorism-related news, terrorists used this handy tool practically for self-branding, introducing their fringe ideas, and conveying their fearful messages to the public (Matthews 2017). This mutually pragmatic approach made the terrorism subject in the media larger than it deserved to be. A dominant terrorism theme relating to al Qaeda and ISIS has constantly been in the media for decades, not only over-extending the reality of terrorism but also instilling the public with unnecessary fear, anxiety, and sense of insecurity. Use of the words 'extremist', 'fundamentalist', and 'terrorist' increased by a factor of ten in the *Daily Telegraph* and six in the *Herald* after 9/11 (Manning 2004; Rane and Hersi 2012).

The *decontextualisation* phase is tacitly achieved in the media. The lack of clear differentiation between terrorism criminals and innocent ordinary Muslims directed a heightened tension of 'terrorism' towards everyday Muslims. Media implicitly targeted all Muslims by associating Islam with violence and 'terrorism'. This meant that every Muslim to some degree was dangerous and prone to violence and terrorism if they followed Islam as a religion. This brazen association put all Muslims under suspicion within the safe boundaries of freedom of speech, which seemingly attacked Islam rather than Muslims. Another tacit strategy for *decontextualisation* was utilising the timing of major attacks and events. When tension was heightened due to terrorism, the censor of deep-seated anti-Muslim hatred was removed by the media, the audience dulled into receiving any accusation without doubting the hateful content. Some headlines from mainstream Australian media in critical times heightened hatred towards all Muslims. Headlines such as 'Denial of Islamic fundamentalism puts us in danger' (Bolt 2014), 'Why does Islam beget violence?' (Bolt 2014a), both following the Martin Place siege in 2014; and the 'Islam must change' headline, giving voice to MP Andrew Hastie, who called for an 'honest debate' on the links between Islamic teachings and 'terrorism' (Herald Sun 2015) at the time of the Paris attacks in 2015, where a group of young Muslim men engaged in a series of coordinated suicide bombings at the behest of ISIS. All these headlines reinforced public opinion that there is fault with Islam and every single follower of Islam.

The *process of Othering* was effectively conducted by linking local Muslims to media portrayals of Muslims as dangerous. In the aftermath of the Paris attacks, when Mufti Ibrahim, a prominent Muslim religious figure in Australia, brought to light some of the push and pull factors, i.e. racism and Islamo-phobia, that could lead to radicalism and militancy, the mainstream politicians and media outlets condemned the mufti for tacitly supporting terrorism and not blaming it. In fact, immediately after the attacks, Mufti Ibrahim publicly condemned them via his Facebook account. The *Daily Telegraph* placed images of the mufti on the cover page, portraying the three 'unwise' monkeys (Christensen 2016) ridiculing him as the 'unwise Mufti' who 'sees no problem', 'hears no concerns', and 'speaks no English' (O'Brien 2015). Prime Minister Tony Abbott further distorted the reputation of respected community leaders and imams by accusing them of appearing apologetic without meaning it (Medhora and Safi 2015). Labelling the Muslim community's respected leaders as hypocrites and hidden supporters of terrorism, both the prime minister and the media further shook the image of everyday Australian Muslims in the public psyche. According to Matthews' (2017) media analysis, negative portrayals of Muslims in Australian media increased by 81per cent following the Paris attacks.

Distortion of Muslims' image by the media in the local context by *categorising*, *decontextualising*, and *Otherising* increased following the declaration of a so-called Islamic State by the terrorist network ISIS in 2014. Australian media triggered anxiety toward the threat of home-grown terrorism by extensively circulating pictures of several Australian-born young men under the ISIS banner. This was followed by police raids in Sydney, Brisbane, and Melbourne by more than 600 police officers. This heightened tension regarding home-grown terrorism, hand in hand with the media as images of hundreds of police officers with dogs storming into houses in three different cities were streamed on Australian news channels, while the visuals were also widely circulated in the media and on social media. These raids claimed to be foiling a plot to commit violent acts in Australia, including a plan to behead a member of the public (ABC 2014). The raids seemingly served to justify the government's countering violent extremism agenda, while increasing moral panic about supposed home-grown terrorism from the Muslim community in Australia.

Around the same time, newspapers peaked in fabricating speculation and false news about home-grown terrorism, placing the entire Australian Muslim community under suspicion. Media coverage of Nouman Ali Haider, shot dead after stabbing two counter-terrorism police officers, was found highly problematic by Katherine Murphy, deputy political editor of the *Guardian*. Murphy published an editorial questioning what agenda Australian media served. While detailing failings of media coverage in the Haider case, Murphy challenged journalists to not abuse their power but to be accountable for it. According to Murphy, the real consequences of irresponsible journalism were reaped by real people:

> How we choose to frame and tell the story has real consequences for real people – for neighbours living alongside neighbours, for the police and intelligence agencies working around the clock to keep communities safe, and for the politicians who must lead at this moment and make critical decisions about community interest and national interest. (Murphy 2014)

Murphy confirmed the media's leading role in shaping anti-Muslim political and public opinion, which drastically impacted on everyday Australian Muslims. Like the Haider case, the December 2014 Lindt café siege in

Sydney by an ill gunman with domestic issues, and the shooting of a police employee in Parramatta by a minor, were quickly labelled acts of terrorism in relation to ISIS without substantiation, while the media further amplified speculation in their coverage.

Apart from introducing terrorism and home-grown terrorism in relation to Islam and Muslims, the media provided ample coverage of far-right groups' accusations and hate speeches against Muslims. According to Latham and Briskman (2017), far-right groups' anti-mosque and anti-halal campaigns and rallies across Australia in 2014–15 gained 'social currency' and 'legitimacy' by those in high office questioning Muslims' trustworthiness, portraying them as outsiders and associating them with terrorism. Receiving wide coverage without any criticism by the media, far-right groups' opposition to mosques and halal food established grounds in the public discourse to associate Islam with 'terrorism', as if mosques were incubators for terrorism and halal food certification a means for funding it. The coverage of Muslim religious institutions and ritual practices in this way reinforced the perception of ordinary Muslims as 'terror suspects'. Accordingly, the role of far-right groups and their anti-Muslim protests were setting subtle normative boundaries about the place of Muslims in Australia (Peucker and Smith 2019). Contamination of the public psyche in relation to Muslims was reflected in the 2016 elections in Australia, with four senators from anti-Muslim Pauline Hanson's ON entering the Parliament. The same year, 2016, was also the triumphant year of Donald Trump being elected as the president of the US.

Under these global and local socio-political conditions, negative portrayal of Muslims in the Australian media has been disproportionately high and hostile. In 2017, media monitoring of five newspapers owned by Murdoch's company News Ltd. found that almost 3,000 articles referred to Islam and/ or Muslims in relation to violence, extremism, terrorism, or radicalism. (One Path Network 2017). As a minority community consisting of just 2.6 per cent of the Australian population, Muslims were over-represented in the media by in excess of eight articles per day and 152 front pages throughout the year in the Murdoch press (One Path Network 2017). Likewise, All Together Now's (ATN) latest analysis of 724 race-related newspaper opinion pieces and television current affairs segments in 2018–20 disclosed that anti-Muslim racism is the most popular racism trend (78 per cent) in the media (ATN 2021). No matter what year and what the sampling size was, ATN's media monitoring reports since 2016 consistently found that Muslims were the most targeted minority community, Muslim women's stigmatisation was the highest in the media (ATN 2019), and being Muslim was repeatedly conflated with 'terrorism' in the Australian media (ATN 2017; ATN 2019; ATN 2020; ATN 2021). The page design of newspapers, selected imagery, and front-page coverage also reinforced the negative portrayal of Muslims by the media (Kabir 2019). Muslims have been depicted by the selected imagery either as outsiders or as an enemy within (Karim 2006; Aly 2007).

The interaction between institutional and interpersonal Islamophobia

The first two sections of this chapter have illustrated how the spread of anti-Muslim sentiments has been orchestrated collaboratively by mainstream and far-right politicians as well as the media and digital media in Australia. This section will discuss the impact of this organisational anti-Muslim racism on the Muslim citizens of Australia.

Institutionally conducted and circulated stigmatisation of Muslims contributes to the increase of everyday anti-Muslim racism. Ewart and Rane (2013) mentioned anecdotal links between negative news media stories and harassment of Muslims in Australia. The symbiotic relationship between international violence or militancy in the name of Islam or at the hands of Muslims and the increase of everyday anti-Muslim racism can be traced in reports analysing Islamophobic hate crimes and incidents in the US (Bridge Initiative Team 2018), UK (Feldman and Littler 2015), and Australia (Iner et al. 2017).

This relationship is captured quite clearly in Australia by tracking the spike time of Islamophobic incidents reported to the Islamophobia Register Australia (Iner et al. 2017). The Register was founded in late 2014, due to a desire to systematically collect and record the increasing anecdotal cases of Islamophobia in the aftermath of massive police raids in Sydney and Brisbane in September 2014. Within the first eleven days, the Register received thirty-three reports of anti-Muslim attacks (five of these occurred in August, at the time of ISIS beheadings, but were reported in September once a reporting platform became available). Thirty-three incident reports in the last eleven days of September coincided with a terror suspect being shot to death by police in Melbourne on 23 September, two days after which the National Security Legislation Amendments Bill (No. 1) was passed by Parliament. Within the same month, the Counter-Terrorism Legislation Amendment (Foreign Fighters) Bill was introduced by George Brandis, attorney-general for Australia. September ended with more police raids in Melbourne (Iner et al. 2017). Further spikes in reported cases were observed during the Lindt Café siege. The Register received the second-largest number of incident reports of 2015 in April, after the Australian teen Jake Bilardi's alleged suicide bombing in Iraq and the media release of a full list of Australian foreign fighters with ISIS in Syria and Iraq. The incident reports were above the annual average again in November 2015, after the Paris attacks, followed by a targeted smear campaign against the grand mufti of Australia. The tension was further heightened by the media release of Attorney-General George Brandis informing the public about a new national terrorism threat advisory system, which was designed to inform the public about the likelihood of an act of terrorism in Australia (Iner et al. 2017). Apart from the heightened tension about terrorism and its media coverage, far-right activism (i.e. nationwide anti-halal and anti-mosque rallies and online campaigns), especially in the last three months of 2015, significantly increased the threat rhetoric of Islamophobic perpetrators. The most popular death threats uttered during this period were killing Muslims by beheading and by halal slaughtering, which was used fifty-three times by perpetrators (Iner et al. 2017).

The *categorisation, decontexualisation*, and *Othering* processes were so effectively orchestrated to portray Muslims as 'terrorists' and criminals that militant groups and individuals fearlessly attacked Muslims at times of overseas terrorism. This level of hate starts with fury and develops further as contempt, dehumanising, disgust, and wanting to kill/harm (Willem and Pligt 2016). This hierarchy of hate illustrates how wanting to harm can be justified without feeling guilt, due to prior preliminary feelings such as dehumanising and disgust. Utilising the blurred lines between 'terrorists' and ordinary Muslims, far-right provocateurs incited violence against the Muslim community by suggesting to massacre, mass murder, as well as to shoot every single Muslim and burn them alive (Iner et al. 2017; Iner et al. 2019). The intensity of hate was also present at the affective level. For instance, according to *Islamophobia in Australia Report-II*, dehumanising came as the second most common feeling or sentiment towards Muslims (19 per cent), followed by disgust (10 per cent), and wanting to harm/kill (9 per cent) (Iner et al. 2019).

Some consistency in the biennial reports of Islamophobia by Iner et al. (2019), whose findings received significant public attention, disclose strong patterns of Islamophobia that are not independent of the socio-politically constructed dangerous Muslim image in the everyday public rhetoric. The two reports confirm that Islamophobia in Australia is part of an everyday routine both for perpetrators and for victims of Islamophobia. According to the analysis of the reported 202 physical cases, Muslims were attacked in commonly frequented places (52 per cent), with shopping centres being the most popular (25 per cent) among all harassment hotspots. Likewise, 60 per cent of cases occurred in guarded and patrolled areas. Although more than half the cases (65 per cent) entailed hate speech, one-quarter consisted of vandalism and physical attacks (Iner et al. 2019).

According to the reports, neither bystanders nor security systems (and guards), for the most part, deterred perpetrators from attacking Muslims publicly. This was apparently due to the inaction and silence of individuals in the face of public harassment of Muslims. Of the 202 physical cases, almost half of the victims mentioned the presence of passers-by. Yet only 14 per cent paid attention to what was happening and within this 14 per cent, only one in three supported the victim against the perpetrator (Iner et al. 2019). Two-thirds of the bystanders withdrawing their support apparently prioritised their own security, and thereby gave perpetrators implicit permission to brazenly hate and publicly attack Muslims. It is possible that passers-by refrained from interfering for reasons of their own safety. Yet the lack of effort to alert security guards or other members of the public after the fact indicates the public's apathy and indifference towards Australian Muslims' safety, as less than half (41 per cent) of the physical cases were later reported to the Register by the bystanders (Iner et al. 2019).

Muslims were not safe even among racialised communities. Although most of the perpetrators in physical cases were white (79 per cent), close to half of the reported physical cases (44 per cent) happened in multiculturally diverse suburbs (Iner et al. 2019). This high percentage indicates two things: silence and inaction by racialised communities, and an exceptional multiculturalism on the part of the white majority, who welcome all minorities except Muslims. This exceptional multiculturalism is captured in the annually conducted Scanlon Foundation Social Cohesion reports. The reports disclose the climbing anti-Muslim racism in contrast to diminishing racism against other minorities (Markus 2018). This result is not independent of consistent and concerted efforts to detach Muslims from Australian national identity and its multicultural legacy, which is agreeable to some members of other racialised communities.

Although conflation of Muslims with terrorism is commonly practised in politics and the media, the harassment language at the time of attacks discloses that the real driver for Islamophobic harassment is Muslims' visibility (45 per cent), rather than terrorism (9 per cent) or associating Muslims with violence (3 per cent) (Iner et al. 2019). This has two implications: terrorism in the public discourse is used as an excuse to demonise Muslims; and Muslimness in the eyes of the perpetrator is perceived synonymously with terrorism (Bakali 2019). Muslim visibility, being the key driver of hate, has seen Muslim women bear the brunt of Islamophobia. Of the women who were attacked (72 per cent of victims), 96 per cent were wearing a hijab. The report findings illustrate the best target profile as unaccompanied hijab-wearing women or mothers who wore the hijab while with their children on their everyday routines like shopping or travelling (Iner et al. 2017; Iner et al. 2019). Neither their profile nor their activities indicate any signs of or affiliations with terrorism. The terrorism debates in politics and media coverage of visual Muslim signifiers, like Pauline Hanson's burqa stunt in Parliament and the frequently used trope of oppressed Muslim women, made the most vulnerable members of the community easy targets for brazen perpetrators. Disappointment was the most common reaction of victims (40 per cent), followed by pretending to ignore the perpetrator (36 per cent). This did not mean acceptance, which was the least-expressed sentiment (7 per cent), but a coping mechanism when left alone and defenceless in public (Iner et al. 2017). This state of mind results in long-term consequences among some victims, such as being unable to leave home alone or to take public transport, sleep difficulty, and hypervigilance (Iner et al. 2017). Apart from the targeted individuals, many from the Muslim community feel the burden of Islamophobia daily, due to the interplay of political, media, and everyday anti-Muslim racism.

Of the 800 participants in a survey conducted by Safi and Evershed (2015) on Australian Muslims' experiences with racism and discrimination, more than two-thirds felt unfairly treated by Australian media, and nearly half expressed the need to regulate their behaviour by changing their manner of dress, outlook, and avoiding certain mosques and certain routes to their workplace. The distress of Australian Muslims about normalised anti-Muslim sentiment has only increased over the course of time. A survey in 2020 among 1,034 Australian Muslims found that media reporting of Islam and Muslims is their top concern (95.6 per cent), followed by discrimination against Muslims (95 per cent), anti-Islam sentiments (94 per cent), and terrorism by right-wing extremists (93.1 per cent). One participant described the impact of anti-Muslim stigmatisation in everyday life as 'slowly making it very hard to survive at work, on the street or anywhere we go' (Rane et al. 2020: 13). Close to one quarter of the participants also felt restricted in practising their religion (Rane et al. 2020).

Conclusion

Australia's historical roots as a settler colonial offshoot of Britain laid the foundation of racialisation in Australia. While overlooking the issues of Indigenous sovereignty, Australian multiculturalism could not escape from the influence of a half-century's White Australian policy (1909–58). White nationalist subjects in Australia have accepted some minorities while rejecting others. The criminalisation of Arabs (especially Lebanese youth) smoothly evolved into profiling Middle Eastern-looking Muslim suspects and criminals in the aftermath of 9/11. Since then, an exceptionalism in multiculturalism has been in force that portrays Muslims as a problem and denies inclusion of Muslims as part of the national entity. This denial is manifested as everyday racism, mostly directed at Muslim women who cover, as well as the systematic discrimination disabling Muslims' socio-economic upward mobility despite their being a highly educated young community (Hassan 2015).

Islamophobia surges as an overt criticism in the political and public discourse. When continuously recycled by political figures ranging from prime ministers to small far-right parties, Islamophobia has a strong impact. When reproduced and extensively circulated by the mainstream media, Islamophobia has widespread repercussions. When conflated with terrorism, especially in times of heightened tension due to violent terrorist attacks, Islamophobia has detrimental effects ranging from inciting online hate, such as the mass killings of Muslims, to executing these actions in real life, as seen in the case of the Christchurch attacks in New Zealand, which left fifty-one dead and forty injured.

Furthermore, the infusion of Islamophobia into the public psyche by the machinery of politics and media has a ripple effect. A spike in ordinary Muslims' harassment is always expected at times of terrorist attacks and polemics about Muslims. There is mass confusion in society about Muslims because of the constant 'enemy within' messaging in media, political, and public discourse. Silence and inaction are the common public response at the time of anti-Muslim harassment and violence. This is interpreted by attackers as permission to hate and harass brazenly. It would appear that an exceptional multiculturalism expelling Muslims from the national imaginary is in force, in tandem with the normalising of anti-Muslim political and media discourse. Nevertheless, a growing public attention to the alarming findings of Islamophobia in Australia is promising and indicates a goodwill from the public to change this trend.

Bibliography

Abdel-Fattah, R. (2017). *Islamophobia and everyday multiculturalism in Australia*, Abingdon: Routledge.

ABC (2014). Anti-terror operation in Sydney and Brisbane 'thwarted' beheading plot, 18 September 18, www.abc.net.au/news/2014–09–18/anti-terror-police-mount-large-scale-raids-in-sydney-brisbane/5752002?nw=0 (accessed 20 June 2021).

ATN (All Together Now) (2017). *Who watches the media: race-related reporting in Australian media*, Sydney: All Together Now, 1–6.

ATN (2019). *Social commentary and racism in 2019*, Sydney: All Together Now.

ATN (2020). *Social commentary, racism and Covid 19*, Sydney: All Together Now.

(ATN) (2021). *Politely racist*, Sydney: All Together Now.

Aly, A. (2007). Australian Muslim responses to the discourse on terrorism in the Australian popular media, *Australian Journal of Social Issues*, 42(1): 27–40.

Bakali, N. (2019). Challenging terrorism as a form of 'otherness': exploring the parallels between far-right and Muslim religious extremism, *Islamophobia Studies Journal*, 5(1): 99–115, doi:10.13169/islastudj.5.1.0099.

Baker, N. (2019). Please explain: the history of Pauline Hanson's One Nation party, SBS News, 30 April, www.sbs.com.au/news/please-explain-the-history-of-pauline-hanson-s-one-nation-party (accessed 25 June 2021).

Barker, R. (2016). Rebutting the ban the burqa rhetoric: a critical analysis of the arguments for a ban of the Islamic face veil in Australia, *Adelaide Law Review*, 37(1): 191–218.

Belot, H. (2016). Labor MP Anne Aly and family receive death threats after Peter Dutton comments, ABC News, 23 November, www.abc.net.au/news/2016–11–23/anne-aly-and-family-receive-death-threats/8050496 (accessed 15 May 2021).

Bleich, E (2011). What is Islamophobia and how much is there? Theorizing and measuring an emerging comparative concept, *American Behavioral Scientist*, 55(12): 1581–600, https://doi:10.1177/0002764211409387.

Bolt, A. (2014). Denial of Islamic fundamentalism puts us in danger, *Herald Sun*, 16 December, www.heraldsun.com.au/news/opinion/andrew-bolt/denial-of-islamic-fundamentalism-puts-us-in-danger/news-story/778a55be1e3800354e61123827340f1d (accessed 5 June 2021).

Bolt, A. (2014a). Why does Islam beget violence? *Courier Mail*, 16 December, www.couriermail.com.au/news/opinion/opinion-why-does-islam-beget-violence/news-story/74edc53c8857d9df85065ccbad195a0e (accessed 10 June 2021).

Bridge Initiative Team (2016). When Islamophobia turns violent: the 2016 US presidential elections, Bridge, 29 November, http://bridge.georgetown.edu/when-Islamophobia-turns-violent-the-2016-u-s-presidential-elections/ (accessed 29 May 2021).

Bridge Initiative Team (2018). Factsheet: Erasing Muslims from the 'West': Islamophobic campaigns across Europe and the US, *The Bridge Initiative* https://bridge.georgetown.edu/research/erasing-muslims-from-the-west%c2%9d-islamophobic-campaigns-across-europe-and-the-us/ (accessed 11 April 2022).

Bridge Initiative Team (2019). Factsheet: The Murdochs and News Corp Australia, 19 November, *The Bridge Initiative*, https://bridge.georgetown.edu/research/factsheet-the-murdochs-and-news-corp-australia/ (accessed 11 April 2022).

Cesari, J. (2011). Islamophobia in the West: a comparison between Europe and the United States. In: J.L. Esposito and I. Kalin (eds), *Islamophobia: The challenge of pluralism in the 21st century*, New York: Oxford University Press, 21–43.

Christensen, N. (2016). Grand mufti sues Daily Telegraph over depiction of him as the three 'unwise' monkeys, *Mumbrella*, 24 April, https://mumbrella.com.au/grand-mufti-sues-daily-telegraph-over-depiction-of-him-as-the-three-unwise-monkeys-362092 (accessed 1 June 2021).

Cole, G. (2017). The systemic marginalisation of Muslim Australian voices: to what extent can Deliberative Democratic theory provide a response? Doctoral dissertation, University of Melbourne, https://minervaaccess.unimelb.edu.au/bitstream/handle/11343/197481/Gcole%20PhD%20thesis%20Systemic%20marginalisation%20of%20Muslim%20voices.pdf?isAllowed=y&sequence=1 (accessed 10 May 2021).

Colic-Peisker, V., Mikola, M., and Dekker, K. (2016). A multicultural nation and its (Muslim) other? Political leadership and media reporting in the wake of the 'Sydney siege', *Journal of Intercultural Studies*, 37(4): 373–89.

Conifer, D. (2016). Prime Minister praises Peter Dutton as 'outstanding Immigration Minister' amid comments about Lebanese community, ABC News, 22 November, www.abc.net.au/news/2016–11–22/turnbull-praises-dutton-amid-comments-about-lebanese-community/8047038 (accessed 8 May 2021).

Costello, Peter (2006). Worth promoting, worth defending: Australian citizenship, What it means and how to nurture it. Address to the Sydney Institute, Sydney, 23 February, www.petercostello.com.au/speeches/2006/2111-worth-promoting-worth-defending-australian-citizenship-what-it-means-and-how-to-nurture-it-address-to-the-sydney-institute-sydney (accessed 6 May 2021).

Dobell, G. (2011). Canberra's 9/11 decade: bureaucracy, *The Interpreter*, https://archive.lowyinstitute.org/the-interpreter/canberra-911-decade-bureaucracy (accessed 10 May 2021).

Dreher, T. (2007). News media responsibilities in reporting on terrorism. In: A. Lynch, E. McDonald, and G. Williams (eds), *Law and liberty in the war on terror*, Annandale, NSW: Federation Press, 211–20.

Earl, G. (2019). Charting 50 years of turning tides in Australian politics, *The Interpreter*, www.lowyinstitute.org/the-interpreter/charting-50-years-turning-tides-australian-politics (accessed 10 June 2021).

Ewart, J. and Rane, H. (2013). Talking about 9/11: the influence of media images on Australian Muslims' and non-Muslims' recollections of 9/11, *Australian Journal of Communication*, 40(1): 137–51.

Ewart, J., Cherney, A., and Murphy, K. (2017). News media coverage of Islam and Muslims in Australia: an opinion survey among Australian Muslims, *Journal of Muslim Minority Affairs*, 37(2): 147–63.

Feldman, M. and Littler, M. (2015). *Tell MAMA Reporting 2014/2015: Annual monitoring, cumulative extremism, and policy implications*, Middlesbrough: Teesside University, www.tellmamauk.org/wp-content/uploads/pdf/Tell%20MAMA%20Reporting%202014–2015.pdf (accessed 18 May 2021).

Gardner, R., Karakaşoğglus, Y., and Luchtenberg, S. (2008). Islamophobia in the media: a response from multicultural education, *Intercultural Education*, 19(2): 119–36.

Ghauri, M.J. and Umber, S. (2019). Exploring the nature of representation of Islam and Muslims in the Australian press, *SAGE Open*, 9(4): 1–9.

Gibson, R., McAllister, I., and Swenson, T. (2002). The politics of race and immigration in Australia: One Nation voting in the 1998 election, *Ethnic & Racial Studies*, 25(5): 823–44, doi: 10.1080/0141987022000000286.

Hage, G. (2012). *White nation: fantasies of white supremacy in a multicultural society*, London: Routledge.

Hassan, R. (2015). *Australian Muslims: a demographic, social and economic profile of Muslims in Australia 2015*, www.unisa.edu.au/siteassets/episerver-6-files/global/eass/mnm/publications/australian_muslims_report_2015.pdf (accessed 16 July 2020).

Herald Sun (2015). Islam must change, 30 November, www.heraldsun.com.au/subscribe/news/1/?sourceCode=HSWEB_WRE170_a_GGL&dest=https%3A%2F%2Fwww.heraldsun.com.au%2Fnews%2Fvictoria%2Fislam-must-change-war-hero-mp-andrew-hastie-leads-radical-push%2Fnews-story%2F039933aae6375358724ad7c63f4ee9e7&memtype=anonymous&mode=premium (accessed 11 May 2021).

Hull, C. (2019). Voters aren't coming to the party because they're in it for themselves, *Canberra Times*, 30 March, www.canberratimes.com.au/story/6005323/voters-arent-coming-to-the-party-because-theyre-in-it-for-themselves/ (accessed 16 June 2021).

Iner, D. et al. (2017). *Islamophobia in Australia Report-I (2014–2015)*, Sydney: Charles Sturt University, 37–85, https://cdn.csu.edu.au/__data/assets/pdf_file/0009/2811960/Islamophobia-In-Australia-Report.pdf (accessed 16 June 2021).

Iner, D. et al. (2019). *Islamophobia in Australia Report-II (2016–2017)*, Sydney: Charles Sturt University, 1–184, https://cdn.csu.edu.au/__data/assets/pdf_file/0008/3338081/Islamophobia-Report-2019-Low-RES24-November.pdf (accessed 23 June 2021).

Jakubowicz, A. (2016). Once upon a time in … ethnocratic Australia: migration, refugees, diversity and contested discourses of inclusion and exclusion, *Cosmopolitan Civil Societies: An Interdisciplinary Journal*, 8(3): 144–67, https://search-informit-org.ezproxy.csu.edu.au/doi/10.3316/informit.891027129327059 (accessed 22 June 2021).

Jennet, G. (2014). Jacqui Lambie says sharia supporters are maniacs who will rape and murder until every woman in Australia wears a burqa, *ABC News*, 22 September, www.abc.net.au/news/2014–09–22/jacqui-lambie-renews-attack-on-sharia-law/5761342 (accessed 22 June 2021).

Kabir, N. (2019). Can Islamophobia in the media serve Islamic State propaganda? The Australian case, 2014–2015. In: D. Iner and J.L. Esposito (eds), *Islamophobia and radicalization: breeding intolerance and violence*, London: Palgrave Macmillan, 97–116.

Karim, H.K. (2006). American media's coverage of Muslims: the historical roots of contemporary portrayals. In: E. Poole and J.E. Richardson (eds), *Muslims and the news media*, London: I.B. Tauris, 116–27.

Kleist, J.O. (2013). Remembering for refugees in Australia: political memories and concepts of democracy in refugee advocacy post-Tampa, *Journal of Intercultural Studies*, 34(6): 665–83, doi: 10.1080/07256868.2012.746172.

Koleth, E. (2010). *Multiculturalism: a review of Australian policy statements and recent debates in Australia and overseas* (Research Paper no. 6), Parliament of Australia, www.aph.gov.au/About_Parliament/Parliamentary_Departments/Parliamentary_Library/pubs/rp/rp1011/11rp06#_Toc275248118 (accessed 12 May 2021).

Latham, S. and Briskman, L. (2017). Political Islamophobia. In: D. Iner (ed.), *Islamophobia in Australia Report-I (2014–2016)*, Sydney: Charles Sturt University, 16–20.

Lentini, P. (2015). Demonizing ISIL and defending Muslims: Australian Muslim citizenship and Tony Abbott's 'death cult' rhetoric, *Islam and Christian–Muslim Relations*, 26(2): 237–52, doi: 10.1080/09596410.2015.1007605.

Manning, P.C. (2004). Dog whistle politics and journalism: reporting Arabic and Muslim people in Sydney newspapers. *Australian Centre for Independent Journalism*, UTS, 1–48.

Markus, A. (2018). *Mapping social cohesion: the Scanlon Foundation surveys 2018*. Scanlon Foundation, Melbourne: Monash University, 1–86, www.monash.edu/__data/assets/pdf_file/0009/1585269/mapping-social-cohesion-national-report-2018.pdf (accessed 18 May 2021).

Maters, A. (2018). Fraser Anning's 'final solution' speech points to a more dangerous threat to Australia. *ABC News – Opinion*, 15 August, www.abc.net.au/news/2018-08-15/fraser-anning-final-solution-more-dangerous-threat/10123350 (accessed 4 April 2022).

Mathew, P. (2002). Australian refugee protection in the wake of the Tampa, *The American Journal of International Law*, 96(3): 661–76.

Matthews, Z. (2017). The media and Islamophobia in Australia. In: D. Iner (ed.), *Islamophobia in Australia Report-I (2014–2016)*, Sydney: Charles Sturt University, 28–33.

Medhora, S. and Safi, M. (2015). Muslim leaders outraged by Tony Abbott's chiding over extremism, *The Guardian*, 23 February, www.theguardian.com/australia-news/2015/feb/23/muslim-leaders-outraged-by-tony-abbotts-admonishment-over-extremism (accessed 2 June 2021).

Morgan, G. and Poynting, S. (2012). Introduction: the transnational folk devil. In: G. Morgan and S. Poynting (eds), *Global Islamophobia: Muslims and moral panic in the West*, Farnham: Ashgate, 1–14.

Murphy, K. (2014). The acid test: Australian journalists must ask what agenda they serve, *The Guardian*, 26 September, www.theguardian.com/world/2014/sep/26/the-acid-test-australian-journalists-must-ask-what-agenda-they-serve (accessed 11 June 2021).

Murphy, K. (2017). Pauline Hanson wears a burqa in Australian Senate while calling for ban, *The Guardian*, 17 August, www.theguardian.com/australia-news/2017/aug/17/pauline-hanson-wears-burqa-in-australian-senate-while-calling-for-ban (accessed 22 July 2021).

National Museum of Australia (n.d.). *White Australia policy*, www.nma.gov.au/defining-moments/resources/white-australia-policy (accessed 14 July 2021).

O'Brien, N. (2015). Paris attacks: Grand Mufti of Australia Dr Ibrahim Abu Mohammed issues clarifying statement condemning terrorism, *Sydney Morning Herald*, 18 November, www.smh.com.au/national/nsw/paris-attacks-grand-mufti-of-australia-dr-ibrahim-abu-mohammed-issues-clarifying-statement-condemning-terrorism-20151118-gl1r36.html (accessed 13 July 2021).

Ogan, C., Willnat, L., Pennington, R., and Bashir, M. (2014). The rise of anti-Muslim prejudice: media and Islamophobia in Europe and the United States, *International Communication Gazette*, 76(1): 27–46.

One Path Network (2017). *Islam in the media 2017*, https://onepathnetwork.com/islam-in-the-media-2017/ (accessed 22 May 2021).

Pauline Hanson's One Nation Party (2019). 'Our Pledge to Western Australia', Facebook, 27 April, www.facebook.com/OneNationParty/photos/2134598953284342 (accessed 11 May 2021).

Peucker, M. and Smith, D. (eds) (2019). *The far-right in contemporary Australia*, Singapore: Springer.

Poole, E. (2016). The United Kingdom's reporting of Islam and Muslims: reviewing the field. In: S. Mertens and H. de Smaele (eds), *Representations of Islam in the News: A Cross-cultural Analysis*, Lanham, MD: Lexington Books, 21–36.

Poynting, S. (2017). The Islamophobic crimes of the past and present. In: D. Iner (ed.), *Islamophobia in Australia 2014–2016*, Sydney: Centre for Islamic Studies and Civilisation, Charles Sturt University.

Poynting, S. (2020). 'Islamophobia kills'. But where does it come from? *International Journal for Crime, Justice and Social Democracy*, 9(2): 74–87.

Poynting, S. and Briskman, L. (2018). 'Islamophobia in Australia: from far-right deplorables to respectable liberals', *Social Sciences*, 7(11): 213–30, doi: 10.3390/socsci7110213.

Poynting, S. and Noble, G. (2003). 'Dog-whistle' journalism and Muslim Australians since 2001, *Media International Australia*, 109(1): 41–9.

Rane, H. and Hersi, A. (2012). Meanings of integration in the Australian press coverage of Muslims: implications for social inclusion and exclusion, *Media International Australia*, 142(1): 135–47.

Rane, H. et al. (2020). Islam in Australia: a national survey of Muslim Australian citizens and permanent residents, *Religions*, 11(8): 1–39.

Roggeveen, S. (2019). Our very own Brexit: response to reviewers, *The Interpreter*, www.lowyinstitute.org/the-interpreter/our-very-own-brexit-response-reviewers (accessed 5 May 2021).

Rumbaut, R.G. (1997). Paradoxes (and orthodoxies) of assimilation, *Sociological Perspectives*, 40(3): 483–511.

Safi, M. and Evershed, N. (2015). Three-quarters of Muslim Australians feel they are unfairly targeted by terror laws, study reveals, *The Guardian*, 16 March, www.theguardian.com/world/2015/mar/16/three-quarters-of-muslim-australians-feel-they-are-unfairly-targeted-by-terror-laws-study-reveals (accessed 13 June 2021).

Said, E.W. and Hitchens, C. (eds) (2001). *Blaming the victims: spurious scholarship and the Palestinian question*, New York: Verso.

Sian, K., Law, I., and Sayyid, S. (2012). The media and Muslims in the UK, *Consultado*, 15: 229–71.

Sky News Australia (2016). Politicians must acknowledge that culture counts – it must be a factor when deciding who we let into Australia, *The Bolt Report*, Facebook, 17 November, www.facebook.com/watch/?v=343440509347418 (accessed 23 July 2021).

Willem, K. and Pligt, J. (2016). *The psychology of radicalization and terrorism*, Abingdon: Routledge.

Chapter 3

The mainstreaming of Islamophobia in United States politics

Todd H. Green

Introduction

By most metrics, Islamophobia in the United States (US) has been on the rise since the al Qaeda attacks of 11 September 2001. In partisan politics and public policy, at the individual and systemic levels, Muslims and those perceived as Muslim have been singled out for exclusion, discrimination, and violence in unprecedented ways in modern US history (Mogahed and Mahmood 2019). A common assumption in public discourse and in the mainstream media is that white conservative Americans in general, and the Republican Party in particular, have a monopoly on Islamophobia. This assumption makes sense on the surface. The Republican Party's platform has depended overtly on anti-Muslim messaging, and most of the egregious anti-Muslim rhetoric and policies since 9/11 have emanated from prominent Republicans.

But it is a mistake to assume that the Republican Party has cornered the market on Islamophobia. It has festered in both major political parties. The mainstreaming of Islamophobia reflects a climate in which support for US imperialism, along with anxiety about whether or how Muslim Americans belong in the cultural and political landscape, resonates across the ideological spectrum, resulting in support both for aggressive military incursions in Muslim-majority regions and for domestic policies that treat Muslims as national security threats. It also reflects the continuation of the historic racialisation of Muslims that has functioned as an extension of the US settler colonial project dating back centuries.

This chapter analyses four key episodes or events since 9/11 that have fuelled the mainstreaming of Islamophobia in US politics: the War on Terror, the 'Ground Zero Mosque' controversy in New York City, the Muslim ban, and Ilhan Omar's election to Congress and the pushback she has received for criticising US–Israel relations. Each episode will be discussed in terms of how it has contributed to the entrenchment of Islamophobia in US politics, along with how representatives from both major parties participated in or responded to each episode in a way that further racialised and 'Otherised' Muslims. Attention will be given to how political conservatives and liberals articulated or promoted Islamophobia in different ways in the post-9/11 era, with the former relying more on traditional Orientalist narratives that presuppose an incompatibility between Islam/Muslims and the US, and the latter expressing confidence that 'good Muslims' – i.e., supposedly moderate or patriotic Muslims who accept US imperialism and cooperate with the national security apparatus – are compatible with the nation's ideals and values. Attention will also be given to what political conservatives and liberals held in common in some of these episodes, most notably broad support for select policies that targeted Muslim lives and civil liberties and that sustained US global dominance at the expense of Muslim populations.

The War on Terror

The US government's response to the 9/11 attacks was to embark on the War on Terror, a global project that involved military invasions of Afghanistan and Iraq but also contained legal, political, and intelligence dimensions on both foreign and domestic fronts. The War on Terror constitutes the horizon upon which all the anti-Muslim episodes discussed in this chapter take place.

The War on Terror also represents the continuation of a US imperialist project seeking political and military hegemony in the Middle East that dates back to the Cold War. The 9/11 attacks themselves reflected ongoing resistance to US imperialism and interventionism in the Middle East from militant Islamist movements that arose in the late twentieth century.

The Bush administration never owned up to its imperialist motives for fighting the War on Terror. What it did instead was justify the war by relying on three Islamophobic tropes, all rooted in a 'clash of civilisations' framework made popular by the likes of Bernard Lewis and Samuel Huntington. The first was that Islam itself was prone to violence and terrorism. Despite initially claiming that '[t]he face of terrorism is not the true faith of Islam' and that 'Islam is about peace', President Bush invoked rhetoric that tied Islam to violence. Not only did he label the war a 'crusade', a term that conjures up images of barbaric Muslims battling heroic Christians, he also relied on phrases such as 'Islamic radicalism' and 'Islamic extremists' to portray the threat posed by militancy (Green 2019: 129–30).

The second trope was that democracy and Islam were incompatible. The initial messaging from the Bush administration was optimistic. Bush assured the neoconservative American Enterprise Institute in 2003 that Iraq was 'fully capable of moving toward democracy and living in freedom' (*The Guardian* 2003). But as popular support in the US and among allies began dwindling after 2005, Bush and his surrogates cast Islam and democracy in opposition to one another. Bush insisted the nation was 'at war with Islamic fascists' and invoked the language of 'Islamo-fascism' to describe the enemy Israel faced in its conflict with Lebanon (Green 2019: 139–40; Huus and Curry 2006).

The third trope was the need to liberate oppressed Muslim women. The trope was used already in making the case for the war in Afghanistan in 2001. At the signing ceremony for the Afghan Women and Children Relief Act, Bush indicated that the Taliban and the terrorists 'were a waking nightmare for Afghan women and their children'. After elaborating on some of the ways Afghan women were oppressed, including prohibitions on laughing loudly and riding bicycles, Bush insisted that liberating Afghan women was essential (The White House 2001a). Just one month earlier, First Lady Laura Bush made a similar argument, with an explicit connection between US military intervention and women's liberation: 'Because of our recent military gains in much of Afghanistan, women are no longer imprisoned in their homes. They can listen to music and teach their daughters without fear of punishment ... The fight against terrorism is also a fight for the rights and dignity of women' (The White House 2001b).

While the Bush administration and its neoconservative operatives were the architects of Islamophobic tropes that justified military incursions into Afghanistan and Iraq, the war effort received significant assistance from Democrats. Democratic congressional representatives gave almost unanimous support for the invasion of Afghanistan. Only one Democrat, and indeed only one member of Congress, voted against the 2001 Authorisation for the Use of Military Force (GovTrack.us 2001). More Democrats opposed the resolution for the Iraq war the following year, in part because the Bush administration's case for war was based on unsubstantiated claims, including that Saddam Hussein was hiding weapons of mass destruction and that he had links to al Qaeda. Even so, approximately 40 per cent of Democrats in the House of Representatives and 58 per cent of Democrats in the Senate voted for the resolution (Clerk.house.gov 2002; Senate.gov 2002). Three out of four future Democratic presidential nominees – Senators John Kerry, Hillary Clinton, and Joe Biden – supported the resolution.

Although not a member of Congress at the time of these votes, the other Democratic presidential nominee in the post-9/11 era, Barack Obama, invested heavily in the War on Terror once he became president in 2008.

This included deploying some 30,000 additional troops to Afghanistan, expanding the war into Pakistan, and ordering over 500 drone strikes that led to upwards of 807 civilian deaths in countries such as Pakistan, Somalia, and Yemen, a number that does not include active battlefields at the time, such as Afghanistan (Perkins and Serle 2017; Kazi 2019: 78; Kumar 2012: 133). Obama, in line with the Democratic establishment, was just as invested in projecting US power over Muslim-majority regions as his Republican counterparts (Kundnani 2015: 6).

In the face of bipartisan support for the War on Terror, Muslims abroad and at home became victims of policies and practices that took aim at their lives and civil liberties. The most significant impact came with the death toll and displacements. According to the Costs of War Project at Brown University, 335,000 civilians have been killed by the various parties involved since the War on Terror began, while 21 million people from Afghanistan, Iraq, Pakistan, and Syria have become war refugees or have found themselves internally displaced (Costs of War Project 2021).

Civil liberties and human rights for Muslim citizens and residents of the US were also casualties of the US-led war effort. The USA PATRIOT Act, passed by Congress in 2001 and applied overwhelmingly to Muslim Americans, expanded the US government's power to employ surveillance and wiretapping without demonstrating probable cause, allowed for secret searches with minimal oversight, and authorised the detention of immigrants based on alleged suspicions of support for terrorism (Cainkar 2009: 123; Kazi 2019: 26). The National Security Entry-Exit Registration System, or NSEERS, was implemented in 2002. It required men aged sixteen to sixty-four from twenty-three Muslim-majority countries, along with Eritrea (which has a significant Muslim population) and North Korea, to register with the US government and to be fingerprinted, interviewed, and photographed. In the first year of the system's implementation, close to 100,000 individuals were registered at their point of entry, while just over 83,000 people already in the US were registered (Department of Homeland Security 2003). Deportation orders were issued to thousands of Muslim and Arab residents as a result of NSEERS (Cainkar 2009: 128; Kundnani 2015: 64).

The government arrested and detained Muslims and Arabs under the guise of national security, often without providing detainees with access to a lawyer or allowing them to talk with their families. In many cases, detainees were never formally charged with supporting or engaging in terrorism. Some of those arrested became subject to extraordinary rendition, or the process of transferring individuals from US custody to countries or locales where they were tortured. The Central Intelligence Agency created secret 'black sites', or unlawful detention centres, to facilitate the torture of terrorist suspects in order to bypass legal obstacles as spelled out in international law and the

United Nations Convention against Torture (Amnesty International 2008). The torture of Muslim detainees also took place in US military prisons such as Abu Ghraib and Guantánamo Bay. The US government, through the US Senate Intelligence Committee, finally admitted in 2014 to employing torture, including waterboarding, ice-water 'baths', mock executions, forced rectal feeding, and sleep and sensory deprivation (Green 2019: 293–4).

Other post-9/11 policies targeting Muslims involved law enforcement surveillance and profiling and 'soft' counter-terrorism efforts known as Countering Violent Extremism (CVE) initiatives. Examples of the former include the Federal Bureau of Investigation's (FBI) use of informants and agents provocateurs to infiltrate Muslim communities and entice law-abiding individuals to participate in a terrorist plot where one did not previously exist, and the New York Police Department's extensive efforts to map, monitor, and spy on Muslim communities and organisations in the New York City metropolitan area (Green 2019: 280–5; Kundnani 2015: 136–7). CVE funnelled money and resources into local communities in an effort to prevent the radicalisation of (mostly) Muslims. The idea was for federal agencies to enlist the help of houses of worship, law enforcement officials, religious leaders, and local schools in identifying which Muslims might be on a path toward terrorism, presumably due to suspect behaviour such as a deepening commitment to Islam or strong opposition to US foreign policy (Love 2017: 110–11; Kundnani and Hayes, 2018: 4–10; The White House 2011).

These policies created a climate in which Muslims 'at home' became symbolic stand-ins for the Muslim enemy abroad. Such a climate fuelled the rise of hate crimes targeting Muslims and those perceived as Muslim. The FBI recorded a 1600 per cent increase in anti-Muslim hate crimes in 2001. While these numbers decreased in 2002, they never dropped back to pre-9/11 levels in all the years after 2001. During presidential election years, anti-Muslim hate crimes often surged, including in 2015 and 2016, when they rose 67 per cent and 20 per cent, respectively, against the backdrop of Republican candidates calling for Muslim ID cards, Muslim registration systems, and a ban on Muslims entering the country (Green 2019: 297–8).

The 9/11 attacks and the War on Terror did not mark the beginning of anti-Muslim hostility and discrimination. As Tazeen M. Ali argues, Islamophobia 'is rooted in anti-Blackness and has been an American reality since the country's inception' (Ali, 2021). From slaves in the colonial context to the Ahmadiyya and Nation of Islam in the twentieth century, Black Muslims in particular have historically been targeted with surveillance, discrimination, erasure, and violence.

What the War on Terror did was to build on this historical trajectory and to pave the way for policies and practices that led to the mainstreaming of Islamophobia in the US political system. This mainstreaming can be seen in two ways. First, the broader US population offered little resistance to the initial war effort or to the curbing of Muslim civil liberties. In the fall of 2001, 80 per cent of Americans supported military action in Afghanistan, while 72 per cent of Americans approved of the invasion of Iraq in March 2003 (Moore, 2001; Newport, 2003). Another poll from 2003 indicated that 74 per cent of Americans believed the Bush administration had not gone too far in curbing civil liberties with the PATRIOT Act and other anti-terrorism provisions (Moore 2003). While support for military action waned in the years that followed, a majority of Americans continued to endorse renewing measures such as the PATRIOT Act (Agiesta 2015).

The second way these policies and practices point to the mainstreaming of Islamophobia pertains to the support they received across the political spectrum. While most of the policies described here were generated by the Republican Party, in part because this was the party that held control of the White House and both chambers of Congress in the immediate aftermath of 9/11, Democrats endorsed many of these policies. A majority of Democrats in both chambers voted for the original PATRIOT Act, while many Democrats joined with Republicans over the years to renew the Act (Kazi 2019: 26). Democrats also gave their support to NSEERs, which was only officially dismantled at the end of the Obama administration in 2016, and to CVE, which was a programme largely developed during the Obama presidency. The Democratic Party, far from keeping Islamophobia in check during the so-called War on Terror, consistently collaborated with Republicans to ensure that the securitising and stigmatising of Muslim populations became a permanent fixture in post-9/11 America.

The 'Ground Zero Mosque' controversy

Although the Republican Party during the Bush presidency developed a number of anti-Muslim policies under the guise of national security, Bush himself occasionally gave nods to the importance of including Muslims and demonstrating respect for Islam. Not only did Bush insist that Islam was a religion of peace, he expressed his conviction that Christians and Muslims worshipped the same God, and praised Muslims for their contributions to American business, education, and industry (Georgewbush-whitehouse. archives.gov n.d.). Such praise and rhetorical niceties faded quickly during the Obama administration in the midst of a controversy in the summer of 2010 surrounding efforts to build an Islamic centre just blocks away from where the World Trade Center towers once stood in Lower Manhattan.

The fight over the so-called 'Ground Zero Mosque', as the planned centre was dubbed by its most extreme opponents, dominated the news cycle for months and ultimately shaped Republican anti-Islam messaging in the 2011–12 election cycle. The Republican Party employed more overt language during the controversy, which painted Muslims as outsiders and antithetical to American identity.

Elements of this strategy were already underway during the 2007–8 elections as some Republican operatives accused Barack Obama, a practising Christian and a Democratic presidential candidate, of being a Muslim. False claims about Obama's Muslim identity were meant to cast doubt on his commitment to and belonging in the US and to pit his presumed Muslim identity against an authentic American identity. The strategy reflected a civilisational discourse that intensified and expanded with the 'Ground Zero Mosque' controversy.

Efforts to build the Islamic centre initially took place outside the media and political spotlight. Investors purchased a vacant property already in July 2009. Among the investors was the Cordoba Initiative, a nonprofit organisation dedicated to interfaith outreach. The idea was to create a Muslim version of a multi-purpose facility comparable to a YMCA (Young Men's Christian Association) or a Jewish Community Centre. Imam Faisal Abdul Rauf of the Cordoba Initiative, whose credentials as a 'moderate Muslim' made him a sought-out figure in various interfaith and government circles, became one of the public voices behind the project (Corbett 2017). He indicated that the centre would 'send the opposite statement to what happened on 9/11' by cultivating tolerance and goodwill between and among diverse Americans (Elfenbein 2021: 38).

The proposed centre, more formally known as the Park51 project, received little attention or pushback until an anti-Muslim blogger named Pamela Geller cried foul on her blog *Atlas Shrugs*. In a blog post in May 2010 titled 'Monster Mosque Pushes Ahead in Shadow of World Trade Center Islamic Death and Destruction', Geller argued that the centre was an insult to Americans, an effort by Muslims to mark their territory in battle. She tied the centre to the 'Islamic jihad' and 'Islamic supremacism' that produced the 9/11 attacks. Geller also teamed up with another anti-Muslim blogger, Robert Spencer, to create Stop Islamization of America and to organise a public rally against the centre. At a 6 June rally, Geller and Spencer compared their resistance to the centre and Islamic supremacism to the American fight against Nazism (Green, 2019: 210–11).

Their efforts to frame the centre as anti-American and a symbol of Islamic dominion generated widespread media coverage and created opportunities for politicians to engage in moral posturing. Republicans took advantage of the controversy to tout not only their patriotic credentials but, in some cases, their presidential ones too. Republican presidential candidate Newt Gingrich argued that building an Islamic centre near Ground Zero was akin to 'putting a Nazi sign next to the Holocaust Museum' (Wyatt 2010). Other Republican candidates fed off the anti-Muslim energy generated by the controversy. Fellow Republican contender Herman Cain stated that as president he would not feel comfortable appointing a Muslim American to his cabinet or as a federal judge, citing efforts by Muslims to engage in a 'creeping attempt … to gradually ease Sharia Law, and the Muslim faith into our government' as the reason (Keyes 2011).

Republican posturing over the Park51 controversy also took the form of highly publicised congressional hearings over the radicalisation of Muslim Americans in 2011. Led by Representative Peter King of New York, who felt the proposed centre was 'very offensive' and who had claimed for years that 80 to 85 per cent of American mosques were controlled by radical imams, these hearings singled out Muslims as particularly prone to extremism. While prominent Democrats, including the first Muslim ever elected to Congress, Keith Ellison, opposed the hearings, the Park51 controversy provided a wider opening for Republicans to present their party as strong in the face of the 'Muslim threat' to the nation (Cury 2021: 64–5).

Republican-led efforts to curtail Muslim civil liberties materialised at the local and state levels in the wake of the Park51 controversy. From California to Wisconsin to Tennessee, opposition to the building of mosques became widespread. This anti-mosque fervour led *Time* to pose the question 'Is America Islamophobic?' on its cover in August 2010. The arguments against mosques were similar to those levelled against the Park51 project, namely that mosques represent a religion bent on domination and conquest and are therefore undeserving of constitutional guarantees for freedom of religion. As Lou Ann Zelenik, a Republican candidate for Congress, indicated in her opposition to the building of a mosque in Tennessee in 2012: 'Islam does not claim to be a religion, but a social and political system that intends to dominate every facet of our lives' (Green 2019: 317).

The Park51 controversy also served as the backdrop to Republican efforts in state legislatures to push anti-sharia legislation. Oklahoma became the first state to attempt to ban sharia law in state courts, in late 2010. That year witnessed some fourteen anti-sharia bills proposed in state legislatures, a number that jumped to fifty-six in the following year and over a hundred between 2012 and 2015 (Elfenbein 2021: 43–4). While most of the bills did not pass, and while constitutional challenges forced conservative legislators to reword the bills to exclude overt references to sharia, the effort was still notable for providing Republicans with high-profile opportunities to promote a message of Islam's incompatibility with American values.

For their part, Democrats struggled to coalesce against the Islamophobic messaging adopted by Republicans. Some prominent Democrats sought to defend freedom of religion for Muslims. President Obama insisted that 'Muslims have the same right to practice their religion as everyone else in this country', and that includes building a house of worship and a community centre in New York City. Obama soon qualified his statement by indicating that he supported the *principle* of Muslims building the centre but did not want to weigh in on the *wisdom* of them doing so (Elfenbein 2021: 38). Many other high-profile Democrats, including Senate majority leader Harry Reid, argued that the proposed centre should be relocated out of sensitivity to the victims of 9/11. While some Democrats were more outspoken in their support, they could not overturn the political consensus that tied Muslims and Islam as a whole to the 9/11 attacks and that saw in the Park51 centre the symbol of extremism and anti-Americanism. This political consensus was mirrored in the broader population. In an August 2010 poll in *Time*, almost half of respondents – 44 per cent – believed the Park51 project was an insult to the victims of 9/11, while 61 per cent were opposed to building the centre. Polls one month later saw opposition to the centre rising to 70 per cent (Elfenbein 2021: 40–1).

The 'Ground Zero Mosque' controversy furthered the mainstreaming of Islamophobia in several important ways. First, the controversy gave birth to what scholars variously refer to as the 'Islamophobia industry' and 'professional Islamophobia' (Green 2019: 205–36; Lean 2017). Extreme anti-Muslim bloggers, pundits, and pseudo-scholars found a more mainstream platform for their views both in the media and in the Republican Party (Bail 2014). Their warnings about a violent, totalitarian religion trying to take over America through stealthy means ultimately went on to shape the messages of Republican presidential candidates and the Republican platform. Second, Islam and Muslims became more overtly singled out for hostility and exclusion in presidential politics, as seen in the messaging by 2012 Republican presidential candidates, along with the hearings and policies promoted by other Republicans. After 9/11, President Bush, at least outwardly, tried to promote a message of respect and inclusion for Muslims. In the aftermath of the Park51 controversy, the notion that Islam was a religion of peace, or that Christians and Muslims worship the same God, was far removed from mainstream Republican discourse. Finally, the controversy pointed to the embedding of an implicit Islamophobia among many Democrats. Those Democrats who opposed building the centre operated within a racialised framework in which Muslims as a whole bore residual guilt for the actions of the 9/11 attackers, hence the decision either to remain silent on whether the centre should be built or to encourage Muslim investors to relocate the project so as not to cause offence to the victims of 9/11.

The Muslim ban

Casting Muslims as a menacing and existential threat to the nation proved popular with the Republican base in the aftermath of the Park51 controversy. This strategy intensified in the 2015–16 presidential primaries against the backdrop of ISIS- (Islamic State in Syria) inspired attacks in the US and Europe. Republican candidate Ben Carson, undoubtedly influenced by the Islamophobia industry, insisted that Muslims should be disqualified from occupying the Oval Office unless they 'reject the tenets of Islam' along with sharia (Bradner 2015). Fellow contender Ted Cruz called for law enforcement 'to patrol and secure Muslim neighborhoods before they become radicalized' (Seipel and Sanders 2016). And Donald Trump, the Republican Party's eventual nominee, flirted with suggestions for Muslim ID cards and Muslim registration systems while adopting the opposite approach to Bush's line on Islam after 9/11 by insisting that 'Islam hates us' (Green 2019: 215–16).

Trump's most egregious and contentious anti-Muslim proposal came less than a week after a December 2015 terrorist attack in San Bernardino, California which left over a dozen dead. At a campaign rally in South Carolina, Trump called for 'a total and complete shutdown of Muslims entering the United States' (Johnson 2015). Opponents labelled the proposal the 'Muslim ban', while Trump and his surrogates euphemistically branded it a 'travel ban'. The branding worked so well that many mainstream media outlets refused to characterise it as a 'Muslim ban' (Green 2018).

Reactions to the initial Muslim ban proposal were predictably critical from Democrats, but many prominent Republicans also voiced concerns. Mike Pence, a presidential candidate who would later serve as Trump's vice-president, called the ban 'offensive' and 'unconstitutional'. The Speaker of the House, Paul Ryan, argued that a religious test for entering the United States was 'not reflective of America's fundamental values' (Stein 2017). Even Cruz, whose anti-Muslim views were no secret, believed Trump's initial proposal was 'not the right solution' to the problem of insecure US borders (Clark and Douglas 2015).

Once Trump won the presidency, his administration went to work on implementing his campaign promise to ban Muslims, or some portion thereof, from entering the country. One week after his inauguration, Trump issued an executive order temporarily suspending refugee admissions and barring immigrants and non-immigrants from seven Muslim-majority countries: Iran, Iraq, Libya, Somalia, Sudan, Syria, and Yemen. Because of lawsuits and federal court rulings that blocked the enforcement of various aspects of the order, the Trump administration revised the Muslim ban two more times, tinkering with its provisions, along with the countries singled out, so that it would circumvent legal objections that the ban was driven by anti-Muslim bigotry. Along the way, various iterations of the ban would continue to face legal challenges and popular resistance in the form of airport protests (Iftikhar 2021: 73–6).

In June 2018, the US Supreme Court, dominated by Republican-appointed justices, upheld the ban. Writing for the majority, Chief Justice John Roberts reasoned that Trump's anti-Muslim statements, including the original promise for 'a total and complete shutdown of Muslims entering the country', were in no way a violation of the constitutional prohibition against an established religion as articulated in the First Amendment's Establishment Clause. Roberts argued that because Trump's executive orders framed the ban in terms of national security, and because the language of the orders did not explicitly single out Muslims by name, the ban must be deemed constitutional (Green 2018).

In a scathing dissenting opinion, Justice Sonia Sotomayor called Roberts and the other majority justices to task for ignoring the obvious intent of the ban. Any reasonable observer, she insisted, could see that Trump's initial campaign promise to ban *all* Muslims, not to mention his many other hostile statements against Islam and Muslims, left no doubt that anti-Muslim animus was driving the ban and that the ban was a clear violation of the Establishment Clause. She likened the greenlighting of the ban to the court's fateful decision in 1944 to uphold President Franklin Roosevelt's executive order allowing for the internment of Japanese Americans during the Second World War under the pretence of national security (Green 2018).

By the time of the US Supreme Court's decision, the Republican leadership had changed its tune. Cruz expressed relief that the court upheld Trump's presidential authority to protect national security. Senator Thom Tillis articulated his gratitude that the court allowed Trump to vet 'bad actors' from problematic countries. Senator majority leader Mitch McConnel, who had previously been hesitant to support the ban, was now fully on board: 'I think the [Trump] administration finally got it right, and the Supreme Court agreed with that' (Jenkins 2018).

Public polling pointed to strong backing for the ban among registered Republicans. In June 2017, a Politico/Morning Consult poll found that 84 per cent of Republicans supported prohibiting visitors from six Muslim-majority countries. Although this was a marked contrast with Democrats, the poll still found that a substantial minority of them – 41 per cent – also supported the ban (Shepard 2017). While not much polling was done after the Supreme Court decision, the ban continued to remain highly popular among the Republican base.

The ban signalled yet another hard-line shift in the Republican Party toward mainstreaming anti-Muslim racism. What initially seemed like an extreme and unpopular proposal from candidate Trump in December 2015 morphed into a policy with broad Republican support by 2017. While the policy had to be tweaked and coded in order to consolidate Republican support, the ban's unambiguous anti-Muslim origins pointed to the reality that blatant Islamophobia had become a fundamental pillar in the Republican Party's platform.

The Democratic Party's leadership never faltered in its opposition to the Muslim ban. Yet its strategy for countering the ban in the 2016 election reflected its continued propensity to mainstream 'soft Islamophobia' through proclaiming support for the 'good Muslim' in the form of the Muslim soldier or the Muslim patriot (or both). Echoing former Secretary of State Colin Powell's invocation of a dead Muslim American soldier in 2008 to counter Republican insinuations that Obama was a Muslim and therefore un-American, the Hillary Clinton campaign called upon Khizr and Ghazala Khan, parents of Captain Humayun Khan, to tell the story of their son's sacrifice in the Iraq war as a means of rejecting the proposed Muslim ban. At the Democratic National Convention (DNC) in August 2016, Khizr Khan made headlines after giving an emotional speech about his son's service in the US military and his death in Iraq. Khan took Trump to task for his proposed Muslim ban, proclaimed unyielding devotion to the US constitution, and chided Trump for sacrificing 'nothing and no one' for the nation.

The Clinton campaign's message via the Khan speech was that the Muslim ban was wrong because it would have prevented 'good Muslims' like Humayun Khan from fighting and dying in US-led wars. The message reflected what Edward Curtis calls 'the myth of the fallen Muslim soldier', or an effort to challenge anti-Muslim bigotry by crafting a new liberal myth in which Muslims are framed as patriots instead of pariahs, in exchange for their willingness to bleed and die on the battlefield for their country (Curtis 2019: 49). As Kazi argues: 'This is what is expected of Muslims who wish to be incorporated into the nation as Americans: unflappable support for the nation's project of empire.' 'Good Muslims', she adds, must 'declare their allegiance to the US military machine' or otherwise offer 'their children as tribute to the war machine' (Kazi 2019: 88, 95).

This conditional belonging for 'good Muslims' found other iterations at the DNC and in the Clinton campaign. In his DNC speech, former president Bill Clinton enthusiastically proclaimed: 'If you're a Muslim and you love America and freedom and you hate terror, stay here and help us win and make a future together' (Wang 2016). Clinton was pushing back against the Muslim ban, yet he seemed to imply that Muslim commitment to the nation and to freedom was in question. If, however, Muslims were willing to prove their patriotism, they could 'stay here' (under the assumption that they were not 'from here') and help 'us' become a better nation. In a debate with Trump just one month before the election, Hillary Clinton tied Muslim inclusion to national security, insisting that the country needs Muslims 'to be part of our eyes and ears on our front lines' in the War on Terror (Hassan 2016). Far from becoming the anti-Islamophobia party, the Democratic Party embraced a platform of provisional Muslim belonging. Muslims could be accepted as American as long as they supported or accepted government policies that stigmatised Muslim populations in the name of national security and the War on Terror.

Ilhan Omar

It might seem odd to label Ilhan Omar, the first Muslim woman of Somali heritage ever to be elected to Congress, as an 'event' that has fuelled Islamophobia in US politics. Yet her election in 2018 proved to be a watershed moment for mainstream political Islamophobia as she became both a lightning rod for intense and relentless attacks from Republicans and the antithesis of the much-desired 'good Muslim' sought by Democrats.

Omar is no stranger to controversy. Her public statements questioning US support for Israel or calling attention to human rights abuses by Israel and the US have landed her in hot water. She has been accused on promoting intolerance, anti-Americanism, and anti-Semitism for tweeting that Israel has hypnotised the world (a tweet from 2012 which she has since deleted), for raising questions about the pressure on US politicians to hold dual allegiance to Israel and the US, for claiming that Republican support for Israel is driven by campaign donations from the American Israel Public Affairs Committee (AIPAC), and for grouping the US and Israel with Hamas and the Taliban as perpetrators of 'unthinkable atrocities'. She also came under fire for characterising 9/11 as a day in which 'some people did something', a comment taken by prominent Republicans as insensitive to the American lives lost in the attacks (Keene 2021).

While Omar is not the only Muslim member of Congress to be accused of anti-Americanism and anti-Semitism – fellow Democrat Rashida Tlaib of Michigan has endured similar accusations for her outspoken support for Palestinian freedom – Omar arguably attracts the most vitriol. In some instances, Omar has walked back or apologised for statements labelled anti-Semitic by her detractors, most notably her tweet in which she suggested that Republican support for Israel was 'all about the Benjamins', a reference to a lyric in a Puff Daddy song about $100 bills that was interpreted as invoking anti-Semitic stereotypes of Jews controlling politics with money. In other instances, she has pushed back against accusations of anti-Semitism, insisting that labelling Muslims as anti-Semitic for criticising Israel is an Islamophobic trope.

Many Republicans find in Omar the presumed embodiment of an intolerant, Jew-hating Muslim and have done everything in their power to invoke this narrative as frequently as possible for political gain. This includes demands for her to be removed from the House Foreign Affairs Committee as punishment for her alleged anti-Semitic comments. It also includes singling her out and demanding out of the blue that she renounce anti-Semitism, such as when Representative Lee Zeldin publicly called upon Omar alone among all members of Congress to condemn an anti-Semitic voicemail he received (Burton 2019).

Republican efforts to cast Omar as anti-Semitic reflect a larger racialised strategy in which Omar and other progressive women of colour in Congress are rendered outsiders to America and are deemed at odds with American values. This strategy appeared to be at work when Trump called upon Omar and Tlaib, along with Alexandria Ocasio-Cortez and Ayanna Pressley, to 'go back and help fix the totally broken and crime-infested places from which they came', despite the fact that all but Omar were born in the US, while Omar herself is a naturalised citizen. This approach was also behind Trump's attacks on Omar at a campaign rally that led an animated crowd to chant 'send her back', a chant Trump seemed to encourage (Hirji 2021: 85).

Some of the Republican fearmongering over Omar has taken more extreme forms. Danielle Stella, Omar's challenger in her congressional re-election bid, suggested that Omar should be tried and hanged for treason (Hirji 2021: 85). Trump himself retweeted a video that took Omar's comments that 'some people did something' on 9/11 out of context and spliced them with images of the 9/11 attacks, all in an effort to paint Omar as sympathetic with terrorism. Omar received a barrage of death threats as a result of Trump's tweet.

For its part, the Democratic Party has struggled to push back consistently on the Islamophobia to which Omar is subjected, at times sending mixed messages. In the case of Trump's video painting Omar as sympathetic to terrorism, two Democratic senators and 2020 primary contenders, Kirsten Gillibrand and Amy Klobuchar, offered an equivocal defence of Omar. While Gillibrand called Trump's rhetoric regarding Omar 'disgusting', she also accepted the Republican interpretation of Omar's initial remarks, that she was being insensitive to 9/11 victims, and rebuked her in a tweet: 'As a Senator who represents 9/11 victims, I can't accept any minimizing of that pain.' Klobuchar chastised Trump for endangering Omar's life, but she added that it is possible to condemn Trump's video and disagree with Omar 'as I have done before' (BBC News 2019). The fact that Klobuchar took the opportunity to clarify that she does not always see eye to eye with Omar, an observation that has nothing to do with the threats upon Omar's life, reflects some of the subtler ways that Omar's Democratic colleagues try to distance themselves from her.

Democratic criticisms of Omar are not always so subtle. At the 2019 AIPAC conference, then Senate minority leader Chuck Schumer lumped Trump and Omar into the same category when it came to anti-Semitism: 'When someone looks at a neo-Nazi rally and sees some "very fine people" among its company, we must call it out. When someone suggests money drives support for Israel, we must call it out' (Ahmed 2019). Schumer's line, which drew applause, reflected a calculated effort to present the Democratic leadership as unyielding in its support of Israel and quick to police any dissent within its ranks.

When Omar listed the US and Israel along with Afghanistan, Hamas, and the Taliban as perpetrators of 'unthinkable atrocities', a group of twelve Democrats issued a joint statement suggesting that her language both 'reflects a deep-seated prejudice' and pushes 'false equivalencies [that] give cover to terrorist groups'. Omar, they insisted, should know better than to compare democracies such as Israel and the US with the likes of terrorist organisations (Sprunt 2021).

What is telling about the statement is that it completely ignores the context of Omar's original concerns as voiced in a conversation with Secretary of State Antony Blinken. Omar was not making in-depth comparisons between the governing philosophies of the nations and organisations she listed. She was asking Blinken where victims of atrocities can go for justice if the US did not want the International Criminal Court to investigate alleged war crimes committed by the likes of Israel and the US.

In light of this context, the outrage from a group of Democrats was little more than manufactured political theatre, particularly given the fact that both Trump and Obama had previously acknowledged that the US had committed torture and potentially other war crimes. Yet it was Omar who was singled out as harbouring prejudice for pointing to US and Israeli atrocities. Why? Elizabeth Bruenig offered a compelling explanation in *The Atlantic*: 'For the Democrats, who seem to believe that their midterm fortunes rest as far from the left as they can possibly tack, knocking out Omar is just a convenient electoral move, and this ridiculous controversy merely a pretext' (Bruenig 2021). What should be added is that this 'convenient electoral move' involved a strategy made popular by Republicans: the Islamophobic insinuation that one of the few Muslim members of Congress is an intolerant, unpatriotic, and terrorist-sympathising troublemaker.

The targeting of Ilhan Omar is significant in understanding the ongoing entrenchment of Islamophobia in US politics for several reasons. First, it highlights the resistance to Muslim belonging in America that has been commonplace in the Republican Party since 9/11. As one of only three Muslim members of Congress, Omar is continually attacked by Republicans as foreign, bigoted, and anti-American, with a soft spot for terrorists. This is certainly because of her Muslim identity, but it's also because she is Black. There is a long history in America of condemning and marginalising Black Muslims who challenge US imperialism and military dominance. As Sylvia Chan-Malik notes, from the time of chattel slavery to the work of freedom fighters such as Betty Shabazz, Malcolm X, and Muhammad Ali, Black Muslims have 'produced counter-narratives of being American that do not rely on, or serve to bolster, US nationalism and exceptionalism' (Chan-Malik 2019). Omar, like many Black Muslims before her, refuses to be complicit in racist and violent policies that target vulnerable populations, nor, as Kamilah Pickett and Su'ad Abdul Khabeer point out, does she accept 'the logic of white supremacy' in which Black and Black Muslim Americans are welcome at 'the proverbial table', but only if 'they don't challenge the status quo and see their seat as a gift which they should be eternally grateful for' (Pickett and Khabeer 2019).

Attacks on Omar also reflect a more concerted effort from Republicans, and at times some Democrats, to levy charges of anti-Semitism whenever prominent Muslim politicians and public figures speak out against Israeli military atrocities or dare to question US support for and military aid to Israel. Efforts to cast Omar as anti-Semitic have been almost relentless and, in the process, Omar's more substantive critiques of US policy in regard to Israel are often ignored or dismissed. This is by design. Charges of anti-Semitism tend to silence criticism of Israel and to shore up the orthodoxies in Washington that underpin US imperialism in the Middle East.

Efforts to discredit Omar also point to the Democratic Party's continued investment in the 'good Muslim' narrative. The case of Omar illustrates what happens when Muslims fail to conform to the model of a 'good Muslim' who accepts or encourages US exceptionalism and militarism. Omar runs afoul of the Democratic Party's leadership precisely on those occasions on which she challenges US imperialism or pushes the US government to do more to protect vulnerable populations from staunch allies such as Israel. She is the wrong kind of Muslim, something the Democratic Party has no qualms in reminding her of when she steps out of line.

Conclusion

Islamophobia shows no signs of receding in US politics. The trend in both major parties since 9/11 has been to rely on Islamophobic strategies and narratives either to galvanise voters or to render Muslim belonging conditional

– or both. The Republican strategy has depended on a civilisational discourse that overtly calls into question the compatibility between Islam and Muslims on the one hand and American identity and values on the other. The Democratic strategy has depended on more implicit and subtle forms of Islamophobia, mostly in the form of creating the category of 'good Muslims' whose support for US imperialism and the national security apparatus qualifies them as acceptable and praiseworthy. And while there are signs that some mainstream politicians, particularly in the Democratic Party, are starting to think more carefully about how to engage constructively and sensitively with Muslim Americans, it is difficult to imagine a robust anti-Islamophobia platform from either party as long as there is ongoing political investment in bolstering and furthering US imperial interests at the expense of Muslim populations abroad and Muslim civil liberties at home.

Bibliography

ABC News (2006). Bush on religion and God, 6 January, https://abcnews.go.com/Politics/story?id=193746&page=1 (accessed 7 July 2021).

Agiesta, J. (2015). Poll: 6 in 10 back renewal of NSA data collection, CNN, 1 June, www.cnn.com/2015/06/01/politics/poll-nsa-data-collection-cnn-orc/index.html (accessed 30 June 2021).

Ahmed, A. (2019). Schumer compares Ilhan Omar to Trump as top Democrats echo GOP's criticism at AIPAC, *Huffpost*, 26 March, www.huffpost.com/entry/schumer-aipac-ilhan-omar-democrats-israel_n_5c9a66cae4b07c88662c7df0 (accessed 1 August 2021).

Ali, T. (2021). Islamophobia, anti-Blackness, and the challenges of healing Muslim–Christian relations in the United States, *Berkley Forum*, 24 May, https://berkleycenter.georgetown.edu/responses/islamophobia-anti-blackness-and-the-challenges-of-healing-muslim-christian-relations-in-the-united-states (accessed 16 August 2021).

Amnesty International (2008). *State of denial: Europe's role in rendition and secret detention* [ebook], London: Amnesty International, www.amnesty.org/download/Documents/52000/eur010032008eng.pdf (accessed 1 July 2021).

Bail, C. (2014). *Terrified: how anti-Muslim organizations became mainstream*, Princeton, NJ: Princeton University Press.

BBC News (2019). Ilhan Omar: the 9/11 row embroiling the US congresswoman, 14 April, www.bbc.com/news/world-us-canada-47923753 (accessed 1 August 2021).

Bradner, E. (2015). Ben Carson again explains concerns with a Muslim president, CNN, 27 September, www.cnn.com/2015/09/27/politics/ben-carson-muslim-president-sharia-law/index.html (accessed 26 July 2021).

Bruenig, E. (2021). What Ilhan Omar actually said, *The Atlantic*, 14 June, www.theatlantic.com/ideas/archive/2021/06/what-ilhan-omar-actually-said/619196/ (accessed 1 August 2021).

Burton, N. (2019). The hypocrisy of Lee Zeldin's attack against Ilhan Omar, *The Forward*, 4 February, https://forward.com/opinion/418702/the-hypocrisy-of-lee-zeldins-attack-against-ilhan-omar/ (accessed 31 July 2021).

Cainkar, L. (2009). *Homeland insecurity: the Arab American and Muslim American experience after 9/11*, New York, NY: Russell Sage Foundation.

Chan-Malik, S. (2019). How Ilhan Omar symbolises the struggle of Black American Muslims, *Middle East Eye*, 6 August, www.middleeasteye.net/opinion/how-ilhan-omar-symbolises-struggle-black-american-muslims (accessed 2 August 2021).

Clark, L. and Douglas, W. (2015). Republicans unify against Trump's Muslim ban, but split over him, *Charlotte Observer*, 8 December, www.charlotteobserver.com/news/politics-government/article48706550.html (accessed 26 July 2021).

Clerk.house.gov (2002). Final vote results for Roll Call 455, 10 October, *US House of Representatives: US House of Representatives Roll Call Votes 107th Congress – 2nd Session*, https://clerk.house.gov/evs/2002/roll455.xml (accessed 1 July 2021).

Corbett, R. (2017). *Making moderate Islam: Sufism, service, and the 'Ground Zero Mosque' controversy*, Stanford, CA: Stanford University Press.

Costs of War Project (2021). Summary of findings. Costs of War, https://watson.brown.edu/costsofwar/papers/summary (accessed 1 July 2021).

Curtis, E. (2019). Blood sacrifice and the myth of the fallen Muslim soldier in US presidential elections after 9/11. In: M. Khalil (ed.), *Muslims and US politics today: a defining moment*, Boston, MA: Ilex.

Cury, E. (2021). *Claiming belonging: Muslim American advocacy in an era of Islamophobia*, Ithaca, NY: Cornell University Press.

Department of Homeland Security (2003). Changes to National Security Entry/Exit Registration System (NSEERS), Federal Register 68, no. 231.

Elfenbein, C. (2021). *Fear in our hearts: what Islamophobia tells us about America*, New York, NY: New York University Press.

Georgewbush-whitehouse.archives.gov (n.d.). Backgrounder: the President's quotes on Islam, https://georgewbush-whitehouse.archives.gov/infocus/ramadan/islam.html (accessed 7 July 2021).

GovTrack.us (2001). H J Res 64 (107th): Authorization for use of military force – House Vote #342 – 14 September 2001, www.govtrack.us/congress/votes/107-2001/h342 (accessed 1 July 2021).

Green, T. (2018). By any other name: why the 'travel ban' really is a Muslim ban, *Religion News Service*, 3 July, https://religionnews.com/2018/07/03/by-any-other-name-why-the-travel-ban-really-is-a-muslim-ban/ (accessed 26 July 2021).

Green, T. (2019). *The fear of Islam: an introduction to Islamophobia in the West*, 2nd edn, Minneapolis, MN: Fortress Press.

The Guardian (2003). Full text: George Bush's speech to the American Enterprise Institute, 27 February, www.theguardian.com/world/2003/feb/27/usa.iraq2 (accessed 1 July 2021).

Hassan, M. (2016). Muslim Americans express disappointment over 2016 debate rhetoric tying Muslims to terrorism, *NBC News*, 10 October, www.nbcnews.com/news/asian-america/muslim-americans-express-disappointment-over-debate-rhetoric-tying-muslims-terrorism-n663431 (accessed 28 July 2021).

Hirji, F. (2021). Claiming our space: Muslim women, activism, and social media, *Islamophobia Studies Journal*, 6(1): 79–92.

Huus, K. and Curry, T. (2006). The day the enemy became 'Islamic fascists', *NBC News*, 5 August, www.nbcnews.com/id/wbna14304397 (accessed 27 June 2021).

Iftikhar, A. (2021). *Fear of a Muslim planet: global Islamophobia in the new world order*, New York, NY: Skyhorse.

Jenkins, N. (2018). Republicans are thrilled with the Supreme Court's decision upholding Trump's travel ban, *Time*, 26 June, https://time.com/5322856/trump-travel-ban-republicans/ (accessed 28 July 2021).

Johnson, J. (2015). Trump calls for 'total and complete shutdown of Muslims entering the United States', *Washington Post*, 7 December, www.washingtonpost.com/news/post-politics/wp/2015/12/07/donald-trump-calls-for-total-and-complete-shutdown-of-muslims-entering-the-united-states/ (accessed 26 July 2021).

Kazi, N. (2019). *Islamophobia, race, and global politics*, Lanham, MD: Rowman & Littlefield.

Keene, H. (2021). Ilhan Omar's long history of controversial statements, *Fox News*, 12 June, www.foxnews.com/politics/ilhan-omar-controversies-anti-semitism (accessed 31 July 2021).

Keyes, S. (2011). Herman Cain tells ThinkProgress 'I will not' appoint a Muslim in my administration, *ThinkProgress*, 26 March, https://archive.thinkprogress.org/exclusive-herman-cain-tells-thinkprogress-i-will-not-appoint-a-muslim-in-my-administration-158c8bead223/ (accessed 21 July 2021).

Khalidi, R. (2004). *Resurrecting empire: Western footprints and America's perilous path in the Middle East*, Boston, MA: Beacon Press.

Kumar, D. (2012). *Islamophobia and the politics of empire*, Chicago, IL: Haymarket Books.

Kundnani, A. (2015). *The Muslims are coming! Islamophobia, extremism, and the domestic war on terror*, London: Verso.

Kundnani, A. and Hayes, B. (2018). *The globalisation of Countering Violent Extremism policies: understanding human rights, instrumentalising civil society*, Amsterdam: The Transnational Institute, www.tni.org/files/publication-downloads/the_globalisation_of_countering_violent_extremism_policies.pdf (accessed 30 June 2021).

Lean, N. (2017). *The Islamophobia industry: how the right manufactures hatred of Muslims*, London: Pluto Press.

Love, E. (2017). *Islamophobia and racism in America*, New York, NY: New York University Press.

Mercia, D. and Lee, M. (2016). How Donald Trump brought Khizr Khan to the DNC stage, CNN, 4 August, www.cnn.com/2016/08/04/politics/2016-election-khizr-khan-donald-trump-muslim-ban/index.html (accessed 26 July 2021).

Mogahed, D. and Mahmood, A. (2019). American Muslim poll 2019: predicting and preventing Islamophobia, ISPU, 1 May www.ispu.org/american-muslim-poll-2019-predicting-and-preventing-islamophobia/ (accessed 16 August 2021).

Moore, D. (2001). Eight of ten Americans support ground war in Afghanistan, Gallup, 1 November, https://news.gallup.com/poll/5029/eight-americans-support-ground-war-afghanistan.aspx (accessed 30 June 2021).

Moore, D. (2003). Public little concerned about Patriot Act, Gallup, 9 September, https://news.gallup.com/poll/9205/public-little-concerned-about-patriot-act.aspx (accessed 30 June 2021).

Newport, F. (2003). Seventy-two percent of Americans support war against Iraq, Gallup, 24 March, https://news.gallup.com/poll/8038/seventytwo-percent-americans-support-war-against-iraq.aspx (accessed 30 June 2021).

Perkins, J. and Serle, J. (2017). Obama's covert drone war in numbers: ten times more strikes than Bush, The Bureau of Investigative Journalism, 17 January, www.thebureauinvestigates.com/stories/2017–01–17/obamas-covert-drone-war-in-numbers-ten-times-more-strikes-than-bush (accessed 28 June 2021).

Pickett, K. and Khabeer, S. (2019). The long history of Black Americans being told to 'go back', Al Jazeera, 24 July, www.aljazeera.com/opinions/2019/7/24/the-long-history-of-black-americans-being-told-to-go-back (accessed 2 August 2021).

Seipel, A. and Sanders, A. (2016). Cruz: 'Empower law enforcement to patrol and secure Muslim neighborhoods, NPR, 22 March, www.npr.org/2016/03/22/471405546/u-s-officials-and-politicians-react-to-brussels-attacks (accessed 26 July 2021).

Senate.gov (2002). On the Joint Resolution (H.J. Res. 114), United States Senate: Roll Call Vote 107th Congress – 2nd Session, www.senate.gov/legislative/LIS/roll_call_lists/roll_call_vote_cfm.cfm?congress=107&session=2&vote=00237 (accessed 28 June 2021).

Shepard, S. (2017). Majority of voters back Trump travel ban, *POLITICO*, 5 July, www.politico.com/story/2017/07/05/trump-travel-ban-poll-voters-240215 (accessed 28 July 2021).

Sprunt, B. (2021). Omar is forced to clarify after Democrats say she equated US, Israel with terrorists, NPR, 10 June, www.npr.org/2021/06/10/1005227610/omar-is-forced-to-clarify-after-democrats-say-she-equated-u-s-israel-with-terror (accessed 1 August 2021).

Stein, J. (2017). Top Republicans denounced Trump's Muslim ban on the trail. Now they support his executive order. Vox, 28 January, www.vox.com/2017/1/28/14424758/ryan-pence-ban (accessed 26 July 2021).

Wang, F. (2016). Muslim Americans react to Bill Clinton's Tuesday night speech, NBC News, 28 July, www.nbcnews.com/news/asian-america/muslim-americans-react-bill-clinton-s-tuesday-night-speech-n618886 (accessed 28 July 2021).

The White House (2001a). President signs Afghan Women and Children's Relief Act, 12 December, https://georgewbush-whitehouse.archives.gov/news/releases/2001/12/20011212–9.html (accessed 27 June 2021).

The White House (2001b). Radio address by Mrs. Bush, 17 November, https://georgewbush-whitehouse.archives.gov/news/releases/2001/11/20011117.html (accessed 27 June 2021).

The White House (2011). Empowering local partners to prevent violent extremism in the United States, https://obamawhitehouse.archives.gov/sites/default/files/empowering_local_partners.pdf (accessed 30 June 2021).

Wyatt, E. (2010). 3 Republicans criticize Obama's endorsement of mosque, *New York Times*, 15 August, www.nytimes.com/2010/08/15/us/politics/15reaction.html (accessed 21 July 2021).

Part II

Islamophobia in former imperial states

Chapter 4

Islamophobia in the Netherlands: constructing mythologies surrounding reverse colonisation and Islamisation through politics and protest movements

Leyla Yıldırım

Introduction

> O Lord, thou hast wrought all these blessings causally through the interference of this kingdom. Therefore, we beg you to repay that interference by lavishing H.M. the Exalted Queen with all salvation; giving her long life and health, with splendid prestige and riches and with all the good that the earth contains, for Her Kingdom. (Kaptein 1998)

This prayer is a supplication or *dua* of salvation written by the well-known Islamic scholar, Sayyid Uthman (1822–1914) from Batavia, and was distributed in lithographed form throughout occupied Java and Madura, present-day Indonesia, to be read in mosques. It was written in honour of Queen Wilhelmina's inauguration as queen of the Netherlands when she became an adult. Such a *dua* was used to express political loyalty. In some cases, the mention or omission of a specific ruler would convey political affiliations. For instance, in the colonial era, when the Ottoman sultan was mentioned, implying pan-Islamism,[1] it would also infer an anti-colonial stance. Indeed, as expected, this religious leader met with protests from the Muslim community in occupied Indonesia, since the *dua* gave a very positive impression of the colonial rulers. The reason behind Sayyid Uthman's action was that he represented the traditional Islamic state philosophy, which assumed that any form of government was better than anarchy. More importantly, when the local ruler demanded fealty from him, he dared not refuse because he did not want to risk his beneficial relationship and personal interests with the colonial ruler (Kaptein 1998). This case illustrates how complicated the relationship between the Dutch state and

Islam has been since the colonial period, which lasted from 1798 until 1949 (Burgers 2010). On the one hand, the Dutch would distance themselves from the religion of Islam on secular grounds, but on the other hand, they would interfere and meddle with the faith leaders for reasons of political expediency.

In this chapter such examples appear several times because this pattern repeats itself from the colonial occupation to the present, vis-à-vis the Dutch state and the Muslim 'Other'. When in the 1990s friction arose among the Moroccan community in the Netherlands about whether or not prayers of salvation should be made for King Hassan II of Morocco, a leading member of the People's Party for Freedom and Democracy (VVD), Frits Bolkestein, intervened by taking the view that mentioning prayers of salvation for the ruler would be an obstacle for the successful integration of that community, and hoped that in the future this would be done for Queen Beatrix (Kaptein 1998). These remarkable words were from the same leader who in the 1990s problematised the religious and cultural background of immigrant communities. He believed that separation of church and state was an essential principle of Dutch values and that Islam was diametrically opposed to this. But on the other hand, in this case, Bolkestein hoped that Muslims would say a prayer of salvation for the elderly queen Beatrix of the Netherlands (Kaptein 1998; Reformatische Dagblad 1997).

Such paradoxes can often be seen in the attitude of the Dutch state towards Islam and Muslims. Normally, due to the adoption of the liberal tradition, the state is expected to be neutral towards religion. But in reality this neutrality has been transient and at times contradictory in regard to the state's treatment of Muslims. The apparent attitude towards neutrality was present in the colonialists' Islam policy in the nineteenth century. The most important architect of this policy was Snouck Hurgronje (1857–1936), the famous adviser on native and Arab affairs who later became a lecturer at Leiden University. He also invented the dichotomy of 'religious Islam' and 'political Islam' (Kaptein 1998). He believed that the state should interfere as little as possible in the religious affairs of Muslims, but political Islam had to be dealt with in a heavy-handed way. In the case mentioned above regarding supplication or *dua* of salvation on Fridays, he indicated that it was not wise to request this from Muslims. He believed that this kind of demand could not be expected from Muslims by their European governors. His advice was not followed on this occasion, but he nonetheless had much influence in the management of colonial policy in the Dutch East Indies. This will be examined in detail in this chapter. Furthermore, the political culture and experiences developed in the colonial period, which continue today, will also be explored in this chapter.

Colonial period

The first encounter of the Dutch people with Indonesians after explorers, was through the government consolidated company, the Dutch East India Company (*Verenigde Oost Indische Compagnie*, VOC). This company was established in 1602 and traded with Indigenous people for many years. In a very controversial way, it was the first major corporation able to wage war, print money, and make economic and political deals. Furthermore, it was empowered to establish colonies, with semi-official powers to punish and imprison people, or to employ prisoners (Steenbrink 2006).

The power of the VOC was dependent on the extent to which it could monopolise the spice trade. Sometimes it maintained its power and monopoly over this trade by means of violence. The company did not allow the local growers of spices to trade their products to other companies. In cases of violation, the farmers were brutally punished. In 1621 the local farmers of Banda violated their agreement by selling their spices to other companies. This was punished by the VOC, who killed all of the farmers, numbering between ten and fifteen people, and allocated their land to VOC farmers who cultivated the land using by imported slaves (Van Reybrouck 2020). Other punishments meted out to disloyal farmers were cutting down their plants or trees (Van Reybrouck 2020).

The VOC continued its corrupt and oppressive management of the colony until the end of 1799. It was at this time that the VOC was declared bankrupt and was taken over by the Dutch government. This move transformed the relationship between the Dutch state and the lands of present-day Indonesia into a traditional colonial settlement. Soon after the takeover, the Dutch state implemented various forms of administration. The first administrative move was called the '*cultuurstelsel*', which referred to the cultivation of the land. The Dutch state decided which product was the best one for export and forced the local people to cultivate it. Locals who did not have fertile ground were forced to work without pay for the Dutch state. This was in fact no different from forced labour (Van Reybrouck 2020). All profits generated from cultivation went to the Dutch state, while the Indigenous population lived in poverty. In 1850 one third of the Dutch state's income came from this *cultuurstelsel*. After 1840 the Dutch state slowly expanded its territory and the whole country came completely under the rule of the Netherlands (Burgers 2010).

Gradually, *cultuurstelsel* began to be criticised for its exploitative nature, and the state doubted its sustainability. However, the state did not want to forego this form of revenue. The middle class of Dutch society argued for a reform of the system, in which forced labour would be abolished and the colonial economic regime would be reduced (Ricklefs 2008). The demand for reform and improvement of the colonies did not mean that expansion of colonial territory was no longer carried out, and gradual expansion continued in a bloody and brutal manner. The Aceh War is an example of this. The costs of these wars were recovered from the local population in the form of taxes (Steenbrink 2006). The longer the Dutch stayed in Indonesia, the more they discovered new sources of income. Once oil was discovered in the colony, the Aceh war was the reason for continued domination over this colony (Ricklefs 2008).

Ethical politics (*Ethische Politiek*)

As already mentioned, people in the motherland began to question the colonial policy, believing that the local population received little or no benefit from colonial rule. The locals profited little from the proceeds, while the same proceeds supplied the economy of the motherland with great wealth. These humanist voices expressed in various European states resulted in the Netherlands moving towards 'Ethical Politics'. This move by the Dutch state was understood as the beginning of a new colonial age (Van Reybrouck 2020). The main principles of the ethical policy were education, irrigation, and integration. In her 1901 speech from the throne to the States-General, Queen Wilhemina emphasised the importance of the Christian mission and the Dutch government's moral responsibility to improve the situation of the local people. God had given the Netherlands a chance to improve the bad situation of this country, she emphasised. From a paternalistic point of view, the Netherlands was seen as a country that was developed, prosperous, and knowledgeable, and this justified domination over the colony. In the view of the Dutch state, this policy was a proof of goodwill on the part of the Netherlands, which differed from other colonial empires with its wish to protect the rights of the colonial subjects by fighting against their exploitation. In his published works, the publicist, jurist, and politician Van Deventer (Van Deventer 1899) voiced the need for a new policy in the colony; this was the '*eereschuld*' ('honour guilt') of the Dutch empire. According to Van Deventer, it was the turn of the Dutch empire to pay back its 'guilt' by compensating its colonial subjects (Touwen 2000). Education was considered a key medium for sustaining this Ethical Politics. It was hoped that the emergence of a highly educated native class, to serve as the future political leaders and administrators, would contribute to the independence of the Dutch East Indies within the Dutch kingdom (Steenbrink 2006). However, theory did not match practice. Many policies could not be implemented, due to population growth and international developments such as the Great Depression, which impacted the economy. Consequently, the empire's promises were unfulfilled (Ricklefs 2008).

Changing perceptions: from Muslims as heretics to a backwards 'Other'

So far, the settlement of the Dutch empire in Indonesia and its colonial policies have been covered. But what about the empire's relationship with Islam? What were the attitudes and perceptions? The position of the Dutch state towards Islam was inconsistent from the outset. The attitude towards Muslims went in parallel with the progress of colonisation. The more territory the Dutch occupied, the more it was seen as a religious victory. From the beginning of colonisation until the nineteenth century, the perception of Islam gradually shifted. It was no longer viewed as a heretical rival to Christianity, but instead it was viewed as a weak and backward religion. Despite these shifting views in Dutch society, some political figures still felt the need to proselytise the Muslim colonial subjects (Steenbrink 2006).

The Ethical Politics was carried out under the prime ministership of Abraham Kuyper, the leader of the Anti-Revolutionary Party (ARP). The ARP believed that the Christianisation of the Indigenous people, both Muslims and the followers of traditional religions, was a priority in the Dutch East Indies. Kuyper was supported by the Anti-Revolutionary Islamologist[2] L.W.C. Van den Berg, who argued for the open evangelisation of the Dutch East Indies based on the superiority of Protestant Christianity. An important article[3] of the ARP's programme stated that the Christian mission should be part of Dutch colonial policy in the Indies. It was their opinion that the Dutch kingdom should not view the Indies merely as a source of income, but that as a 'Christian people' it also had a 'moral obligation' to the Indigenous peoples, both in the proclamation of God's Word and in the funding of local education and healthcare (Jungman and van Iterson 1918). However, as elsewhere, missionary work often also took place within Christian education and healthcare. For Van den Berg, the heretical Islamic religion was a fundamental obstacle to progress (Van den Berg 1907). This was a common supremacist ideology of the colonial powers that justified their existence in colonised lands, the attitude that Western civilisation, as a 'developed' civilisation, was tasked with tutoring colonial territories (Said 2003). This idea was even present in the ideas of Karl Marx, who saw the colonial presence as something positive because it would educate feudal societies into civilised societies (Katz 1990).

Van Deventer opposed the policy of Abraham Kuyper and, as a liberal, advocated a strict separation of church and state. According to Van Deventer, a neutral government was essential for the success of the Ethical Politics. He argued that an overly strong Christian presence, especially coming from the government, would make the Muslim population of the Dutch East Indies resistant towards the colonial authority (Touwen 2000). He even went further by claiming that even Christian education posed a possible risk to the fledgling peace in the archipelago (Van Deventer 1911).

These debates and policies also had an effect on the study of Islam at Dutch universities, where the approach shifted from religious to scientific study of Islam as a historical and anthropological phenomenon (Steenbrink 2006). During the colonial period, some scholars played an important role in the development of colonial policies. One prominent scholar was Snouck Hurgronje. What was exceptional about him was not only his scholarly writings but his influence on colonial policy and politicians. As Edward Said pointed out, the growing contacts between European powers and the Orient led to a partial interweaving of the academic study of the Orient and colonial politics (Said 2003). Although European academics were generally not part of the colonial apparatus – with exceptions such as Hurgronje – imperialist expansion offered new research opportunities, such as the discovery of unknown territories, peoples, and cultures. Their inquiries were used in developing new colonial policies. However, Hurgronje's legacy also signified the culmination of the most controversial and disputed era of Orientalism, namely the degeneration of Islamology into a colonial auxiliary science. He believed that Islam could best be studied in its natural habitat, and decided to go to Mecca with a subsidy from the Dutch state. To be able to enter Mecca, he converted to Islam and took the name Abd al Ghaffar. The Dutch state wanted to observe the situation in the pilgrim city because it was afraid that colonial subjects would adopt radical ideas there (Vrolijk and van Leeuwen 2014: 121–2). Due to political instability in Arabia, Hurgronje cut short his journey in Mecca and returned to the Netherlands.

In 1888, he asked the government to provide him with a researcher's post in Indonesia to survey the potential revolt movements. The government offered him a job as an adviser and required him to investigate the Bantam revolt and the role of pilgrims from Mecca in the revolt. The Dutch government believed that there was a connection between Islam and the resistance of its subjects (Benda 1958). Hurgronje avoided working openly for the Dutch authorities and lived in the archipelago under his pseudonym Abd al Ghaffar. He married the daughters of two Muslim scholars from prominent West Javanese families and lived like 'a native' Muslim[4] (Van Koningsveld 1985). In 1891, the Dutch authorities sent him to Atjeh, where he continued his work as a 'native' under his 'Muslim name'. The information he provided helped the Dutch authorities to hold down the revolt and resistance to the Dutch settlers (Vrolijk and van Leeuwen 2014: 121–2). But the harsh action of the Dutch military weakened the relationship between Hurgronje and the Dutch authorities, so he decided to return to the Netherlands and continue his job as lecturer at Leiden University (Vrolijk and van Leeuwen 2014: 121–2).

Hurgronje held to liberal positions in his recommendations, especially with regard to religious education. He believed that the Dutch state should act neutrally in terms of the content of religious education. He advocated for education on a neutral basis because, according to him, Islam was a religion that was not able to adapt to the developments of the modern age. Education would help Muslims to emancipate and liberate themselves from their religion (Steenbrink 2006). The colonial government had attempted several times to mix colonial education with the existing Islamic education, but these attempts had mostly failed (Steenbrink 2006).

At home, the discourse centred on the Dutch state's mission to educate its subjects to be civilised. As already mentioned, Islam was seen as a political force, and pan-Islamism was seen as the most pressing topic for policy makers and the colonial administration. Jihad (resistance or militaristic struggle) was considered by Hurgronje as a 'backward doctrine', which Muslims needed to give up if they wanted to attain to the level of modern society. He criticised the previous colonial politics and proposed a more conscious politics. His thinking on conscious politics matched well with the Ethical Politics of the colonial administration. He considered the Aceh war as a war against political Islam that had to be fought. Victory would lead to the modernisation of the country and closer relations with the Netherlands (Jung 2010). He strongly believed that when the colonial government replaced the exploitative policy with development policies, the Indigenous population would rise to the level of Dutch society, which would strengthen the ties between the colony and the motherland (Steenbrink 2006).

There has always been a contradiction between the ideals of Hurgronje and his actions. He generally advocated for the separation of religion and politics, but his advice to the colonial government consistently led to more government interference in the affairs of Muslims (Steenbrink 2006). His interventions with the Islamic faith went so far that the Office of Native Affairs was seen as the precursor of the Indonesian Ministry of Religious Affairs. Although Hurgronje's political ideal held that the state had to be neutral, in practice this could not be realised. For example, the colonial government appointed the religious judges, the leaders and preachers of the main mosques, and passed judgments and rulings on matters related to marriage and inheritance, which are religious institutions in Islam (Steenbrink 2006). Hurgronje advocated for a neutral position towards religion, but in the case of resistance to the colonial government this neutrality shifted towards hard intervention. This side of Hurgronje was mostly seen in the Aceh war, where he advised the colonial government to be robust in supressing the rebellion. He problematised this rebellion as 'political Islam' and advocated for eliminating this way of thinking (Poorthuis and Salemink 2011). Ultimately, Hurgronje believed that when the influence of Islam was weakened, its political role would also be weakened (Kaptein 2014). In order to achieve this, the colonial administration must have a dedicated focus on educating its subjects. However, his goal was not achieved. Instead of Indonesian Muslims' desire for independence, which he called 'political Islam', being weakened, it became stronger, and education did not prevent the independence of Indonesia from the Dutch occupation (Jung 2010). It is impossible to discuss the Dutch colonial rule over Indonesia without considering Hurgronje's influence, because he had a direct impact on colonial administration and daily life in the archipelago.

The colonial administration considered political Islam as a threat for the colonial order, and believed that all resistance to the colonial administration was inspired by political Islam. They were afraid that pan-Islamism would overflow to the Dutch Indies, and because of this they even tried to restrict the Hajj pilgrimage to Mecca, since they believed that pilgrims would meet pan-Islamists and would return with 'fanatic' and revolutionary ideas (Kaptein 2014). The Dutch government's conception of an Islamic policy was based on the fear of political Islam. This policy, which was officially approved by the colonial government, aimed to give Muslims complete freedom in matters of faith and worship, and to strictly prosecute and suppress any politically based movements which were inspired by pan-Islamism, the caliphate, and jihadism. Hurgronje, who also advocated for the establishment of a peaceful and voluntary union of the Dutch and Indonesian people in the future, wanted Indonesian Muslims to overcome the period of rigid dogmatism and catch up with European civilisations and the era of modern liberal thinking. He hoped that with the spread of Western education the Muslims would eventually adopt Western culture, and considered it a moral duty for the Dutch to lead in this. But Hurgronje's ideal failed because the improvement in the education system led to a stronger critical consciousness on the part of Indonesians under colonial rule, which led to the revolution and independence (Steenbrink 2006).

Postcolonial period and continuities

After the Second World War, the Netherlands was no longer a colonising country, but one that received immigrants. Independence for the colonies resulted in large swaths of migration. The biggest migrant influx was after the Second World War. This great wave of migration brought guest workers to the Netherlands, and was composed mainly of migrants from Muslim-majority countries.

Until 1970, there was no clear policy in place regarding the status of immigrants. They were expected to return to their homelands: the Moluccans[5] would return to Indonesia and the guest workers were expected to return to their home countries (Kaya 2009). One of the reasons for not developing a policy before 1970 was that the Dutch state did not want to be a migrant-receiving country. Fears of overpopulation were always emphasised, and the immigration of guest and colonial workers was seen as exceptional. But after 1980 immigrants were no longer framed as guest workers or colonial migrants, but as permanent settlers labelled as 'cultural minorities' or 'ethnic minorities' (Scholten 2011). After 1980 more family unification took place and permanent stays became the new normal, which resulted in a change of status among the guest workers. The guest workers were no longer labelled as 'guests', but as migrants who had a right to stay in the Netherlands. The policies that were developed aimed to create social and economic emancipation for the immigrants, but differentiated them from the rest of Dutch society (Scholten 2011). As such, the idea that they could one day return was seemingly always a possibility, as they were constructed as a distant 'Other' within the state. The initial focus was on the integration of these migrant workers, while retaining the Dutch culture and language.

From guest worker to Muslim

In the 1990s the integration policies and perceptions towards immigrants shifted towards an assimilationist approach. During this period, immigrants were not only discussed in the context of national developments, but also in terms of the impact that immigration was having on an international level. There was much focus on the cultural and religious backgrounds of immigrants, especially those coming from Muslim-majority nations. Muslims in the Netherlands initially settled there for economic reasons, and their priority was finding work and earning money to support their family and relatives in their countries of origin. But, with the arrival of their families in the Netherlands, followed by permanent settlement, they started to have other concerns as well. Some of these concerns were religious needs that should be accommodated (Kaya 2009). Meanwhile, Muslim migrants established institutions like mosques, schools, and even universities (Scholten 2011). Thus, they became more visible in Dutch society and paternalistic attitudes that had developed in the colonial period towards Muslims in the Dutch Indies began to resurface, but this time under the polemics of integration.

Domestic as well as international incidents such as the death of Pim Fortuyn and, later, Theo van Gogh placed Muslims at the centre of discussions in local media and politics (Scholten 2011). Integration was no longer about learning the Dutch language, opportunities in the labour market, and the emancipation of immigrants. Rather, the discourse centred mainly on the cultural and religious background of the immigrants. It was not enough to master the Dutch language and thereby to be able to function better in society, but Dutch values and norms had to be adopted as well. Islam was portrayed as an obstacle, and the profile of a well-integrated immigrant could not go hand in hand with preserving Islamic identity. We see here a resurgence of the colonial attitude towards Muslims that saw Islam as an obstacle to adapting to modern society. Islam as a religious identity had to be abandoned if one wanted to integrate well and be accepted by Dutch society. This became the mainstream discourse on which the integration debate was centred. Politicians such as Frits Bolkestein gave speeches and wrote articles about the integration of minorities, with special attention to the Muslims. Parts of his speeches were published in the newspaper NRC Handelsblad (Bolkestein 1991). He emphasised that Islam was not only a religion but also a way of life, which was at odds with the liberal values of the separation of church and state (Shadid and Koningsveld 1995). Freedom of speech, which, according to Bolkestein, was non-existent in Muslim-majority countries, had to be protected. These liberal values should be upheld not only in Europe and North America, but all over the world. There was no such thing as compromise, he emphasised, when there was a clash with Islam. In the case of a clash, liberal ideals had to be defended (Scholten 2011). Bolkestein adopted a misogynistic attitude by making remarks like 'Muslim girls are allowed to wear a headscarf if they want to, even if that headscarf is intended for much more than just a head covering' (Bolkestein 1991). Here he was implying that the way Muslim women were perceived within Muslim cultures was a blemish on the reputation of Islam. He rehashed imaginaries and mythologies surrounding the 'oppressed' Muslim woman, perpetuated throughout the colonial period. He capitalised on tropes relating to the position of women in Islam and explained how liberal values can liberate them.

In the late 1990s and early 2000s, Muslims were attacked much more explicitly by politicians such as Pim Fortuyn. Integration debates in those years were used to stigmatise Muslims. In these debates, the idea that the integration of Muslims had failed was always present, and this was blamed on their religion. This was in spite of the fact that there were studies on the goals achieved by integration policies, which showed that Muslim immigrants were by and large successful (Scholten 2011). However, the prevailing political discourse in the Netherlands proclaimed that immigrants, especially Muslim immigrants, were expected not only to master the language and to participate in society, but also to abandon their religious beliefs and to adopt a critical attitude towards their faith. The criterion for a well-integrated Muslim became the degree to which they were less 'Islamic' and adopted a more critical attitude towards Islam. Similar viewpoints can be traced back to the Dutch colonial history in administering Muslim-majority lands. The colonial government in the Dutch Indies tried to promote a type of Islamic thinking, which they considered 'deradicalised' and apolitical, uncorrupted by Islamic polemics from the Middle East. To achieve this end, they entered into alliances with local ethnic and religious groups and tried to influence local Islamic education. The pilgrimage to Mecca, at the behest of Hurgronje, was regulated to prevent the growth and spread of supposed transnational radical Islamic ideas. The pilgrims would be interrogated after their return to examine whether or not they were under the influence of the 'fanatics' of political Islam (Jung 2010).

In the late 1990s and early 2000s, integration discourse shifted from cultural emancipation to a cultural assimilationist approach. After Bolkestein, it was Pim Fortuyn who succeeded in bringing assimilation to the centre of political debate. Noteworthy in Fortuyn's rhetoric was the dichotomy of liberal Muslims who were acceptable to him and fundamentalist or political Islam that was not acceptable and compatible with Western values (De Koning 2016). Furthermore, Fortuyn introduced the idea of the so-called Islamisation of the Netherlands, which posed a threat to Dutch identity. He proposed an ideal image of Dutch identity as being secular, modern, and liberal – against all of which values he presumed Islam was in contradiction. These were the values and rights that had been achieved from the 1960s and needed to be protected against the Muslim threat (De Koning 2016). Fortuyn created an atmosphere of openly targeting Muslims under the pretext of criticism of Islam, presenting Islam as a problem and reinforcing an 'us' (Dutch/Western culture) against 'them' (Islamic culture) that represented 'backwardness' and a threat to Dutch values and norms. He called for an ideological struggle against Islam. This ideological struggle was about convincing Muslims to accept the core values of modernity (Fortuyn 2001). After Fortuyn's assassination by an environmental activist, his 'ideological' struggle against Islam was continued by another politician, Geert Wilders.

After Fortuyn, this harsh atmosphere and tone towards Muslims became even louder. Islamophobic statements started to become normalised in political and public discourse (Berger 2014). The most vocal Islamophobic leader was Geert Wilders, the most prominent figure after Fortuyn in Dutch politics. He was not only popular in the Netherlands but was seen as a vanguard against the tidal wave of Islamisation sweeping across Europe. He also worked with other European and American far-right political figures and groups (Hafez 2014). Fortuyn had warned against the Islamisation of the Netherlands, but Wilders took these warnings a step further by proposing the de-Islamisation of the Netherlands. He advocated that 'our' (Judeo-Christian) identity and traditions were in danger, due to the Islamisation of society. In his party programme he advocated for closing mosques, banning the wearing of headscarves, banning the Qur'an, closing Islamic schools, and imprisoning radical Muslims as a preventive measure. He also wanted to close the borders to migrants from Islamic countries (Butter, Valk, van Oord 2021). In 2018, he tried to introduce his party's proposals as an initiative Bill in Parliament, calling the proposed legislation the 'Islam Act'. He outlined Islam as a totalitarian ideology and listed several bans on Islamic expressions (Butter, Valk, van Oord 2021).

Wilders and his predecessor, Fortuyn, created a public and political discourse that influenced all layers of society. In this context, T.A. Van Dijk (Van Dijk 2008) notes that the discourse used by some elites influences individuals in society. These political elites work for certain institutions and are therefore part of them. In this context, a vicious circle is created in which the elite uses racist discourse about refugees and migrants being a danger to society. Individuals are influenced by this and these individuals are in turn part of the institutions where policies are developed. As a result, racist policies are developed and introduced. This discourse not only influences policy, but also leads to interpersonal forms of Islamophobia.

Since 2015, there has been a growth in far-right groups such as Pegida across Europe and in the Netherlands. These groups regularly hold protest actions against refugee reception and against the construction of mosques. Pegida has also carried out attacks on mosques in the form of pig auctions and posters calling for de-Islamisation (Yildirim 2018). Social media is the medium where they assemble and announce their actions. Studies show that these groups are gradually becoming violent and are starting to arm themselves. Consequently, the number of armed attacks against minority groups, particularly Muslims, are growing in the Netherlands (Yildirim 2018). Another worrying point is the growth of their influence on the political and social landscape. Their intimidating actions against Islamic institutions and mosques are labelled and normalised in the media as protest actions. Some political parties even have ties with these groups, and their ideas are given a platform via these political parties (Bakali 2019).

Since the 1990s there has been an open resistance on the part of both politicians and the public with regard to Muslim institutions and the growth of Muslim migrants in the Netherlands. Certain international developments, such as the attack on the World Trade Center on 11 September 2001 and the murder of Theo van Gogh, have gradually normalised the way in which this resistance manifests itself. As already mentioned, there is a continuity in the distinction between acceptable and unacceptable Islam, tracing its roots to the colonial period. Sometimes this has been expressed by certain politicians or opinion makers, but these distinctions are repeated in other shapes and forms. Policy makers and the government are also increasingly inclined to make this distinction. In the modern era, and particularly since 2000, labels have been developed to categorise Muslims – labels such as radical Muslim, Salafist, liberal Muslim, and others. Muslims who do not shake hands with women, or Muslim women who wear a niqab have been labelled as Salafists by the government and not considered to fit into Dutch society (Fadil, De Koning, Ragazzi 2019). As Martijn de Koning and Nadia Fadil have pointed out that 'several scholars have noted how this focus on Islam and Muslims as threats to social cohesion has triggered a securitization of Islam and Muslims and "an Islamization of security"' (Fadil, De Koning, Ragazzi 2019: 11). As such, 'any debate on Islam focuses on the threat it represents, and any debate about security is reduced to Islam. This makes Islam the centre stage in public debates and policies concerning national security' (Fadil, De Koning, Ragazzi 2019: 11).

From the earliest years in which immigrant policy was developed in the Netherlands, we can see the assumption of a potential of clash of cultures on backgrounds. This is noticeable in the following quote in the Wetenschappelijke raad voor het Regeringsbeleid (WRR) Report of 1979 (The Scientific Council for Government Policy) (Penninx: 1979 xxii):

> Very important aspects of our Western culture such as individual freedom and equality are under attack from another culture in a manner which is sometimes militant. In those cases of confrontation where a compromise in practice is not possible, no choice exists but to defend our culture against competing pretentions.

In a study by Butter, Valk and van Oord (2021), it was found that the majority of the archives of the Dutch Parliament are filled with documents in which Muslims are profiled as a security problem or as 'Others' whose norms and values are diametrically opposed to 'our' norms and values. It is worth noting that the same study points out that after 2010 more attention was paid to Muslim discrimination in Parliament. This came from members of Parliament who were predominantly from left-wing parties and who had Islamic backgrounds themselves (Butter, Valk, van Oord 2021).

Since the early 2000s, Islam and Muslims have been an important issue during election campaigns. They are often mentioned in the context of security and prevention of radicalisation. Restrictions on certain religious expressions, such as face coverings and building mosques, have even been included in party programmes. After 2017, these restrictions were also included in the election programmes of liberal parties. Despite some pushback from political elites, there are still a majority in Dutch politics who portray Muslims as a great danger to society. The popularity and growth of Islamophobic political parties since the early 2000s makes it attractive for other parties to go along with their ideas. Furthermore, they are becoming so popular that they are also gaining influence in developing legislation relating to anti-terrorism and radicalisation laws that increasingly target Muslims at an institutional level.

For example, the burqa ban reflects the consequence of this Islamophobic discourse at an institutional level. In 2005, Geert Wilders submitted a motion in the Dutch Parliament in which he demanded a ban on face-covering clothing in public places. Since then, it has always been on the political agenda. In the beginning, people wanted to limit the ban to certain areas, but later, when the Party for Freedom (PVV: Party of Geert Wilders) took part in the minority government of the VVD and the Christian Democratic Appeal (CDA) in 2011, this changed. The PVV came up with a new proposal in which the face covering would be banned from 2013. It took some time to implement this law, but in 2020 the legal ban was officially introduced. The underlying idea of this law was, according to its developers, safety and communication. It was emphasised that in the Netherlands, looking each other in the face is an important norm, and to do otherwise would create feelings of insecurity (Abaaziz 2020). Furthermore, the government was of the opinion that face-covering clothing could be a hindrance to service and safety. Not surprisingly, in a time of global pandemic, it turned out to be impossible to enforce this law. Although the text of the law was stated in neutral terms, it was aimed at a specific group. This was fairly obvious, as the National Government website described the ban as a 'burqa ban' or 'niqab ban' (Abaaziz 2020). Other laws and policies have been introduced that have had similar results to the burqa ban. The laws and policies are formulated in a neutral way, but the target is often Muslims. An example is the law on the 'prohibition of non-anaesthetised slaughter', in which Islamic ritual slaughter and kosher slaughter are targeted. Furthermore, the parliamentary 'investigation into foreign funding of religious institutions in the Netherlands' can also be mentioned. In the course of this investigation, only Islamic institutions were called to account in Parliament. This investigation took place in response to a television report on Islamic institutions receiving foreign funding.[6] With the help of the media, an atmosphere was created in which it seemed that these Islamic institutions had a lot to hide and were under foreign influence. Few alarm bells were raised by these overt anti-Muslim media representations, as it reinforced the type of discourse created by Islamophobic politicians who had passed legislation and policies which targeted Muslims in the Netherlands.

Conclusion

Considering the development of the perception of Islam and Muslims from the arrival of the Dutch explorers in the East Indies in 1595 until the end of the nineteenth century, there was a shift from an image of Islam as a heretical religious movement to Islam as an outdated, medieval system whose primitive followers should be re-educated to become modern citizens. In the 1990s, under the influence of international development, Islam was placed at the centre of debates on immigration and integration which saw open resistance to the arrival of Muslim immigrants and the existence of Muslim institutions. During this period, the discourse on integration no longer revolved around inclusion and emancipation of the migrants into society through education and participation, but an assimilationist integration model became more prevalent. This ensured that integration of Muslims depended on the extent to which they internalised Dutch values and norms. The dominant idea in the colonial period, that Islam was an obstacle to the 'civilised' Muslim, continued in these integration debates.

Both international and national developments led to the rise of Islamophobia. Politicians such as Bolkestein, Pim Fortuyn, and, later, Geert Wilders owed their popularity to the stigmatisation of Muslims. Muslims were held responsible for the problems that arose in the economic and social spheres of Dutch and European societies. Categorisations such as 'political Islam' and 'religious Islam' that existed in the colonial era were continued by Fortuyn with the 'acceptable Muslim' and 'non-acceptable Muslim'. Later on, these categorisations had no meaning at all to Wilders. For him, Muslims had to abandon their religion altogether if they wanted to be considered civilised people.

Consequently, one can say that there is great continuity in the policy and perception of Muslims in the Netherlands. Islam was perceived as a heretical religion under colonial rule. But with the arrival of colonial subjects after decolonisation and guest workers in the 1960s, Islam was viewed as a religion that existed in a realm of 'Otherness'. From the 1990s, a strong anti-Islam movement started to develop in Dutch politics as a result of major historical moments such as the Islamic revolution in Iran, the Iraq–Iran war, the 9/11 attacks, the invasion of Iraq and Afghanistan through the War on Terror, as well as the murders of Pim Fortuyn and Theo van Gogh. There is a recycling of the colonial images of Islam, which are linked to contemporary representations of Muslims by Dutch politicians. The popularity these images experience ensures that other political parties also adopt their ideas. Consequently, a vicious cycle is created in which anti-Islam attitudes are normalised, which in turn influences the policies developed to discriminate against Muslims.

This chapter has argued that traces of colonialism continue to persist in the present day. The Dutch state still behaves as an occupier (Wekker 2016). Colonialism and racism are closely intertwined. The colour line considered by Raymond Kennedy as the core of colonialism also has its validity for the Netherlands. According to Kennedy (1945), the colonial administration created a hierarchical division in which the white European was at the top. One can still see marks of this structure in modern Netherlands and policy towards Muslims.

Notes

1 Pan-Islamism is a political movement that emerged at a time when colonialism was spreading in Muslim countries. Jalal al-din al-Afgani is considered the developer of this ideology. Its main aim was to restore political strength in Muslim countries by reuniting all the Islamic countries (Ummah) under one country and one leader (Caliph). Later, inspired by this movement, some Muslims opposed colonial rule in their countries. As a result, the movement was considered a danger to colonial power.

2 In the Netherlands a person is called an Islamologist when they have studied Islamology, which is the study of the laws, culture, religion, history, and philosophy of Islam.

3 Article 18 of the party programme, see more in Jungman and van Iterson (1918).

4 He kept his marriages secret from the Dutch authorities, who would not accept this commitment as legal. Worth noting here is that he was likely to have behaved as a Muslim in his daily activities, otherwise he would not have been able to marry the daughter of a Muslim scholar (for more details, see Van Koningsveld 1985).

5 Moluccans were the first group immigrants from the East Indies to the Netherlands who were forced to stay in the Netherlands after the independence. They mainly consisted of the descendants those who had worked for the Dutch government as soldiers. The Dutch government promised them their own independent republic but did not follow through because they lost control over the islands.

6 For more information see the research report: Hoorens et al. (2020).

Bibliography

Abaaziz, I. (2020). *Zwartboek Boerkaverbod: een Pleidooi voor de afshaffing van het 'boerkaverbod'*, Stichting Meld Islamofobie, https://collectieftegenislamofobie.nl/wp-content/uploads/2022/02/Eindrapportage-Weerbaar-tegen-moslimdsicriminatie-en-hatecrime-220211-def-1-1.pdf (accessed 1 April 2022).

Bakali, N. (2019). Challenging terrorism as a form of 'otherness': exploring the parallels between far-right and Muslim religious extremism, *Islamophobia Studies Journal*, 5(1), 99–115.

Benda, H.J. (1958). Christiaan Snouck Hurgronje and the foundations of Dutch Islamic policy in Indonesia, *The Journal of Modern History*, 30(4): 338–47.

Berger, M.S. (2014). The Netherlands. In: J. Cesari (ed.), *The Oxford Handbook of European Islam*, Oxford: Oxford University Press.

Bolkestein, F. (1991). Islamitische immigranten moeten integreren. In: *NRC Handelsblad*, 10 September, www.delpher.nl/nl/kranten/view?identifier=KBNRC01:0 00029462:mpeg21:p009&coll=ddd (accessed 10 April 2022).

Burgers, H. (2010). *De Garoeda en de Ooievaar: Indonesie van Kolonie tot Nationale Staat*, Leiden: KITLV Uitgeverij, https://ewoudbutter.nl/2021/05/10/vierde-monitor-moslimdiscriminatie-is-uit-agendering-moslimdiscriminatie-en-moslimhaat-blijft-bittere-noodzaak/ (accessed 10 November 2021).

Butter, E. (2016). *Over immigratie, integratie, dicriminatie en tegengaan van radicalisering*, Utrecht: Movisie, www.kis.nl/sites/default/files/bestanden/Publicaties/verkiezingsprogrammas-politiek-over-diversiteit-inclusie.pdf (accessed 24 March 2022).

Butter, E., Valk, I., and van Oord, R. (2021). *Monitor moslim discriminatie: vierde rapportage met speciale aandacht voor discriminatie op de arbeidsmarkt*, Amsterdam: University of Amsterdam.

De Koning, M. (2016). *Een Ideologische strijd met de Islam: Fortuyns gedachtegoed als scharnierpunt in de radicalisering van moslims*, Uithoorn: Karakters Uitgevers B.V.

Fadil, N., De Koning, M., and Ragazzi, F. (2019). Radicalization: tracing the trajectory of an 'empty signifier' in the Low Lands. In: N. Fadil, M. De Koning, and F. Ragazzi (eds), *Radicalization in Belgium and the Netherlands: critical perspectives on violence and security*, London: I.B. Tauris, 3–26.

Fortuyn, P. (2001). *De islamisering van onze cultuur. Nederlandse identiteit als fundament*, Uithoorn: Karakter Uitgevers.

Hafez, F. (2014). Shifting borders: Islamophobia as common ground for building pan-European right-wing unity, *Patterns of Prejudice*, 48(5): 479–99.

Hoorens, S. et al. (2020). *Onderzoek naar buitenlands financiering van religieuze installingen in Nederland*, Cambridge: Rand Europe, www.rijksoverheid.nl/documenten/rapporten/2021/02/22/onderzoek-naar-buitenlandse-financiering-van-religieuze-instellingen-in-nederland (accessed 24 March 2022).

Jung, D. (2010). Islam as a problem: Dutch religious politics in the East Indies, *Review of Religious Research*, 51(3): 288–301.

Jungman, J.A. and van Iterson, F.K. (eds) (1918). *Parlement en kiezer. Jaarboekje 1918–1919*, Den Haag: Anti-Revolutionaire Partij Program van Beginselen Art.

Kaptein, N.J.G. (2014). *Islam, colonialism and the modern age in the Netherlands East Indies: a biography of Sayyid 'Uthman (1822–1914)*, Leiden: Brill.

Kaptein, N. (1998). Islam en politiek in Nederlands-Indië: Een islamitische heilbede voor Wilhelmina ter gelegenheid van haar inhuldiging, *Indische Letteren*, 13: 167–76, www.dbnl.org/tekst/_ind004199801_01/_ind004199801_01_0019.php#133 (accessed 4 April 2022).

Katz, S. (1990). The problems of Europocentrism and evolutionism in Marx's writings on colonialism, *Political Studies*, 38(4): 672–86.

Kaya, A. (2009). The Netherlands: from multiculturalism to assimilation. In: A. Kaya (ed.), *Islam, migration and integration: the age of securitization*, London: Palgrave Macmillan, 116–40.

Kennedy, R. (1945). The colonial crisis and the future. In: R. Linton (ed.), *The science of man in the world crisis*, New York: Columbia University Press.

Penninx, R. (1979). *Etnische Minderheden*, Den Haag: Staatsuitgeverij.

Poorthuis, M. and Salemink, T. (2011). *Van harem tot Fitna: Beeldvorming van de Islam in Nederland 1848–2010*, Nijmegen: Valkhof Pers.

Reformatische Dagblad (1997). Moslim moet voor Beatrix bidden, 22 May, www.digibron.nl/viewer/collectie/Digibron/id/tag:RD.nl,19970522:newsml_d73272d5154222b79817920fa15353a78153c1e432400a40d233d8d5 (accessed 12 April 2022).

Ricklefs, M.C. (2008). *A history of modern Indonesia since c.1200*, New York: Palgrave Macmillan.

Said, E. (2003). *Orientalism*, London: Penguin.

Scholten, P. (2011). *Framing immigrants' integration*, Dutch Research–Policy Dialogues in Comparative Perspective, Amsterdam: Amsterdam University Press.

Shadid, W.A.R. and Koningsveld, P.S. (1995). *De mythe van het islamitische gevaar. Hindernissen bij integratie*, Kampen: Uitgeverij Kok.

Steenbrink, Karel A. (2006). *Dutch colonialism and Indonesian Islam: contacts and conflicts, 1596–1950*, Amsterdam: Rodopi.

Touwen, L.J. (2000). Paternalisme en Protest, Ethische Politiek en nationalism in Nederlandse-Indie, *Leidschrift: Nederlands-Indië*, 15(3): 67–94.

Van den Berg, L.W.C. (1907). 'Javaansch Christendom', *De Gids*, 71: 4.

Van Deventer, C.Th. (1899). 'Een eereschuld', *De Gids*, 63(4): 205–57.

Van Deventer, C.Th. (1911). 'De oplossing der islâm-quaestie in Nederlandsch-Indië', *De Gids*, 75: 103–16.

Van Dijk, T. (2008). Elite discourse and institutional racism. In: C.M. Teasley, *Transnational perspectives on culture, policy and education: redirecting cultural studies in neoliberal times*, New York: Peter Lang Publishing Inc., 93–112.

Van Koningsveld, P.S. (1985). Snouck Hurgronje: Een moslim of niet? Een vergeten kwestie uit de koloniale geschiedenis, *Tirade*, 29: 296–300.

Van Reybrouck, D. (2020). *Revolusi: Indonesië en het ontstaan van de moderne wereld*, Amsterdam: De Bezige Bij.

Vrolijk, A. and van Leeuwen, R. (eds) (2014). *Arabic studies in the Netherlands. A short history in portraits, 1580–1950*, Leiden: Brill.

Wekker, G. (2016). *White innocence: paradoxes of colonialism and race*, Durham, NC: Duke University Press.

Yildirim, L. (2018). Islamophobia in the Netherlands, National report 2018. In: E. Bayrakli and F. Hafez (eds), *European Islamophobia report 2018*, Istanbul: SETA, 589–620.

Chapter 5

Criminalising Muslim political agency from colonial times to today: the case of Austria

Farid Hafez

Introduction

While Austria has a long history of incorporating Islam in the political system based on the Islam Act of 1912, which allowed Muslims to be recognised as a religious denomination alongside fifteen other churches and religious communities (Potz and Schinkele 2016), this regulation has to be seen at the backdrop of long-standing efforts to domesticate Muslims by cutting them off from their transnational ties to the Ottoman Caliphate at the time and making them loyal to the Austro-Hungarian Empire. By this means the perception was created of the 'good Muslim' – manifested in the white, Bosnian Muslim who embraced the modernisation project of the Empire – vis-à-vis the 'bad Muslim', the orientalised Turkic Bosnian Muslim, whose loyalty was still aligned to Istanbul rather than Vienna (Hafez 2014). While the 1912 Islam Act was still regarded as relatively 'tolerant', the Islam Act of 2015 has introduced clear legal discrimination that has given rise to several policies that aim at securitising and controlling Muslims.

While some segments of the Muslim population in Austria have protested against the Islam Act of 2015 (Hafez 2017a), as well as much other legislation that has been implemented thereafter, the reactions of state institutions and their allies in academia have tried to delegitimise and defame voices of dissent (Hafez 2019). This has culminated in the establishment of a state-funded institution, the Documentation Centre for Political Islam (Dokumentationsstelle Politischer Islam), which attempts to map out what the Austrian government has called 'political Islam', a classification which excludes Muslim organisations from Austrian civil society and deprives them of state funding as such organisations are accused of shrouding their real, undemocratic agenda in secrecy (Hafez 2020b).

This chapter investigates how Muslims are framed as a security threat[1] to the liberal order, delegitimising their agency for equal treatment as colonial as well as postcolonial subjects. These (anti-)Islam policies are an attempt to uphold the liberal white order, which is secured by the modern nation-state, defending the privileges of whiteness, property ownership, and gender norms against racialised 'Others', be that in the colonial times of the Habsburg monarchy or today by referring to the 'War on Terror'.

This chapter pays particular attention to discussing how the notion of pan-Islamism during the colonial period and political Islam in contemporary times has been used to justify extraordinary means, assuming that these forms of Islam have been an existential threat to the political order. This will be accomplished by going back to archives of the Habsburg monarchy, including exchange letters between the colonial periphery and the power centres, as well as analysing political programmes, speeches, press releases, and institutions in contemporary times.

Before doing so, some observations are needed on Austria's role as a colonial empire in order to contextualise its colonial politics towards its Muslim populations in Bosnia and Herzegovina. In a later section, the chapter provides a detailed analysis of how the notion of 'political Islam' was introduced by politicians, institutions of knowledge production, and the intelligence agency in the postcolonial era in order to criminalise Muslim-ness and Muslim political agency.

Colonial governance of Muslim subjects in the empire

In terms of colonialism and racism, Austria is not unique among its European counterparts, where there are denials of the existence of racism which are connected to the historical and scholarly neglect of racism in Europe from the colonial period to the present (El Tayeb 1999). While, formally speaking, the Austro-Hungarian Empire was a latecomer to the project of colonialism and acquired a Muslim-populated colony only in 1878, governing and occupying colonial territory officially for only forty years (Sauer 2012), Austrian colonists were in close dialogue with other colonial projects (Loidl 2012). The colonial experience impacted on Austrian society as well. The arts and popular culture, trade and migration regimes, knowledge production, and especially anthropology and geography were deeply connected to the Austrian colonial project. Key ideological notions such as race (Hamann 2015) that would take on a formative role in the coming years, especially informing the Nazi regime, were developed during the era of colonialism

(Grosse 2005). Some scholars have also traced the origins of the Nazis' genocidal politics to the brutal Kaiserreich's colonial wars in Africa (Zimmerer 2005; Madley 2005; Kühne 2013). Nevertheless, the Austrian public has been quite ignorant about the history of Austrian colonialism. As such, the Austrian historian Walter Sauer has mentioned how the societal perception of Austria as having had no colonial burden has become one of Austria's *Lebenslügen* – a national lie – not only to distance Austria from National Socialism, but also to create links to an emerging postcolonial world for political and economic gains (Sauer 2011). Within this context, Fatima El-Tayeb argues that Europe largely

> continues to imagine itself as an autonomous entity ... untouched by 'race matters' ... a colour-blind continent in which difference is marked along lines of nationality and ethnicity. Others are routinely ascribed a position outside the nation, allowing the externalisation and thus silencing of a debate on the legacy of racism and colonialism. (El-Tayeb 2008: 658)

She further claims that this can be achieved by excluding colonialism, which leads to the externalisation of its postcolonial populations from the list of key events that have shaped contemporary Europe (El-Tayeb 2008). This, among other factors, makes the Muslim embody the position of a religious and cultural rival to Christianity and situates enlightened Europe opposite the African migrant, who is Europe's external other.

Also, the history of German *völkisch* (ethno-nationalist) anti-Semitism, which led to the annihilation of six million Jews in the Holocaust, initially resulted in a denial of guilt. This later led to depoliticisation through the creation of a culture of remembrance in which *völkisch* anti-Semitism was framed as an isolated phenomenon, without engaging in critical reflection on contemporary racism in Austria and Germany. This is what the historian Astrid Messerschmidt termed the 'post-Nazi' era in Germany (Messerschmidt 2017). In this context, many scholars in Austria and Germany and elsewhere have pointed to the commonalities between anti-Semitism and Islamophobia (Hafez 2016b; Younes 2016).

Bosnia and Herzegovina are the only case of an obvious colony of the Austro-Hungarian Empire (Donia 2007). The land was handed over to the Austro-Hungarian monarchy following the Congress of Berlin in 1878. At first, the dual monarchy met fierce opposition from the Muslims of Bosnia and Herzegovina, who waged a weaponised jihad against the Austro-Hungarian invaders. Religious dignitaries were prominent leaders of the armed resistance, which was enthusiastically embraced by the masses. While it took the monarchy only a few days to take Sarajevo, the empire's 170,000-strong army took three months to take control of the entire province (Donia 2007: 23). Apart from an estimated 65,000 to 150,000 people who fled, there were discussions among the remaining population about the religious obligation to leave a country that was under control of non-Muslim rulers (Bougarel 2018). While initially the dual monarchy envisioned installing a regime that favoured Catholics, the Muslim leaders of the resistance were all arrested and executed within a few days. The colonial administrators also 'saw themselves as missionaries of a cultural revival that would end the backwardness and particularism that they believed bedevilled Bosnia's peoples' (Donia 2007: 1).

Following the occupation, the urban elite chose to compromise with the new imperial elites, while the rural Bosnian leaders called for independence and autonomy in their religious affairs, which was modelled along similar campaigns by the Serb Orthodox community (Okey 2007: 74–91). The provincial government regularly interfered in the religious affairs of Bosnian Muslims (Rustemović 2019). One of the most symbolic and crucial contestations was around the spiritual investiture (*menšura*) to the office of Reis-ul-Ulema (President of the Bosnian Muslim scholars) by the Sheikh-ul-Islam (chief mufti) of Istanbul. While Bosnian Muslims worked for such an investiture (Bougarel 2018), the long-time colonial administrator in charge, Benjámin von Kállay, understood this as 'making the Mahometans an autonomous national political unit with an administrative body, and thus a political factor equivalent to a "state within the state"' (Bougarel 2018: 19–20). He fully rejected what he feared to potentially become a 'Mahometan political nation' (*mohamedanische politische Nation*). The local administrator was told by Kállay that the sultan should have no power to interfere in religious affairs, because this would give him de facto sovereignty (Rustemović 2019: 26–7). The colonial empire implemented repressive measures such as banishing the leading voice of the autonomy movement, designating him a non-authorised emigrant after leaving the country. Others were imprisoned. At the same time, strategies were employed to best counter the political agency of Muslims. One could read in the Austrian press in 1908 on the issue of the *menšura*:

> Finally, it should be mentioned that the pan-Islamic current can also be felt in Austria-Hungary in Bosnia and Herzegovina. Its spiritual carriers have not yet shown their faces. They are probably also to be found in a secretly operating religious-political brotherhood, which is connected with religious-political circles in Constantinople. This movement appears in Bosnia in the so-called 'Menšura question', which is unmistakably pan-Islamic in character. (Quoted in Rustemović 2019, 30)

Only after many years of contestation and the death of the most powerful finance minister in charge of Bosnia and Herzegovina, Benjámin von Kállay, both parties concluded in 1909 that three candidates should be elected for the post of Reis-ul-Ulema by a spiritual electoral curia, whose names would be submitted to the regional government. Then, the emperor would appoint one from among the three candidates. In a final step, the spiritual electoral curia had to write a petition to the Sheikh-ul-Islam for the enactment of the *menšura* in the name of the person appointed by the emperor as Reis-ul-Ulema, via a diplomatic route through the embassy of the dual monarchy (Rustemović 2019: 28–31). This flip-flopping reveals several interesting aspects. On the one hand, there is the dominant role of the dual monarchy, which never vanished. On the other hand, there is the strengthened position of the Muslim movement, as seen in its political self-organisation and the allies it used to gain more independence, from the Serb-Orthodox, from whose struggles they learned, to the Ottoman Empire, to the Hungarians, who sympathised with them because of their own marginal role and nationalist ambitions within the dual monarchy. The pressure exerted by Muslims in Bosnia gave them some victory and autonomy when Bosnia was annexed in 1909, and also created the basis for the Islam Act of 1912, which recognised Muslims as a religious community in the Austrian part of the empire.

Postcolonial governance: saving Muslims from 'political Islam'

While Austria has a long history of incorporating Islam in the political system based on the Islam Act of 1912, which allowed Muslims to be recognised as a religious denomination alongside other religious communities, it was due to economic and diplomatic foreign policy considerations that Muslims were able to build on this legacy and re-establish the legally recognised Islamic Religious Community in 1979 (Hafez 2016a; Dautovic 2019). Demographically, Muslims did not play a major role in Austria for the next thirty years. The 9/11 attacks and the ensuing War on Terror were not taken as opportunities to politicise anti-Muslim grievances by the governing conservative Austrian People's Party ÖVP (Österreichische Volkspartei) and the far-right Freedom Party of Austria (FPÖ, Freiheitliche Partei Österreichs), due to the ÖVP's decision to not problematise Islam but, rather, to present the Austrian government as a non-racist one. This was especially important, given the diplomatic pressure on the Austrian government following the inclusion of a far-right party into government and the subsequent diplomatic boycott by the then remaining fourteen European Union member states (Hafez 2010).

But this understanding changed fundamentally after 2015. When the far-right FPÖ was in opposition again, it started focusing on Islam as a threat in 2005. Step by step, other political parties started co-opting this discourse, first and foremost being the conservative ÖVP. But while the FPÖ rallied against the religion of Islam as a threat, the ÖVP under Sebastian Kurz presented a much more differentiated discourse in the public sphere, arguing that it wanted to protect Muslims, was not against Islam, and was only against 'political Islam'. By introducing the notion of 'political Islam' into the public discourse, the ÖVP managed to distance itself from the blatant anti-Muslim discourse coming from the FPÖ, while at the same time criminalising every sign of Muslimness in a more sanitised language. As in many other countries in Europe, in the course of the War on Terror, 'Islam' – as an indefinite object, an imaginary, and not an ontological reality – has been turned into a security threat. By using the notion of 'political Islam', the ÖVP managed to fundamentally reshape the state's politics towards Muslim communities.

The notion of 'political Islam' is based on a similar concept developed by Germany's state authorities, especially the interior ministry, which implemented a law-and-order policy vis-à-vis the domestic Muslim population in the wake of the destruction of Manhattan's Twin Towers on 11 September 2001. The security apparatus criminalised many Muslim organisations by labelling them 'legalistic Islamists'. The secret service of the German Ministry of the Interior defines legalistic Islamism as follows:

> The vast majority of Islamists in Germany are 'legalists'. This term is used for members of Islamist organisations in Germany who strive to impose ideas of social and individual life based on Islamist ideology whilst abiding by the law. However, their goals are not reconcilable with the free democratic basic order. Officials and supporters of these organisations engage in lobbying to achieve their aims, intensively using the possibilities provided by the German legal system ('march through the courts'). They intend to obtain complete and permanent freedom for their members to live their lives in accordance with sharia. This, however, may lead to the development of parallel societies, which hinder integration. It is also possible that legalist Islamists promote the further radicalisation of (young) Muslims. (Bundesamt für Verfassungsschutz 2015)

As the secret service explicitly admitted, this approach included most Islamist (read Muslim) organisations in the definition. Thus, observations about large Muslim civil society organisations were included in the annual report of the secret service, the *Verfassungsschutzbericht* (Report on Constitutional Protection). The repercussions of being mentioned in these reports entailed social marginalisation and ineligibility for state funds. As a consequence, Muslims began to refrain from participating in Muslim civil society organisations so as to avoid being surveilled or becoming a state target (Öktem 2013: 46). In a welfare state like Germany, where the state plays a rather strong role in fields such as education, health, and public policy, an existing trend of class–ethnicity divides (Faist 1995) has expanded to encompass religious divides. The Ministry of the Interior also introduced several programmes such as the German Islam Conference (Deutsche Islamkonferenz, DIK), which was premised on racialising Muslims and framing them as security threats (Hernández Aguilar 2017). Many years after the German secret service had introduced this notion of 'legalistic Islamism', the ÖVP followed the same concept, but employed another term, 'political Islam'.

Introducing 'political Islam' in Austrian discourse

The term 'political Islam' that was introduced by the ÖVP was addressed more comprehensively for the first time in two subchapters of its election programme of 2017, called 'Showing zero tolerance towards political Islam' and in 'Preventing parallel societies':

> Political Islam is a combination of religious fundamentalism and political extremism and as such is a breeding ground for violence and terrorism. It aims to undermine our values and ways of life. Islam has no place in our society – we must fight radicalization, violence and terrorism with all means. (ÖVP 2017)

The danger of political Islam, according to the election programme, is three-fold: political Islam is a 'breeding ground for violence and terrorism [...] a totalitarian system with the ambition to produce parallel legal systems', and promoted from abroad to 'undermine our values and way of life' (ÖVP 2017: 23). This trend goes hand in hand with a discourse that has pursued a project of creating an 'Austrian/European-style Islam' (Hafez 2018), especially by Sebastian Kurz since his position as state secretary in the Federal Ministry of the Interior from 2011 onwards. The 'Islam of Austrian character' constitutes the other side of the coin of a negatively framed 'political Islam'.

Several institutions, from academia (Hafez 2020a) to policy-driven quasi-state institutions have been central in shaping the discourse on Islam. One of these is the Austrian Integration Fund (ÖIF, Österreichischer Integrationsfonds), which is a fund of the Republic of Austria that 'used its platform to promote anti-Muslim views through speakers and reports. The ÖIF supports the anti-Muslim policies of the Austrian People's Partys' (Bridge Initiative Team 2020b), and targeting 'political Islam' is part of its agenda. It organised several panels on 'The Influence of Political Islam' (ÖIF 2019), and similar panel discussions, where panellists argued that Islamophobia was a means of 'political Islam' to prevent reforms of liberal Muslims, saying: 'Political Islam strives to take over the Muslim community in Europe. In the process, ideas for reform or justified criticism are immediately dismissed wholesale as "Islamophobic"' (ÖIF 2020).

With continuous knowledge production over many years, several politicians of the ÖVP repeatedly framed 'political Islam' as the greatest threat to Austrian society. The ÖVP's general secretary argued, 'The poison of political Islam must not endanger our society [...] Violent clashes, territorial conflicts and parallel justice are on the agenda according to executive officials and judges' (Krone 2018). By using terminologies like 'poison', those who are framed as proponents of 'political Islam' are dehumanised, which justifies any extraordinary means against them. If Muslims are framed as carriers of poison or poisonous, every measure can be taken to protect oneself from them. This allows political leaders to justify political measures to be taken against this allegedly dangerous group of people. For Chancellor Kurz, tackling 'political Islam' meant to monitor Islamist associations, Islamist ideology on social media, and segregation in the realm of education (Renner 2019). This is essentially a way of criminalising thought and self-organisation, legitimising surveillance, and intimidating Muslim organisations and not going after criminal activities. While the intelligence services have minimal institutional contact with churches and religious communities, Muslims are the only religious group where the intelligence services regularly meet and surveil community leaders. Based on these securitised structures, the further institutionalisation of surveillance is not a far stretch.

Political 'answers' to 'political Islam'

A major shift in the legal regulation of Islam was the Islam Act of 2015. It was used by the governing parties, then the ÖVP and the social democratic SPÖ (Sozialdemokratische Partei Österreichs), as a means to fundamentally restructure the position of the state vis-à-vis the legally recognised Islamic Religious Community (IGGÖ) (Hafez 2017b). The state gave itself a stronger position in relation to the IGGÖ and gave preference to the IGGÖ over other Muslim associations, which previously were free to act under the Law of Association and now had to be organised under the Islam Act (Dautović and Hafez 2019). While protest came primarily from the Muslim civil society, the state-near IGGÖ seemed to be comfortable with this position (Hafez 2017a). Although members of Parliament of the governing parties, especially the SPÖ, reiterated that this was no law regulating issues regarding security, the head of the ÖVP's parliamentary faction drew parallels and made connections between the militant organisation ISIL (Islamic State in the Levant) and the Islam Act, arguing that it was an 'appropriate response to Islamism' (Hafez and Heinisch 2018). Based on this new law, the state also felt more empowered to interfere in Muslim religious affairs. In March 2017, the Federal Law on the Prohibition of the Concealment of the Face in Public (Anti-Facial Disposal Act) followed. The law that prohibited the face veil was praised as enabling 'the exchange between all people living in the public space' (Hafez 2018). The outspoken far-right politician Kurz stated that 'total veiling' was 'a symbol of antagonism and political Islamism and we resolutely fight it' (Hafez 2018). He further said, 'we stand by our European values, such as equality between men and women. We will continue to defend them unperturbed' (Hafez 2018). This reflects an old pattern that goes back to the colonial governing of Muslim women in France and elsewhere (Fanon 2003), where the white male saviour pretends to advocate freedom for women, while simultaneously he controls her identity by defining what to wear and what not to wear (Abu-Lughod 2013).

Things became even harsher following the inception of the new coalition of ÖVP and FPÖ (2017–19), where 'political Islam' for the first time became a focal point of governance. During this period, numerous laws were implemented to battle 'political Islam'. The FPÖ parliamentary group's party leader, Johann Gudenus, proposed a new Act that forbade political Islam, which was to be implemented in mid-2019 (APA 2019). Ultimately, the legislation did not pass, as the coalition dissolved. This failed legislation was reintroduced following the murder of four people in Vienna by a former ISIL sympathiser in November 2020. The socially more liberal and nominally not far-right Greens, now in coalition with the ÖVP, pushed against this move and watered the Bill down to ban 'religiously motivated extremism', while Integration Minister Raab (ÖVP) still declared during the presentation of the law that it was directed against 'political Islam' (Gaigg and Schmidt 2020). Until that point, there was no clear definition of 'political Islam' offered by the government, while at the same time one could infer from the implemented policies what the government actually meant by the term. Under the auspices of this policy and the broad brush encompassed by 'political Islam', individuals wearing a hijab, or people administering the affairs of a local mosque, could be potentially targeted. During the ÖVP–FPÖ coalition, the government announced that eight mosques would be closed to fight 'political Islam'. The chancellor framed the government's initiative as a means to protect ordinary Muslims from 'political Islam' (Gigler and Jungwirth 2019). This statement reflects two dimensions: on the one hand, the ÖVP does not want to appear blatantly racist, although its policies are de facto criminalising Muslimness. On the other hand, the ÖVP gives space to all those collaborative 'good Muslims', who support these policies while being assured that they would hurt only the 'bad Muslims'. Sanctimoniously, Minister Blümel (ÖVP) argued that it was 'no contradiction to be a believing Muslim and a proud Austrian' (Gigler and Jungwirth 2019). Following a complaint by the mosques, the Viennese Court of Administration ruled six months later that this initiative was against the law (ORF Wien 2019). In the same year, the government also decided to ban the hijab in public elementary schools and expressed its intention to extend this legislation to high schools, universities, and public service. This decision was repealed by the Constitutional Court in December 2020. Nevertheless, the battle against 'political Islam' continues to be a topic at the forefront of Austrian politics.

While the Austrian domestic intelligence service, the Federal Office for the Protection of the Constitution (BVT, Bundesamt für Verfassungsschutz und Terrorismusbekämpfung) had in the past used the terminology Islamism and jihadism in its annual report dating back as far as 1997, only in 2019 was the notion of 'political Islam' introduced. Furthermore, the content of the report deviated from previous as well as future reports. For the first time, the legally recognised IGGÖ was presented not as an ally against extremism but as an organisation from which risks emanate. The report presented three types of problematic manifestations: while the first two speak of jihadist and thus violent expressions of so-called Islamic extremism, the third speaks of explicit non-violent Islamic movements. According to the report, while these movements denounce the democratic constitutional state, they cooperate with parties, associations, and non-governmental organisations to have social and political impact. This could lead to a 'strategic infiltration with the aim of shaping and regulating the society according to social beliefs of the "caliphate" and "shari'a"' (ORF Wien 2019: 17). Here, political participation is framed as potential infiltration. According to this report, Islamists use education, social welfare services, and the organisation of cultural life in order to create a 'counter-society'. The goal is to prevent 'assimilation', which then becomes the very goal of the intelligence service itself. Never before had any Austrian state agency made such an indictment in an official document. Saying this, the BVT clearly went beyond its own scope, discussing not only security threats in society, but also laying down a social agenda. While it alleges that Islamists have an agenda of creating an alternative society, it appears this state agency itself follows a clear programme of making Muslims invisible. This major shift in the bureaucracy suggests that the discourse started by the ÖVP has found its way deep into the state authorities.

This tendency found its peak in the proclamation to create a monitoring centre that tracks religious extremism, conducts research, and archives and documents it (ORF 2019), which was only done when the Greens joined a coalition with the ÖVP as the junior partner in 2020. The Documentation Centre for Political Islam was established in July 2020 and presented by the minister of the interior, Susanne Raab, alongside two scholars, Mouhanad Khorchide (Bridge Initiative Team 2021c) and Lorenzo Vidino (Bridge Initiative

Team 2020a), all well-known propagators of the ÖVP's recent anti-Muslim policies. The Documentation Centre has been presented as 'part of the national strategy of extremism prevention and deradicalisation' (Wiener Zeitung 2020) with an annual budget of €500,000. According to Minister Raab, the Documentation Centre allows 'for the first time in Austria [...] to independently and scientifically deal with the dangerous ideology of political Islam and offer insights into the previously hidden networks' (Krone 2020). The board includes many unabashed and well-known anti-Muslim authors like Khorchide, Vidino, Susanne Schröter (Bridge Initiative Team 2021a), and Heiko Heinisch (Bridge Initiative Team 2021b). The Centre was presented by the minister as a pioneering project for Europe. Raab declared that the Centre will publish

> an overview map of problematic networks and associations in Austria that can be attributed to political Islam. The aim is to make visible structures, actors and goals of the representatives of this dangerous ideology. Financial, organisational and ideological connections (abroad) are also to be investigated and disclosed.

One year after the establishment of this Centre, the so-called 'Islam Map' was heavily criticised in public for presenting a map that showed all 623 Muslim associations and their addresses during a press conference of the Documentation Centre (Farzan 2021). From the beginning, the Documentation Centre claimed to present a 'detailed analysis of the individual networks operating in secret' (Farzan 2021). During the Centre's presentation in 2020, Khorchide argued that political Islam was 'wrapped with a cloak of democracy'. He further suggested that the proponents of political Islam would engage in *taqiyya* – dissimulation or denial of religious belief in the face of persecution – by masking their 'inwardly' values. According to this logic, whatever Muslims do, they cannot be trusted. While Susanne Raab reaffirmed that this monitoring centre was not directed against Islam as a religion, Muslim activists argued that it might become an 'institution of surveillance' (Religion ORF 2020). And one could add here that it might become an institution of criminalising Muslimness, when regular reports were produced insinuating that Muslims and their institutions were waging a war by integrating themselves into the system. If Muslims are not trusted, and their intention and their social activities are fundamentally questioned, they become 'Otherised' subjects, whose agency is framed as a fundamental opposition to the existing order. Hence, they have to be criminalised in order to be excluded from the resources of the power structures.

In November 2020, the interior minister (ÖVP) announced that a raid had been carried out against thirty people, including the author of this present chapter (Siddiqui 2021). According to the interior minister, this was aimed at 'cutting off the roots of political Islam' (The Local 2020). Eight months later, the Higher Court of Graz ruled that the raid was illegal (Thalhammer 2021). When the defendants accused of 'terrorist organisation' and 'terrorism finance' were interrogated following the raids, they were asked questions that had little to do with violence and militancy, but more to do with an Orientalist perspective on Islam and being Muslim with political views. The accused were routinely asked questions like: how many non-Muslim friends do you have? Do you visit a mosque, and if yes, which mosque? What do you think about the caliphate? What do you think about peace with Israel? Should kids raised in Austria be educated to become martyrs? Do you want to introduce sharia? Do you know the Protocols of the Elders of Zion? What do you understand by the term 'Islamophobia'? In your opinion, is this term justified? If so, please explain why and what do you understand by this term? Are Muslims suppressed in Austria? Is Islamist global terrorism possibly the reason for fears emanating from Islam or is it the oppression, especially of women or people of other faiths, by the norms of the sharia? May your son marry a Christian, unbeliever, or a Jew? Do you designate your son's spouse? What does the term 'Kuffare' (sic) mean for you? Are Christians for you Kuffar? Is one allowed to kill in the name of God? Do you and your wife and your kids observe the prayer times?[2]

One could write a whole book about the above questions. Clearly, they reveal the Orientalised perspective of the authorities. But first and foremost, they show how much imagined personal religious practices and perspectives have become a target of the state. Criminalising 'political Islam' has become a means to manage how Muslims ought to think, what political views they are allowed to have, and, lastly, whether they are allowed to contest inequalities, as the above question regarding Islamophobia suggests. There is no space for Muslim agency to combat Islamophobia or to think about and discuss Islamic concepts. In a nutshell, the notion of 'political Islam' manifests the imagination of a Muslim threat that has to be managed for security reasons.

This tendency goes so far as to criminalise thought rather than actions. Shortly after the militant attack in November 2020, Chancellor Kurz pledged to proclaim 'political Islam' a criminal offence. This legislation, which was heavily criticised by human rights associations like Amnesty International Austria (Amnesty International Austria 2021), is designed to criminalise thought, not actions. This Bill was implemented in the summer of 2020 and has the potential to criminalise Muslim agency that does not fit into the assimilationist paradigm or criticises current policies of the Austrian state.

Conclusion

In colonial as well as postcolonial politics regarding Islam and Muslims, one can see how governments interfered in the religious affairs of Muslim subjects. In colonial Bosnia, the central government feared that Muslims were working towards achieving autonomous status as a religious minority that was seen as a threat to the political order of the Empire. In postcolonial Austria, the ÖVP under the leadership of Sebastian Kurz denied Muslims equal treatment before the law with regard to religious autonomy.

The most powerful colonial governor, Benjámin von Kállay, feared the 'Mahometan political nation', and the media stirred up fear of a pan-Islamic movement working in secrecy. The colonial empire implemented repressive measures such as banishing leaders of the autonomous movement or imprisoning central actors. In postcolonial Austria, the ÖVP introduced the notion of 'political Islam' to portray Muslim religiosity and Muslim agency as a security threat. When proclaiming to fight 'political Islam', Austrian governments banned the hijab, closed mosques, and raided the homes of Muslim civil society leaders and critical anti-racist scholars including the author of this chapter.

With the latest idea to make 'political Islam' a criminal offence, the ÖVP is taking a step towards regulating not only socio-political agency, but ideas. While the annual report published by the Austrian secret service, BVT, reveals how hegemonic the discourse on 'political Islam' has become, the Documentation Centre for Political Islam was established to monitor, surveil, and subsequently criminalise Muslim associations. Lastly, the questions from the raid against alleged proponents of 'political Islam' reveal that these institutions, rather than targeting violence, are simply criminalising religious and political thought, as well as religious practice.

In a larger picture, these measures should be read as a further step in curtailing freedom of expression and freedom of religion, while heading towards the creation of more authoritarian structures by the nation-state in Austria and Europe.

Notes

1 Echoing Alison Howell and Melanie Richter-Montpetit's critique of classic securitisation theory as structured by Eurocentrism, civilisationism, methodological whiteness, and anti-Black racism, I use securitisation here as a word to simply name how Muslims are imagined as a threat (Howell and Richter-Montpetit 2020).
2 The questions are taken from the files of the investigation. Some of them can also be accessed online via: Arabischer Palästina-Club, Politisch motivierte Razzia und

Gesinnungsfragen bei BVT-Vernahmen, www.facebook.com/permalink.php?story_fbi
d=1760584047452617&id=1060883244089371 (accessed 15 November 2020).

Bibliography

Abu-Lughod, L. (2013). *Do Muslim women need saving?* Cambridge, MA: Harvard University Press.

Amnesty International Austria (2021). 'Anti-terror-package': a highly problematic quick shot ('Anti-Terror-Paket': Ein problematischer Schnellschuss), *Amnesty International Austria*, 26 January, www.amnesty.at/presse/anti-terror-paket-ein-problematischer-schnellschuss/ (accessed 4 April 2022).

APA (2019). 'Gudenus will Gesetz gegen politischen Islam bis Mitte 2019', *Der Standard*, 16 December, https://mobil.derstandard.at/2000094068620/Gudenus-will-Gesetz-gegen-politischen-Islam-bis-Mitte-2019 (accessed 5 September 2019).

Bougarel, X. (2018). *Islam and nationhood in Bosnia-Herzegovina: surviving empires*, London: Bloomsbury.

Bridge Initiative Team (2020a). Factsheet: Lorenzo Vidino, 22 April, *The Bridge Initiative*, https://bridge.georgetown.edu/research/factsheet-lorenzo-vidino/ (accessed 4 April 2022).

Bridge Initiative Team (2020b). Austrian Integration Fund (Österreichischer Integrationsfonds, ÖIF), *The Bridge Initiative*, 4 November, https://bridge.georgetown.edu/research/factsheet-austrian-integration-fund-osterreichische-integrationsfonds-oif/ (accessed 4 April 2022).

Bridge Initiative Team (2021a). Factsheet: Susanne Schröter, *The Bridge Initiative*, 13 January, https://bridge.georgetown.edu/research/factsheet-susanne-schroter/ (accessed 4 April 2022).

Bridge Initiative Team (2021b). Factsheet: Heiko Heinisch, *The Bridge Initiative*, 3 March, https://bridge.georgetown.edu/research/factsheet-heiko-heinisch/ (accessed 4 April 2022).

Bridge Initiative Team (2021c). Factsheet: Mouhanad Khorchide, *The Bridge Initiative*, 15 March, https://bridge.georgetown.edu/research/factsheet-mouhanad-khorchide/ (accessed 4 April 2022).

Bundesamt für Verfassungsschutz (2015). Islamist organisations, www.verfassungsschutz. de/en/fields-of-work/islamism-and-islamist-terrorism/figures-and-facts-islamism/ islamist-organisations-2015 (accessed 4 April 2022).

Dautovic, R. (2019). 40 Jahre seit Wiederherstellung der IRG-Wien. In: F. Hafez and R. Dautovic (eds), *Die Islamische Glaubensgemeinschaft in Österreich. 1909–1979–2019: Beiträge zu einem neuen Blick auf ihre Geschichte und Entwicklung*, Vienna: New Academic Press, 99–123.

Dautović, R. and Hafez, F. (2019). Institutionalizing Islam in contemporary Austria: a comparative analysis of the Austrian Islam Act of 2015 and Austrian Religion Laws with special emphasis on the Israelite Act of 2012, *Oxford Journal of Law and Religion*, 8(1): 28–50.

Donia, R. (2007). 'The proximate colony. Bosnia-Herzegovina under Austro-Hungarian rule', www.kakanien.ac.at/beitr/fallstudie/RDonia1.pdf (accessed 4 April 2022).

El Tayeb, F. (1999). 'Blood is a very special juice': racialized bodies and citizenship in twentieth-century Germany, *IRSH*, 44: 149–69.

El-Tayeb, F. (2008). 'The birth of a European public': migration, postnationality, and race in the uniting of Europe, *American Quarterly*, 60(3): 649–70.

Faist, T. (1995). Ethnicization and racialization of welfare-state politics in Germany and the USA, *Ethnic and Racial Studies*, 18(2): 219–50.

Fanon, F. (2003). Algeria unveiled. In: P. Duara (ed.), *Decolonization perspectives from now and then*, Abingdon: Routledge, 60–73.

Farzan, A.N. (2021). Muslim groups in Austria fear attacks after government publishes map of mosques, *Washington Post*, 29 May, www.washingtonpost.com/world/2021/05/29/austria-islam-map/ (accessed 4 April 2022).

Gaigg, V. and Schmidt, C.M. (2020). Antiterrorpaket: Neuer Straftatbestand zielt auf religiöse extremistische Verbindungen ab, *Der Standard*, 16 December, www.derstandard.at/story/2000122537911/ministerrat-will-umstrittenes-anti-terror-paket-beschliessen (accessed 4 April 2022).

Gigler, C. and Jungwirth, M. (2019). Regierung überprüft 61 Imame und schlie.t sieben Moscheen, *Kleine Zeitung*, 8 June, www.kleinezeitung.at/politik/innenpolitik/5442906/Jetzt-live_Regierung-plant-Ausweisung-von-40-Imamen-und (accessed 5 September 2019)

Grosse, P. (2005). What does German colonialism have to do with National Socialism? A conceptual framework. In: E. Ames, M. Klotz, and L. Wildenthal (eds), *Germany's colonial pasts* (Nebraska: University of Nebraska Press, 2005), 115–34.

Hafez, F. (2010). Österreich und der Islam – eine Wende durch FPÖVP? Anmerkungen zur Rolle von Islamophobie im politischen Diskurs seit der Wende. In: F. Baker and P. Herczeg (eds), *Die beschämte Republik: Zehn Jahre nach Schwarz-Blau in Österreich*, Vienna: Czernin Verlag.

Hafez, F. (2014). Gedenken im 'islamischen Gedankenjahr'. Zur diskursiven Konstruktion des österreichischen Islams im Rahmen der Jubiläumsfeier zu 100 Jahren Islamgesetz, *Wiener Zeitschrift für die Kunde des Morgenlandes*, 104: 63–85.

Hafez, F. (2016a). Ostarrichislam. Gründe der korporatistischen Hereinnahme des Islams in der Zweiten Republik, *ÖZP – Austrian Journal of Political Science*, 45(3): 1–11.

Hafez, F. (2016b). Comparing anti-Semitism and Islamophobia: the state of the field, *Islamophobia Studies Journal*, 3(2): 16–34.

Hafez, F. (2017a) Austrian Muslims protest against Austria's revised 'Islam Act', *Journal of Muslim Minority Affairs*, 37(3): 267–83.

Hafez, F. (2017b). Debating the 2015 Islam law in Austrian Parliament: between legal recognition and Islamophobic populism, *Discourse & Society*, 28(4): 392–412.

Hafez, F. (2018a). Alte neue Islampolitik in Österreich? Eine postkoloniale Analyse der österreichischen Islampolitik, *ZfP – Zeitschrift für Politik*, 65(1): 22–44.

Hafez, F. (2018b). Islamophobia in Austria: National Report 2017. In: E. Bayraklı and F. Hafez, *European Islamophobia report 2017*, Istanbul: SETA, 49–84.

Hafez, F. (2019). Muslim civil society under attack: the European Foundation for Democracy's role in defaming and delegitimizing Muslim civil society. In: J. Esposito and D. Iner (eds), *Islamophobia and Radicalization*, Cham: Palgrave Macmillan, 117–37.

Hafez, F. (2020a). Rassismus im Bildungswesen: zur Disziplinierung des muslimischen 'Anderen' im Bildungswesen am Beispiel des Diskurses zu islamischen Kindergärten in Österreich. In: M. Oberlechner, R. Heinisch, and P. Duval (eds), *Nationalpopulismus bildet? Lehren für Unterricht und Bildung*, Frankfurt am Main: Wochenschau Verlag, 100–22.

Hafez, F. (2020b). Institutionalizing the surveillance of Muslim activism in Austria, *The Bridge Initiative*, 15 September, https://bridge.georgetown.edu/research/institutionalizing-the-surveillance-of-muslim-activism-in-austria/ (accessed 4 April 2022).

Hafez, F. and R. Heinisch (2018). Breaking with Austrian consociationalism: how the rise of rightwing populism and party competition have changed Austria's Islam politics, *Politics & Religion*, 11(3): 649–78.

Hamann, U. (2015). *Prekäre koloniale Ordnung: Rassistische Konjunkturen im Widerspruch. Deutsches Kolonialregime 1884–1914*, vol. 21, Bielefeld: Transcript Verlag.

Hernández Aguilar, L.M. (2017). Suffering rights and incorporation. The German Islam Conference and the integration of Muslims as a discursive means of their racialization, *European Societies*, 19(5): 623–44.

Howell A. and Richter-Montpetit, M. (2020). Is securitization theory racist? Civilizationism, methodological whiteness, and antiblack thought in the Copenhagen School, *Security Dialogue*, 51(1): 3–22.

Krone (2018). Politischer Islam darf Bürger nicht gef.hrden, *Kronen Zeitung*, 1 October, www.krone.at/1780687 (accessed 5 September 2019).

Krone (2020). Dokumentationsstelle nimmt Extremismus ins Visier, *Kronen Zeitung*, 15 July, www.krone.at/2192166 (accessed 29 November 2020).

Kühne, T. (2013). Colonialism and the Holocaust: continuities, causations, and complexities, *Journal of Genocide Research*, 15(3): 339–62.

Loidl, S. (2012). Colonialism through emigration: publications and activities of the Österreichisch-Ungarische Kolonialgesellschaft (1894–1918), *Austrian Studies*, 20: 161–75.

Madley, B. (2005). From Africa to Auschwitz: how German South West Africa incubated ideas and methods adopted and developed by the Nazis in Eastern Europe, *European History Quarterly*, 5(3): 429–64.

Messerschmidt, A. (2017). Rassismusthematisierungen in den Nachwirkungen des Nationalsozialismus und seiner Aufarbeitung. In: K. Fereidooni and M. El (eds), *Rassismuskritik und Widerstandsformen*, Wiesbaden: Springer, 855–67.

ÖIF (2019). ÖIF-Diskussion zu Islam in Europa: 'Muslime müssen in Europa geltende Werte und Gesetze leben', *OTS*, 23 January, www.ots.at/presseaussendung/OTS_20180123_OTS0166/oeif-diskussion-zu-islam-in-europa-muslime-muessen-in-europa-geltende-werte-und-gesetze-leben (accessed 5 September 2019).

ÖIF (2020). Bruckner: 'Berechtigte Religionskritik und antimuslimische Haltungen nicht vermischen', *Österreichischer Integrationsfonds*, 5 February, www.integrationsfonds.at/newsbeitrag/podiumsgespraech-bruckner-5144 (accessed 29 November 2020).

Okey, R. (2007). *Taming Balkan nationalism: the Habsburg 'civilizing mission' in Bosnia, 1878–1914*, Oxford and New York: Oxford University Press.

Öktem, K. (2013). Signale aus der Mehrheitsgesellschaft. Auswirkungen der Beschneidungsdebatte und staatlicher Überwachung islamischer Organisation auf Identitätsbildung und Integration in Deutschland, Oxford: Zentrum für Europastudien and Oxford University, September, http://tezhamburg.files.wordpress.com/2013/09/signale-aus-der-mehrheitsgesellschaft.pdf (accessed 4 April 2022).

ORF (2019). Offenbar Beobachtungsstelle gegen Extremismus geplant, *ORF*, 12 January.

ORF Wien (2019). Gericht: Moscheenschließung rechtswidrig, *ORF Wien*, 14 February, https://wien.orf.at/v2/news/stories/2964549/ (accessed 4 April 2022).

ÖVP (2017). Der neue Weg. Ordnung and Sicherheit 3/3. *Das Programm der Liste Sebastian Kurz – die neue Volkspartei zur Nationalratswahl 2017.*

Potz, R. and Schinkele, B. (2016). *Religion and Law in Austria*, Alphen aan den Rijn: Kluwer Law International.

Religion ORF (2020). IGGÖ-Kritik an Dokustelle für 'politischen Islam', *ORF*, 15 July, https://religion.orf.at/v3/stories/3004988/ (accessed 29 November 2020).

Renner, G. (2019). Beobachtungsstelle neu. Ein D.W für Islamisten! Oder: Wie die Regierung schnell zurück zu ihrem Lieblingsthema kommt, *Kleine Zeitung*, 3 March, www.kleinezeitung.at/meinung/5588894/Beobachtungsstelle-neu_Ein-DOeW-fuer-Islamisten-Oder_Wie-die (accessed 19 December 2019).

Rustemović R. (2019). Die Rolle der Autonomiebewegung der bosnischen Muslime bei der Anerkennung des Islams in der Habsburgermonarchie. In: Rijad Dautović und Farid Hafez (eds), *Die Islamische Glaubensgemeinschaft in Österreich. 1909–1979–2019 Beiträge zu einem neuen Blick auf ihre Geschichte und Entwicklung*, Vienna: New Academic Press, 19–44.

Sauer, W. (2011). Auf dem Weg zu einer Kolonialgeschichte Österreichs, *Den Nil aufwärts. Österreich in Geschichte und Literatur*, 55(1): 2–5.

Sauer, W. (2012). Habsburg colonial: Austria-Hungary's role in European overseas expansion reconsidered, *Austrian Studies*, 20: 5–23.

Siddiqui, U. (2021). Muslim Austrian academic shares tale of gunpoint raid, *Aljazeera English*, 4 March, www.aljazeera.com/news/2021/3/4/muslim-professor-reveals-raid-in-austria (accessed 4 April 2022).

Thalhammer, A. (2021). Operation Luxor: Razzia laut OLG Graz rechtswidrig, *Die Presse*, 3 August, www.diepresse.com/6016465/operation-luxor-razzia-laut-olg-graz-rechtswidrig (accessed 4 April 2022).

The Local (2020). Police in Austria raid dozens of 'Islamist-linked' addresses, *The Local*, 9 November, www.thelocal.at/20201109/police-in-austria-raid-dozens-of-islamist-linked-addresses/ (accessed 4 April 2022).

Wiener Zeitung (2020). Job advertisement for the board of the documentation center for Political Islam, *Wiener Zeitung*, www.wienerzeitung.at/amtsblatt/aktuelle_ausgabe/artikel/?id=4409041 (accessed 29 November 2020).

Younes. A.-E. (2016). Race, colonialism and the figure of the Jew in a new Germany. Dissertation, Berlin: Graduate Institute of International and Development Studies.

Zimmerer, J. (2005). The birth of the Ostland out of the spirit of colonialism: a postcolonial perspective on the Nazi policy of conquest and extermination, *Patterns of Prejudice*, 39(2): 197–219.

Chapter 6

Islamophobia in the United Kingdom: the vicious cycle of institutionalised racism and reinforcing the Muslim 'Other'

Tahir Abbas

Introduction

This chapter provides an overview of the salient features of Islamophobia in the United Kingdom (UK). It explores how the concept is related to ongoing issues of racism, orientalism, and social exclusion, all of which are perpetuated by a deepening sense of ethnic nationalism, which is exclusionary to both indigenous-born minorities who are citizens of the state and outsiders, including white and Christian groups that herald from European Union (EU) Christian-majority nations. This virulent nationalism aims to determine an idea of Englishness that remains rooted in existing class and ethnic inequalities, compounded by the Brexit discourse and the UK's eventual withdrawal from the EU. The COVID pandemic has revealed the extent of structural Islamophobia, with Muslim minority groups significantly more likely to catch the virus and die from it; this being a function of existing patterns of exclusion and disadvantage that impact on Muslim minority experiences in the UK, but also because of racial and ethnic inequalities that continue to plague the health service of the country. The chapter explores a series of issues in relation to exclusion and racialisation that have ongoing and lingering effects which result in Islamophobia. First, the issues of migration, settlement, and adaptation in the post-war period with regard to the experiences of Muslim minority groups in the global North, in particular the UK, are explored. Second, Islamophobia as understood and practised implies creating 'extremism' among disaffected Muslim minorities, but also disillusioned ethnic majorities. Third, this in turn has the effect of inducing Islamophobia and therefore perpetuating a cycle of violence and extremism, as will be discussed. Fourth, it is possible to eliminate the negativity associated with the representation of Muslims in society, and some suggestions are provided. In conclusion, it is argued that the perpetual nature of the cyclical dynamics of Islamophobia and radicalisation creates significant challenges without real opportunities for moving forward. The issues rest at the level of political elites who purposely take advantage of a divide and rule perspective. This is combined with an economy that continues to divide people based on those with existing levels of privilege, as compared with new and current minority groups who face considerable downward pressures on their social mobility and, therefore, their sense of inclusion and participation in society.

Migration, settlement, and adaptation

The period immediately after the Second World War led to the mass migration of Muslims to Europe, America, and Australia (Abbas, 2017b). Driven by the economic needs of various nations undergoing rapid transformation, the emergence of groups from Muslim nations led to patterns of economic, political, and cultural subjugation that have remained resilient in the intervening years. One such community in Europe is the Turks, who came to Europe as immigrant labour, in particular to Germany and Denmark, where opportunities arose in the motor and vehicle manufacturing sectors. Many of the Turks who immigrated came from the less-developed sending regions of Anatolia. These workers possessed little by way of formal education or skills before arrival, resulting in their enduring marginalisation due to the lack of opportunity to up-skill once the motor-industrial sector of the economy began to deteriorate in the 1970s. This was a pattern repeated for Pakistanis working in the heavy engineering sectors in the UK and Denmark, with Moroccans and Algerians facing similar problems in the major industrial cities of France.

Although nervousness exists around the integration of Muslim minority communities into post-industrial societies, the matter of Islam re-entering European society has also been an issue. Over time, Muslim minority groups established themselves through attempts at integration, hoping to achieve economic and social mobility, plus political and cultural assimilation. However, the demands placed upon various states concerning particular religious needs and wants created tension among the majority (Fetzer and Soper 2005). Many decades later, these Muslim groups are still occupying lower socio-economic positions. In the case of Britain and France, issues of historical colonialism endure in defining the locale of social relations between the Muslim minority and non-Muslim majority groups during the phases of immigration and integration, although this did not apply to Turks in Germany (Küçükcan 2004). Despite these historical distinctions, racial and ethnic exclusion is persistent and systematic for different Muslim minorities across Western Europe (Amiraux 2005). The end of economic immigration during the early 1970s resulted in a process of family reunification as the primary means of moving from Muslim lands into Western Europe. This episode also witnessed the Arab oil crisis of 1974 and the emergence of confrontations such as the Iranian Revolution and the Soviet invasion of Afghanistan (Peach and Glebe 1995). In more recent periods, another layer in this new-found emergence of Islam in Europe relates to how Muslims arrived as refugees and asylum seekers, as seen during the 'Balkanisation' of former Yugoslavia in the 1990s. This has continued since the War on Terror, the Iraq war, and in the aftermath of the Arab Spring and the fall of the Islamic State, which has displaced countless Muslims due to oppression, political unrest, and violence.

The processes of deindustrialisation, globalisation, and neoliberalism have gone hand in hand since the events of 9/11. Alongside them, a notable shift to the political right has also emerged across a whole host of Western European nations. Along with Britain, France, and Germany, nations such as the United States, Canada, and Australia are struggling with the question of how to deal with their own so-called 'Muslim problem' (Ahmed and Donnan 1994). Caused by their geographical concentration into poorer parts of towns and cities, the visibility of Muslim groups adds to apprehensions framed by elites promoting the 'unassimilability' of Muslims, combined with a focus on the security threat of Muslims. Discussions on Muslims living 'parallel lives' have also abounded during this time (Phillips 2006), resulting in polarisations between the words of political elites and the realities facing Muslim communities in towns and cities across nations (Abbas 2019). These concerns have led to the emergence of questions relating to community, identity, integration, and equality. The prevailing political discourse, however, routinely rejects the question of the potential assimilability of Muslims in Europe. Since the early 2000s, political actors and commentators have raised distinct challenges in response to various acts of terrorism conducted by European-born Muslims of South Asian, Middle Eastern, or North African backgrounds.

Young men implicated in these attacks have presented their acts of violence in the name of Islam, despite the palpable but under-reported outcries by Muslims everywhere. Solutions identified by states converge on pressing the need for deeper loyalty to a set of dominant cultural values, which are undefined. Simultaneously, Muslims face widespread surveillance of groups in society, with securitisation of the question of multiculturalism. The 'clash of civilisations' thesis, first expounded in the late 1980s but still widely propagated today, dominates this rhetoric. It has convinced many on the political far-right that their apprehensions have materialised with regard to the unavoidable clash between Islam and the West, with the origins of conflict inherent only in Islam, not the West. Despite these discourses, a 'myth of return' is no more (Anwar 1979). Muslims in Western Europe and North America are a part of the fabric of their new societies. They are engaging with the political process and continuing to advance their positions in education and employment within diverse urban centres. Most Muslims support open-minded religious and cultural norms and values. They are also becoming increasingly confident, despite all the political and cultural challenges they face (Anwar 2008; Norris and Inglehart 2012; Schumann 2007).

The media is swift to associate Muslims with dissent and implicate them in the 'clash of civilisations'. This approach neutralises attempts to underscore the ongoing impacts of globalisation and neoliberalism. It permits media power to continue to concentrate on fundamentalism and extremism as the principal drivers of hostilities. An ongoing example is the question of the hijab, which frames Muslim women as suppressed by Muslim men and the faith of Islam. However, it also drives public interest onto the apparent unassimilability of Muslims in secular liberal democracies. French politics routinely resist the hijab, and during the 2000s, France actively banned the niqab (the 'face veil'). These actions convey more about France than about its Muslims, in particular, how the policy pertains to associate an entire Muslim community seemingly unable to adhere to the norms and values of *liberté, égalité,* or *fraternité.* It takes the focus away from most French Muslim women who do not wear any kind of headscarf. Disapproving representation of Islam and Muslims, therefore, reproduces the power relations between Muslims and non-Muslims, objectifying an entire community of communities. Through tokenism, selectivity, and the inherent bias attuned to supporting the status quo, the formulation of curiosity about Muslims is through the frame of anxiety, dissonance, and difference, affecting Muslim–non-Muslim relations in significant ways.

Europe and Islam share a significant history where violence and conflict have characterised the interaction, but an immense appreciation of the 'Other', the latter regularly forgotten. Over the centuries, Muslims were colonised, and when the 'masters' left, the once-colonised arrived in the 'mother country' to struggle for the crumbs of the cake their ancestors had effectively gathered the ingredients to bake. Islamophobia intensified during these periods of contact and demonisation. Because of this experience, particular features are remarkably resistant to change, for example, given how part of English social and economic history is still so important to national identity. With global events in Muslim lands dominating the geopolitical landscape since the end of the Cold War, Islamophobic discourse permeates society at every level. Meanwhile, Muslim umbrella organisations compete for authenticity and a seat at the table of the same power that feeds its thinking from the inkwells of the right-wing think-tanks and media-savvy politicos whom they seek to challenge. As to intellectual impact, policy development, and the resultant action of these endeavours, little emerges save from extensive community engagement and limited hurried policy responses fine-tuned to appeal to the middle ground (Mandeville 2009). Islamophobia is enacted at the level of the individual, community, organisational, and societal, and it is local and global (Morgan and Poynting 2016).

Islamophobia as constructing 'Muslim extremism'

Islamophobia has been in existence since well before the events of 9/11. Although it emerged as a concept used by academics and policy makers during the 1990s, the reality of Islamophobia is as old as Islam itself. It is based on a reimagining of the Orient, a reconceptualising of the 'Other', and a reframing of the discourse of difference across societies that emphasises an 'us' and 'them', the civilised and the uncivilised, the familiar and the unfamiliar, the insider and the outsider, the West and the rest. Nonetheless, events have also had a role in reshaping the discourse. Muslims began to enter the imagination of Western political, cultural, and intellectual discourse during the Rushdie affair in Britain in 1989 (Weller 2013). This event raised to the fore concerns over the supposed unassimilability of Muslim groups who were previously considered 'ethnic' or 'Asian' as part of the post-war 'new commonwealth' migration instigated by the British government, initially in the late 1940s and utilised until the late 1950s, when popular opinion revealed racism at the core of society (Shaffer 2008). These disquiets have existed ever since then, but they have also taken on a new lease of life. Since the events of 9/11, not only have reported incidences of violence and aggression towards Muslims in Britain increased but the wider majority population has shown a tendency of greater prejudice towards Muslims. These events are not mere historical backdrops but, in fact, have real implications for the Muslim experience and perceptions of Muslims by the dominant 'Other'. The events of 9/11 did not fundamentally change the world. Rather, they confirmed an existing set of prejudices and discriminations that further accelerated their impacts, in the process transforming binary identities into rigid categories of self and 'Other', Muslim and non-Muslim, Islam and the West (Poynting and Mason 2007).

The nature of globalisation, neoliberalism, and the endorsement of capitalism across swathes of Middle Eastern and Asian Muslim territories invariably leads to social divisions and political polarities that destabilise nations and create the conditions for social conflict and problematic ethnic relations.

Part of this dilemma is a consequence of wider global historical trepidation about the nature of relations between groups based on colour and power, but a significant part is also because of the 'Muslimness' of Muslims to act appropriately. Islamophobia is not a given or an absolute. It is a relative experience dependent on context, opportunity, and design. Muslims across the world have been on the global political map as victim communities, suffering from patterns of oppression and underdevelopment attributed to systems of the West. An extensive real and significant historical circumstance exists in appreciating the dynamics that operate in many nations, and among different Muslim minority communities, but the occasion for change from within is omitted, unless the West ameliorates, thereby reinforcing Orientalist tropes about the Muslim 'Other'.

Some find it difficult to accept the 'R' word. Racism is a concept that completely disappeared from the popular vernacular on understanding differences in society. A greater focus is on notions of values. Today, much of all of this refers to the intractable problem that emerges from being British and being European, as regularly expounded by the dominant hegemonic media and political elite. Race has disappeared from the agenda, not by accident, but by design. Anti-racism had its heyday in the late 1970s, but then meandered. By the 1980s, multiculturalism was the buzzword, as if it would solve the problems of racism. However, while multiculturalism raises awareness of differences, it did not fight racism, structural discrimination, or ethnic inequalities in practice. After 9/11, multiculturalism in Western Europe refers to a security agenda that isolates Muslims and immigrant groups. Here, Muslims are treated as a racial group, where anti-Islam hatred replaces the defining characteristic of racism. Racism, moreover, is different from racialism, which is the idea that we are all tribalistic. A strong undercurrent suggests that it is acceptable to be anti-racist, but there are Muslim-specific issues that worry 'us' about 'their values'. It results in blindness to the deeper structural factors that lead to discrimination and a desire to focus on culture, or multiculture, as a means to fight racism, which is almost impossible because racism or equality are not about culture. This Islamophobia as new-found anti-Muslim racism has become the dominant hegemon that divides 'us' and 'them'. This critique is an implicit misrecognition of Muslim minorities in Western Europe (Lentin and Titley 2012). Moreover, Islamophobia has driven far-right social, community, and political activism across Western Europe. From the English Defence League, Britain First and National Action in Britain, to the National Front in France, to the Party for Freedom in the Netherlands, to the Northern League in Italy, to the Pax Europa Citizens' Movement in Germany, far-right groups have entered the popular imagination in local area communities and in national politics (Abbas 2017a). The racialisation of Muslims through the political and media manufacture of Muslims as monsters goes beyond 'managing extremists' as such, to the more general signifier of Muslims as 'extremist'.

Extremism as manifestations of Islamophobia

It is important to consider issues of social structure and identity politics when attempting to understand the nature of radicalisation and extremism among those who engage in far-right extremism as well those drawn to Islamist extremism. In the current political climate, the projection is that violent radical Islamism is a reality of Muslim communities, in which lie all the problems and all the solutions. That far-right and Islamist extremists are similarly problematic with distinctively related issues, as the path towards radicalisation is local and urban in nature and outcome, is largely true. A need exists to recognise that these kinds of extremisms are two sides of the same coin, where limiting one will invariably reduce the other. Both perspectives feed off the rhetoric of the 'Other', compounded by elite discourse that looks to maintain a divide and rule approach to dealing with differences in society, combined with the issue of the diminished status of white working-class communities in general terms. A greater understanding of the linkages, interactions, and symbiosis between these two oppositional but related extremisms is crucial. This is especially the case in the current epoch, where a post-truth, post-normal world has gained ascendancy, with experts derided and the status quo prevailing.

In 2017, there were five UK terrorist attacks, with thirty-five people dead and many others injured. The security services thwarted nine further potential attacks, including one targeting Downing Street and the prime minister. At the same time, Islamophobia is becoming virulent and more aggressive than ever. While investment goes into counter-terrorism and countering violent extremism projects, these attacks keep happening. This is the hyper-normalisation of Islamophobia and radicalisation, yet we are no closer to solving either of them. With critics of all hues silenced, the average citizen is confused. This is also an age of rampant disinformation, and there seems to be no escape from it. The current wave of anti-Islam 'fake news' or disinformation began after the events of 9/11, although it is clear that Orientalism and Islamophobia have a much longer history in the West. The 'weapons of mass destruction' led to the illegal invasion of Iraq, when much of the world argued, with millions demonstrating in cities all of the world, that Saddam Hussain was no threat to the West and going into Iraq was a folly that would cost countless lives and destabilise the region. After numerous pressures derailed the Arab Spring in Egypt, the attacks on Libya and Syria led to the disruption of the entire Middle East and North Africa (MENA) region and the emergence of the Islamic State, whose origins lie in Western attempts to arm Sunni rebels in opposition to President Bashar al-Assad. The era of UK fakery heightened during the Brexit campaign. Based on huge distortions of fact, it divided a nation into two, leaving a country stranded.

So-called ethnic 'ghettos', where specific Muslim groups are sometimes found living, rarely out of choice, are not a reflection of communities necessarily choosing to live among themselves. Instead, their experience reflects the failures of government policy to implement integration and equality policy and practice. At the same time, former 'white' working classes have also suffered because of deindustrialisation, technological innovation, and globalisation, and face ongoing cultural, economic, and political disenfranchisement because of it. For most Muslims, they keep their ethnic, faith, and cultural norms and values as solace, which some majorities may regard as a retreat into regressive practices. However, though they also suffer from marginalisation in society, ostracised 'white' groups have the history of their nation, whether imagined or real, and the co-ethnic partisanship of the dominant hegemonic order at their disposal. Combined with this gloomy condition, the dominant political discourse continues to blame the assailants for their 'values' or 'crises of identity', rarely scrutinising the workings of wider society to appreciate the holistic character of social conflict. Routinely instrumentalised are issues to do with freedom of expression, or categorising values as alien, all of which ensure that the focus is on the terrorists. Attacks from 2015 to 2017 by takfiri-jihadis in London, Paris, Berlin, Nice, Barcelona, and Sydney were all carried out by the sons of immigrant minorities caught between cultures. Rather than supported and developed as individuals and communities in society, through mechanisms not always of their agency, the far fringes of marginalised groups vented their frustrations back towards the centre. All these attackers were the insiders-outsiders of society.

Structural crises affect Muslim groups in the Muslim world and the West. Many of the pre-migration sending countries still have difficulty with trust in the political process, habitually needed for stable democracies. Material and economic issues are also underdeveloped. As young people become vulnerable, they also become outraged. Many of the young men and women who ended up in the Islamic State had little or no real appreciation of Islam at all. In this respect, young people want to develop a sense of themselves for a whole host of reasons, but where a specified political Islam provides a pre-prepared model it is necessary to accept how the lived experience in the West contributes to pushing young people towards extremism. To look at the structure of societies and their popular culture is vital, where structural disadvantage is measurable, conflated by the extreme centre of the political spectrum, which pushes out dissenting voices to the periphery. Opportunities are limited in a climate where the 'us' and 'them' dichotomy designed by the powerful affects the most powerless. Those who want to give the impression that everything else affecting people associated with these categories is insignificant in determining both the push and the pull wish to place the spotlight on Islam and Muslims.

Those gravitating towards zones of conflict in the Middle East do so because of push and pull factors, but other individuals are also vulnerable. Huge generalisations are dangerous; such is the power of the media that even right-minded people can end up overstating the crises, fuelling a perennial cycle of fear, hate, and violence. Many other struggles affect Muslim communities across the globe, but misinformation routinely promulgated by self-serving interests fuel protestations on all sides. Muslims have far greater struggles than merely violent extremism. Moreover, around the world today Muslims are the victims of violent extremism more than any other group. Shi'as, Sufis, Christians, and Jews are all subject to its might. Religion justifies, but conundrums of integration, alienation, power, authority, and social class cannot be underestimated. Ill-informed policy making has its unintended consequences. In many of the instances of Muslim-originated violence found in Western Europe in the last few months alone, the role of the policing, security, and intelligence services remains unclear – not in how they managed to prevent these atrocities or otherwise, but in how many of the young men involved in the violence were on their radars, and in some cases had been picked up and mistreated by the authorities.

Reducing the stigmatisation of Muslim communities

While policies to counter violent extremism have been in play since the beginning of the War on Terror, there remain ongoing challenges in relation to impact and effectiveness, to such an extent that some of these policies are seen as doing more harm than good. For example, one of the most widely criticised aspects the UK's countering violent extremism programming has been the Prevent strategy. The Prevent strategy forms a branch of the UK's overall countering violent extremism policy, referred to as Channel. Prevent was aimed at identifying individuals who may be on a trajectory towards violent extremist activity and preventing such individuals before they engaged in these activities. In 2015 the programme was instituted on a statutory basis. This required people working in the public sector, such as teachers, nurses, and other healthcare professionals, to report individuals who they suspected were vulnerable to radicalisation. Not doing so could involve institutional repercussions (Younis 2021). The Prevent strategy did not claim to target any specific ethnic or religious groups; however, in practice it overwhelmingly targeted Muslim communities. According to data collected by the UK government in 2018, 'Islamist extremists' were seventeen times more likely to be referred to Prevent than individuals engaging in 'far-right' extremist activities (Home Office 2018). Despite representing approximately only 5 per cent of the UK population, Muslims accounted for 65 per cent of the referrals to the Prevent programme. Recent data indicates that 95 per cent of the Muslim referrals to Prevent required no further Channel intervention (Butt 2019). In other words, 95 per cent of the Muslims referred to Prevent were falsely identified and did not pose a threat. Muslims were forty to fifty times more likely than non-Muslims to be referred to this programme, roughly a quarter of these referrals being youth under the age of fifteen (Butt 2019). The Prevent strategy has disproportionately targeted Muslim communities, and consequently has had far-reaching effects in these communities. Many Muslims in the UK feel stigmatised because of the wide net cast by this programme. Muslim parents have felt the need to think twice about how they educate their children about Islam, and may even encourage them to engage in self-censorship out of fear that they may be flagged through this programme. These concerns are legitimate, as Muslim children as young as four years have been misidentified by Prevent (Kundnani 2014).

How is it possible, then, to counter violent extremism through a multi-layered, multifaceted approach that reduces stigmatisation and resistance? The latter is reproduced unwittingly by the present approach to countering violent extremism, especially in Britain and in other parts of Western Europe. The dominant, negative, discourse on the role of religion in society, in particular among Muslim communities in the West, has a profound effect at many different levels. The problems of stigmatisation are further illustrated below (Abbas, 2021).

First, it creates the impression that Muslim communities are homogeneous, powerless, and entirely unable to organise themselves in response to the challenges of violence through extremism. It takes away their agency and narrows the lens through which state–community relations are formulated. If governments in Western Europe and North America wish to talk to their Muslim communities only about terrorism and radicalisation, it disengages groups who encounter their own internal ethnic, sectarian, and cultural divisions and conflicts. It also raises suspicion that governments are interested only in a type of liberal Islam that is pro-integration, based specifically on values and nurturing identities rather than the structural realities affecting communities.

Second, while narratives of exclusion and victimisation exist within the wider context of Muslim communities who are in the process of integrating into majority society, one cannot ignore the fact that a great deal of evidence supports their claims, which is ignored or simply disregarded. A particular discourse on the 'left behind' concerns the aspirations and social mobilisations of what could be described as former white working-class communities (Beider 2015). This is well documented in research on social inequalities and social immobility (Dorling 2019). It is no surprise, therefore, that many Muslim migrants who came to the West, particularly into Western Europe as part of a post-war migration process, now as third and even fourth generations, also experience genuine instances of economic and cultural alienation. One emphasis on the part of state actors is to draw attention to cultural questions within communities with respect to concerns such as the treatment of women, female genital mutilation, or grooming of vulnerable young women. This potentially further alienates a significant body of people looking to the state for answers to struggles which they collectively suffer as communities and neighbourhoods.

Third, while there is a presumption that it is the religious narrative that encourages vulnerable young people to turn to violent Islamist radicalisation to generate solutions to their worldly struggles, analysis of social media from the militant group the Islamic State of Iraq and Syria (ISIS) suggests that less than 10 per cent of its recruitment output refers to religion alone (Zelin 2015). Rather, the likes of ISIS focus on grievances, which are rooted in the experience of Muslims in Western European and North American societies. Recruiters play on the injustices of racism, exclusion, vilification in the media, political marginalisation, and cultural isolation. It is not simply enough to provide counter-narratives but it is necessary to work towards models of social equality that encourage social cohesion, building trust and confidence in the institutions of the state and the workings of society more generally.

Fourth, it is almost impossible for researchers, policy makers, and activists to encourage governments to shift the huge juggernaut that is the dominant trend of neoliberal economics across the Western world. Nor is it possible to prop up states that are close to collapse (or have 'gone rogue'), therefore leading to insecurity and injustices meted out by the arms of these various states. There is, however, room to work with grassroots civil society organisations. Such groups are committed to challenging violent extremism within their communities, building social and political trust in the process. Moreover, these community groups undergo the brunt of criticism from within their communities for 'selling out'. They also encounter the challenges of capacity and resource limitations facing small organisations competing for investment in a marketplace that is crowded and squeezed, due to limitations in the availability of funding in general.

Fifth, a specific way to counter the narratives is by empowering Muslim communities in the West through Islam. This is not a suggestion without merit. During the 1980s, the German government invested a great deal of thought in developing a system of Islamic education for the growing number of German-born Turks who confronted the brunt of racism and discrimination at one level. At the other level, these Turks encountered intergenerational disconnect from parents whose cultural values were attuned to their lives in the sending regions before migration. The German initiative was a well thought-out programme that aimed to introduce Islamic education funded by the state. It was abandoned, due to various political pressures, but only after Helmut Kohl's government spent three years investigating the topic, generating the research, and producing the policy guidelines (Berglund 2015).

Conclusion

We live in post-normal times, which suggest that a whole host of issues of social, political, cultural, and geological nature are shifting at enormous rates. They are also moving at a rate beyond our abilities to know the nature of their course with any degree of confidence. Policy makers, communities, and individuals across the world are unable to come to terms with the vastness of change and the endless uncertainty it brings. Observation of human phenomena can provide us with a view that individuals today can influence the futures of tomorrow – challenging the instruments of power to determine a positive social change. While we can say with reasonable predictability that we will get most of the predictions reliably wrong, one thing that is always foreseeable is that change is inevitable.

The Muslim population in the global North, especially in the UK, is undergoing a dramatic transformation of its socio-economic profile, where increasing residential urbanisation and clustering is observable in some of the older towns and cities across nations. While a specific problem of the underachievement of young Muslim men in education is a concern, the relative overachievement of young Muslim women in education is not always realised in terms of labour market participation rates. Therefore, gender equality is a priority, but not just to empower women, which is an urgent issue, but also to empower men who face all sorts of crises of masculinity in the context of neoliberal globalisation and hyper-localisation. The rise in the profile of dual-income middle-class Muslim households, with both heads possessing advanced tertiary education, from established universities, is important, but a Muslim brain drain also exists because of the pressures of racism, discrimination, and cultural marginalisation that lead to suppression of social mobility and a deep sense of under-appreciation.

Muslims in the UK are young, with one in three under the age of fifteen, which is consistent with Muslim world population profiles. This dynamic has not shifted since the mid-2000s. Two-thirds of all the people on the move in the world today are Muslims, and conflicts in the world today are often in Muslim-majority countries. When these lands are the most affected by capitalism, Muslims face the greatest consequences of the destabilisation of capitalism. In addition, while it is inevitable that Islamophobia can drive different radicalisations that create further Islamophobia, it is important to break this cycle, reverse-engineering the process that leads to harmful consequences. But before this can happen, Muslim communities need to firmly own Islamophobia and define it from within, which does mean the need to engage with the state in meaningful dialogue to challenge its workings effectively. Speaking truth to power disrupts the speed, scope, and scale of the uncertainty faced today. However, we also live in times of great ignorance, surpassed by heaps of arrogance. The consequences of globalisation and unfettered capitalism are palpable. The dominant hegemon that is the present world order is bereft of any new ideas, partly based on the failures of ideas of all kinds, as political Islam and Western liberalism both have collapsed. One has a consequence for the 'Other', and the maintenance of these 'Self'–'Other' identities perpetuates ongoing conflict.

In the case of Muslims, the problems of the hyper-masculinity of men and the unreconstructed nature of patriarchy that exists within households are at odds with wider society, where a gradual decline of masculinity and the improving nature of gender equality continue in earnest in the UK (Abbas 2019). A divergence appears between the Muslim male mind within the home and the workings of wider society with respect to the role and position of Muslim women *and* women in general. Moreover, the 'Self'–'Other' dichotomy remains a powerful force in the minds of people who believe in the absolute truth of their knowledge, but without the wisdom or an ability to think outside of their self-contained, self-sealed boxes. This is an issue within all societies and all aspects of society, including those with privileged access to power, status, and the ability to define an image of society based on their self-image. These ongoing trends suggest that there will remain challenges of a socio-economic and socio-cultural nature, given the wider forces of hyper-capitalism and neoliberal globalisation, and, while they remain unchecked, Muslim minorities face all sorts of internal challenges as well as the ongoing effects of unreconstructed patriarchy. They are at real risk of lagging further behind the curve. Assimilation is not an inevitability, but further integration is desirable to gain the power, position, and potential to bring about positive change to the collective human existence. Revolution can exist within an evolution. In this space, the decolonising of minds, especially that of the Muslim male, is crucial.

The ideals of diversity, difference, and the notion of a mosaic society are all amiable, but these terms mean nothing without equality, without which peace cannot occur. As soon as one tribe regards itself as prized in comparison with another, it is the beginning of every dispute. This reality is as old as history, hard-wired into human existence. That is, human beings do not face a challenge from another group to affirm the need for tribal identities. The natural environment and the need to subsist have created a predisposition to survive while simultaneously in competition with the other. In the seeds of existence lies the basis of human destruction. Conflict has been a feature of human history since the beginning of human existence. Conflict resolution, therefore, is the need to solve problems without amplifying them. Too often, counter-terrorism and countering violent extremism policy has concentrated on the wrong end of the spectrum, squeezing out the role of failed integration and foreign policy in the MENA region. Muslims nevertheless need to remember that they are not without agency; otherwise, other interests will define the debate. Muslims can (a) play an active part in limiting extremism by avoiding narratives that Muslims are always victims, (b) stop using Islamophobia as a way to limit the debate on internal cultural issues when they arise, and (c) actively re-examine and reinterpret Islamic scriptures, taking the power to imagine and reveal the faith from the limited perspectives defining the dominant space.

Since the events of 9/11, the response on the part of certain Muslim individuals and groups involved in countering militancy has been to decry the institutions and the individuals involved. However, there is a great deal of nuance, as these divisions are not equally split between the idea of a world separated by light and dark, or that evil and good forces are in a constant battle. External forces have broken down Islam as a faith tradition, with many nations seeking to take full advantage of the resources available to them through colonialism, imperialism, and, today, globalisation. However, the main problem with such a perspective is that it denies Muslim agency, which is to say that Muslims are not innocent bystanders in a vacuum, allowing all to be done unto them without a response. It is important to believe, even if the reality may suggest a contradictory perspective, where confidence and trust in politics is at an all-time low, that Muslims have a positive role to play in society. While a proportion of upwardly-mobile, professional, technologically savvy, internationally travelled, well-read British Muslims represent the paradigm of Generation M – a mobilisation on the part of Muslims engaging actively with the halal economy (Janmohammed 2016), many Muslim groups, having lost their confidence, remain suspicious of what they regard as a betrayal by the state.

Collective ownership of the problem and the solutions can lead to patterns of violence and militancy abating in the light of improved relations, interactions, and engagements between and within communities, combined with an open, informed, and meaningful mode of engagement with the state.

Moreover, the state needs to move on from the inadequate perspective that ideology is the cause and the solution to extremism and terrorism, for this only worsens existing problems, not solves them.

Bibliography

Abbas, T. (2017a). Ethnicity and politics in contextualising far right and Islamist extremism, *Perspectives on Terrorism*, 11(3): 54–61.

Abbas, T. (ed.) (2017b). *Muslim diasporas in the West*, 4 volumes, Abingdon: Routledge.

Abbas, T. (2019). *Islamophobia and radicalisation: a vicious cycle*, London and New York: Hurst and Oxford University Press.

Abbas, T. (2021). *Countering violent extremism: the international deradicalization agenda*, London: Bloomsbury-Academic.

Ahmed, A.S. and Donnan, H. (eds) (1994). *Islam, globalisation and postmodernity*, Abingdon: Routledge.

Amiraux, V. (2005). Discrimination and claims for equal rights amongst Muslims in Europe. In: Cesari J. and McLoughlin, S. (eds) *European Muslims and the secular state*, Farnham: Ashgate, 25–38.

Anwar, M. (1979). *The myth of return: Pakistanis in Britain*, London: Heinemann.

Anwar, M. (2008). Muslims in Western states: the British experience and the way forward, *Journal of Muslim Minority Affairs*, 28(1): 125–37.

Beider, H. (2015). *White working-class voices: multiculturalism, community-building and change*, Bristol: Policy Press.

Berglund, J. (2015). *Publicly funded Islamic education in Europe and the United States*, Washington DC: The Brookings Project on US Relations with the Islamic World, Analysis Paper No. 21, April.

Butt, S. (2017). *Islam21.com: News*, 9 November, www.islam21c.com/news-views/judgement-released-dr-salman-butt-vs-uk-government/ (accessed 8 August 2019).

Butt, S. (2019). Anti-extremist policy targeting UK Muslims successfully appealed, *TRT World: Opinion*, 11 March, www.trtworld.com/opinion/anti-extremist-policy-targeting-uk-muslims-successfully-appealed-24844 (accessed 8 August 2019).

Cesari, J. (2004). *When Islam and democracy meet: Muslims in Europe and in the United States*, Basingstoke: Palgrave Macmillan.

Dorling, D. (2019). *Inequality and the 1%*, London: Verso.

Fetzer, J.S. and Soper, C.J. (2005) *Muslims and the state in Britain, France and Germany*, Cambridge: Cambridge University Press.

Home Office (2018). *Individuals referred to and supported through the Prevent Programme, April 2017 to March 2018*, London: National Archives.

Janmohammed, S. (2016). *Generation M: young Muslims changing the world*, London: I.B. Tauris.

Küçükcan, T. (2004). The making of Turkish-Muslim diaspora in Britain: religious collective identity in a multicultural public sphere, *Journal of Muslim Minority Affairs*, 24(2): 243–58.

Kundnani, A. (2014). *The Muslims are coming: Islamophobia, extremism, and the domestic war on terror*, New York: Verso.

Lentin, A. and Titley, G. (2012). The crisis of 'multiculturalism' in Europe: mediated minarets, intolerable subjects, *European Journal of Cultural Studies*, 15(2): 123–38.

Mandeville, P. (2009). Muslim transnational identity and state responses in Europe and the UK after 9/11: political community, ideology and authority, *Journal of Ethnic and Migration Studies*, 35(3): 491–506.

Morgan, G. and Poynting, S. (eds) (2016). *Global Islamophobia: Muslims and moral panic in the West*, London: Routledge.

Norris, P. and Inglehart, R.F. (2012). Muslim integration into Western cultures: between origins and destinations, *Political Studies*, 60(2): 228–51.

Peach, C. and Glebe, G. (1995). Muslim minorities in Western Europe, *Ethnic and Racial Studies* 18(1): 26–45.

Phillips, D. (2006). Parallel lives? Challenging discourses of British Muslim self-segregation, *Environment and Planning D: Society and Space*, 24(1): 25–40.

Poynting, S. and Mason, V. (2007). The resistible rise of Islamophobia: anti-Muslim racism in the UK and Australia before 11 September 2001, *Journal of Sociology*, 43(1): 61–86.

Schumann, C. (2007). A Muslim 'diaspora' in the United States? *The Muslim World*, 97(1): 11–32.

Shaffer, G. (2008). *Racial science and British society*, Basingstoke: Palgrave-Macmillan.

Weller, P. (2013). *A mirror for our times: the Rushdie affair and the future of multiculturalism*, London: Continuum.

Younis, T. (2021). The psychologisation of counter-extremism: unpacking PREVENT, *Race & Class*, 62(3): 37–60.

Zelin, A. (2015). Picture or it didn't happen: a snapshot of the Islamic State's official media output, *Perspectives on Terrorism*, 9(4): 85–97.

Chapter 7

'French-style' Islamophobia: from historical roots to electioneering exploitation

François Burgat

Introduction

The tensions and rifts between France and the Muslim world, whether domestic or regional ones, may be analysed as resulting from various historical dynamics. The most important of these rifts is an internal one. It is by far the most structural – and the most decisive. Above all, it is rooted – unsurprisingly – in the contemporary, post-Revolutionary history of French society. This rift has, however, been made more explicit, amplified, and 'state-ified' by recent political power struggles, particularly since 2018. Like many of their European counterparts, for several decades, French political forces had thrown themselves into defiant electioneering one-upmanship against their fellow citizens descended from Muslim immigration. Since 2018, this posture has no longer been the sole preserve of extreme-right opposition forces. It has become the position of a quasi-majority of the political field. Far more consequentially: it has become the policy of the government of President Emmanuel Macron. In what follows, this chapter will examine the historical roots of Islamophobia in the French context, as well as how the issue of Muslims and Islamophobia has become deeply politicised in France.

Tensions rooted in France's Christian, revolutionary, and colonial histories

France's Christian heritage

France was historically referred to as the 'Church's eldest daughter', a title derived from that of 'eldest son' of the Church that was bestowed upon the first baptised kings of France. The very first dividing line between 'the Muslims' and today's France encompasses a classical rivalry between dogmas. Since at least the Crusades, the competition between Christendom and Islam has carried weight in the Western imaginary in general and the French imaginary in particular. For at least two reasons, however, this religious dynamic no longer appears to be the most decisive cause that has fuelled the Islamophobic wave of the early twenty-first century. This is, firstly, because twenty-first-century France is more de-Christianised than it is Christian (Roy, 2019). Churches have become increasingly abandoned; few now wish to become priests or monks; and the consequences of multiple scandals have demonstrated a severe decline in the nation's affiliations with the Church. Secondly, with regard to France's Muslim population, Christian spaces appear far less systematically hostile than are non-religious or 'laïc' (secular) ones. In practice, across the boundary between the Christian and Muslim faithful, and beyond the common denominator of faith, certain conservative societal stances even converge – in particular concerning the family, procreation, or homosexuality.

The 'defence of laïcité'

The second aspect of the current tensions is the one that is most explicit and deeply rooted in France today. It differs quite radically from the first, already mentioned. The adepts of ambient Islamophobia no longer consider Islam as a foreign dogma and a rival to the endogenous Christian dogma. Rather, rightly or wrongly, they consider it an expression of the resurgence in the public sphere of a certain kind of religiosity. Namely, the type of religiosity opposed by the revolutionaries of 1789, then by their successors of the Third Republic, who in 1905 wrote the 'Law on the Separation of Churches and State' to solidify 'laïcité', or state secularism, in France. This is the dynamic that embodies the political rhetoric of France's relationship with Islam and Muslims today. Alone among the nations of Europe, in order to enter the era of Republican political modernity, Revolutionary France passed through the stages of disavowal, then of expulsion from public space, of the all-powerful Church that the monarchy had for so long instrumentalised in order to perfect its own absolute power.

As I shall argue, the rhetoric of exclusionary laïcité is likely not the key dynamic of the tension that opposes French society to the Muslim presence within it. But it is the most widespread and the most explicit. One reason for its current centrality is, however, that this rhetoric of the 'defence of laïcité' often serves as a façade – a sanitised pretext – to the third of the three dynamics of the French version of anti-Muslim tension, which will be discussed in the following section. This dynamic is much less respectable.

As such, it is harder to put forward explicitly in public debate. It is at the core of the French fixation on such emblematic questions as the Muslim veil. This 'defence of *laïcité*', which has become almost an obsession, is far from being the key dynamic of our 'French-style Islamophobia'. Yet it remains important to spell out its effects – and, more so, its rhetorical functions.

This French dividing line emerges rather simply. It is at the core of the impossible acceptance of Muslim identity and of the legitimacy of the specific demands of Muslims with respect to their French national environment. It is in the name of 'the protection of *laïcité*' that the most heavily media friendly of political and intellectual elites are unable to conceal a singular fact. This is that, among Muslims in France and elsewhere, the interaction between their belonging to communities of religion and of citizenship may operate differently to the relationship between Catholicism and absolutist monarchical power as it appears in the national narrative of these elites. The *laïciste* activist Elisabeth Badinter, and so many others with her, in some sense rejects that a Muslim feminist who refuses to remove the outward markers of her religious belonging may belong to the national community. In doing so, above all, Badinter refuses to admit that the political agenda of a Muslim socio-political actor might be capable of being somewhat specific with respect to those of her French counterparts. Together with a large part of the *laïciste* intelligentsia, she is unable to accept that the process of political modernisation – in the sense of overcoming the limits of the exercise and the transmission of the absolutist and hereditary powers of those of the past – might follow a different trajectory than the rejection of any display of religion in public space. She refuses to understand that, unlike a woman of Christian tradition, a feminist Muslim woman, a descendant of colonised peoples, might indeed be part of a group struggling against a patriarchal and macho Mediterranean culture that is sometimes also instrumentalised by religion – but that she can also legitimately hold a stake in an initiative of self-differentiation, of demarcation and of resetting at a distance of a Western culture that for a time disqualified the signs of the 'non-Western' identity of her cultural belonging and Muslim religion.

'Can s/he really be one of us, s/he who does not critique their religion as we do?'[1] Anglo-Saxon societies have answered the question in the affirmative – without even feeling the need for a parliamentary debate of the kind the French are so fond of. The British very swiftly considered that a bearded Sikh and a veiled Muslim woman may be Her Majesty Elizabeth II's policemen and women. To mitigate possible tensions, Canada encouraged veiled women to join the prestigious Royal Canadian Mounted Police. In 2005, faced with interreligious riots, and to smooth the ability of Muslim women to become rescuers at sea – a symbol of belonging to the Australian nation – Australian authorities chose to promote the covering 'burkini', a type of modest swimwear that covers the arms and legs. This was the same burkini that, a few years later, French authorities attempted to ban from public beaches. And when, in France, the clothing store Decathlon decided to add jogging suits that included a hijab to its catalogue, it was in France – and from France only – that a vigorous protest campaign was launched.

As important as it may be, in the field of government communications in particular, this differentiated perception of the stakes of religious belonging for citizenship that the Revolution, then the post-Revolution's assertion of *laïcité*, established is insufficient to grasp the third dynamic of the current Islamophobic tensions. This is, in my mind, the most decisive. We move now to its roots, not in the Christian aspect of France's history, nor in its revolutionary history – but in France's colonial history.

From Islam abroad, to Islam 'at home': the groundswell of decolonisation

France's relationship with the world of Islam has a long strained and contentious history. From the post-Revolutionary Napoleonic expedition (1798) to the second of the great waves of migration after the Second World War – whose members, as opposed to those of the first wave, did not mean to return to their home countries – France's early encounters with Islam and/or with Muslims took place on 'Muslim territory'. At the end of the 1950s, Islam and Muslims vis-à-vis the French state irresistibly shifted from the realm of foreign affairs, to which they had been exclusively circumscribed – into the domestic affairs space. From the Napoleonic expedition to decolonisation, and despite the colonial fiction of a 'French' Algeria, Islam was the religion of societies whose common denominator was that they related to France through a relationship of indirect or direct submission and alienation. Not only did the encounter between France and Islam take place in Muslim lands, but it was burdened by a balance of power that was wholly in favour of the French. From the 1960s, a second, major, official wave of migration was requested by French authorities to answer major manpower needs for reconstruction. This saw immigrant workers from North or sub-Saharan Africa settle on French soil, this time permanently, where, for the first time, they were resettled with their families. At the heart of the very territory of the former colonial power began, first, a slow rise in the visibility of ethnicity (Arab and Black migrants), then, increasingly, the presence of the Muslim faith. For a decade or two, the political representation of this Muslim component of the French nation was short-circuited through communitarian institutions that were directly controlled by the countries of origin of Muslim migrants, of which the Paris Great Mosque is the archetype. The only public voice in the media of France's Muslims was the voice of the authoritarian regimes of their parents' home countries. Then a shift in state policy began to occur, where institutional mechanisms, which represented Muslims, were hijacked to serve the interests of the French state. In keeping with colonial practice, these institutional mechanisms were systematically operationalised through manoeuvres of all kinds. This was even more the case in the media, where figures were promoted as the 'representatives of Muslims' who were, in reality utterly divorced from the community that they claimed to represent, a small collection of Muslim spokespersons whose common denominator was their posture of criminalising the overwhelming majority of their co-religionists,[2] and whose overexposure was precisely inversely proportional to their reach within the community that they supposedly represented.

Despite the multiplicity of such fetters, and albeit very slowly, France's Muslims benefited from various forms of citizen 'empowerment'. With the second, then the third generation, even with a failing educational system, a solid minority among them were able to reach higher education and, in so doing, mastered the art of speaking to the media. France, the colonial power whose architects had for so long freely erected churches and other markers of sovereignty in the lands of the Muslim 'Other', was unable to prevent the opening of places of worship that asserted and made explicit the presence of Muslims within the intimate space of France's own territory. Hence, the descendants of the peoples marginalised by colonisation, little by little, acquired the linguistic, intellectual, and social resources that enabled them to insert themselves into public debate, and to fulfil their part in it. There, French Muslims began to demand two things. First, the right to take part in writing their painful common history. Second, and very importantly, they began to demand the rights pertaining to the citizen 'equality' of which their nationality proclaims that they are the bearers. The latter part of these rights is tied to the practice of their Muslim religion in the workplace or at school and, more broadly, in the public arena. It is very obviously there that – concealed beneath the mask of the rhetoric of 'the defence of *laïcité*' – the French reaction of rejection catalysed.

The long march of Islamophobia

From the end of the 1980s onwards, this process of 'the defence of *laïcité*' generated a series of clashes that political forces gradually sought to claim ownership of. First the far-right; then the so-called 'Republican' right; then, last but not least, whole swatches of the left – especially the so-called 'Vallsist' left, named after Manuel Valls, the second-to-last of the prime ministers (2014–16) appointed by President François Hollande. Consequently, one of the more contemporary features, which radically differs from previous generations of the French political landscape, has been adherence by a considerable part of the members of the Socialist Party to issues that are dear to the far-right. This transformation manifested itself in 2016 with the creation of the 'Republican Spring' movement, whose 'defence of *laïcité*' very swiftly took on a specifically Islamophobic tone. From there on, the battle of ideas has taken place under two banners: on one side, the assertion of the citizenship rights of practising Muslims; on the other, the rhetoric of the 'defence of *laïcité*'. The first skirmishes occurred around the so-called 'Muslim' strikes at the Renault factory in Billancourt in the 1980s (Bougarel and Diallo, 1991). From 1989 onwards, the foremost pretext for these confrontations was the never-ending quarrel over the wearing of the Muslim veil in schools (Confluences Méditerranée, 2006). This emblematic issue gave rise to a first legislative response – which was as foundational as it remains to this day unique in Europe – prohibiting the wearing of the veil in secondary schools in 2004. The quarrel then spread outside the school walls. An equivalent injunction was then attempted towards mothers accompanying their children's school outings. It also spread to the wearing of other forms of clothing – more specifically, to the wearing of the 'burkini' in swimming pools. Next came the prohibition on the wearing of the full veil (niqab) in public spaces, through the Law of 11 October 2010, which came into effect on 11 April 2011. Only this specific prohibition was exportable: it has become a dominant one in Europe. Identical spasms of political and media jousting regularly occur over holding prayers in public – something that in reality was made necessary by the absence of places of worship, or the inadequate size of available indoor prayer spaces in France; and over specific diets, in particular the question of the serving of pork in school canteens. Each came with the same procession of sectarian excesses. France's twenty-four-hour news channels have fallen into the hands of the far-right. They have made of such controversies their primary subject of focus, their 'bread and butter', if you will.

From the 1980s onwards, the international stage then regularly and decisively interfered in representations of the nature and role of Islam within French society. This conflation swiftly came to constitute such a reservoir of political-rhetorical tools that, gradually, no segment of the national political spectrum now resists the temptation – and the ease – of electioneering on this terrain.

From far-right Islamophobia to state Islamophobia

From October 2020, the tensions rooted in France's revolutionary history, and more so in its colonial history, were brutally exacerbated by the electioneering requirements of the budding 2022 presidential campaign. For the first time in France's contemporary history, a would-be centrist president crossed the Rubicon of adopting a position that had for so long remained circumscribed to the far-right associated with the Le Pen family. Regardless of their political leanings, all of Macron's predecessors had fought this posture. Paradoxically, Macron himself had sold his voters the promise that he would erect an unpassable barrier against this far-right position.

In 2018, in the wake of the unsettling defiance of thousands of largely working-class demonstrators wearing *gilets jaunes*, or yellow vests, as a sign to protest economic injustice in France, President Macron was awakened to the fact that he would not be re-elected in 2022 by the same centre-left votes that had lifted him to the presidency in May 2017. The social tension demonstrated by the *gilets jaunes* protests convinced him that it was only on the far-right (which had for several decades made spectacular electoral progress) that he could hope to find new voters. It is well known that France's far-right stock-in-trade is to blame society's problems (unemployment, deficits, insecurity, identity, etc.) on the 'last-comers' in the chronology of migration. In France, after the Italians, the Spanish, or the Poles, these were political or economic refugees from North Africa, the Comoros Islands, or the south of the Sahel. As such, this generation of migration was very largely made up of Muslims. On 2 October 2020, in the small city of Les Mureaux, Macron – with his mind-set fixed on campaigning for re-election – delivered a speech against 'separatism'. This was the new denomination – later dropped – of the 'Muslim' ill accused of breaking the harmony of French society and endangering its future. In this speech, Macron made explicit a spectacular turn to the right in his actions and, more so yet, in his communications. As spelled out in its preamble, the goal of the draft law that was passed on 23 July, after having been re-christened 'Law To Reinforce Republican Principles', was theoretically aimed at 'fighting separatism and attacks on Citizenship' and 'providing answers to communitarian self-isolation and the development of radical Islam, by reinforcing the respect of Republican principles and by amending the law on religious worship'.

Islam, a religion 'in crisis across the entire world'?

Emmanuel Macron in his 2022 re-election campaigning sought to cling to his utopian desire to reconcile opposites 'in tandem' (*'en même temps'*, his 2017 campaign mantra): the humanist and inclusive ambitions derived from the traditions of the left – *and* the segregationist shortcuts associated with the traditions of the right. When he presented this project, Macron paradoxically cited a challenge that quite clear-sightedly identified the roots of the malaise of part of French society. (The rest of his speech, and his actions that followed, swiftly moved away from this very fleeting illumination.) At the time, he acknowledged:

> We have ourselves built up our own separatism. The separatism of our suburbs and housing projects, the ghettoisation that our Republic [...] allowed to develop [...] we have built up a concentration of impoverishment and hardships [...] We have concentrated educational and economic difficulties in certain areas of the Republic [...] We have thereby ourselves created neighbourhoods where the promises of the Republic are no longer fulfilled.

A few measures aside,[3] and even before the law was passed, however, it was not this component of his speech – the one imprinted with realism and clear-sightedness – that the president put into practice. Quite the opposite. Rather, the president put into action a culturalising and essentialising problematic. This consisted of making a de-territorialised 'Islam' bear the full weight of responsibility for the tensions causing rifts in French society. Indeed, according to Macron, 'Islam' was purportedly 'in crisis in the entire world'. Very swiftly, this rhetoric of the description and, more so, the criminalisation of 'separatism' appeared to directly lean on the contents of a collected volume, *The conquered territories of Islamism*, published a few months earlier, edited by a political scientist named Bernard Rougier. This book had very swiftly and massively been promoted by the governmental press. In the distant wake of the theories of Bernard Lewis (the inventor of the theory of the 'Clash of Civilisations', whose popularity among the American neo-cons is well known), and in line with the insinuations long since adopted by Gilles Kepel and his colleague Bernard Rougier, the range of Muslim and non-Muslim targets of French Republican opprobrium was dramatically expanded.

In the absence of statistics that could quantify the phenomenon that Rougier described, the thesis he suggested – and that he largely suggested to his research team – is unprovable as such (as he describes it, his research team was made up of 'French citizens of North African or sub-Saharan origin, from working-class neighbourhoods', whom he has chosen to protect by keeping them anonymous (Esmili 2020)). It is, moreover, very heavily contradicted by the work of many French, British, and American scholars, including those close to the seat of power or to the Central Intelligence Agency, including the prominent American scholar Marc Sageman, for example (Gabon 2020). In reality, Rougier's approach draws on an ancient and well-known stratagem. This consists of portraying the consequences of dysfunctions in 'French coexistence', which are old as they are well known, in an exclusively alarmist way, while considerably exaggerating them, and without any statistical toolkit to assess these claims. Rougier thus sets up an 'Islamist ecosystem' that, like a rolling carpet, purportedly and inevitably leads to the 'terrorism' of all Muslims who merely wish to assert their cultural and religious belonging with a certain visibility – or even just to exercise their right to take part in national debate from an oppositional perspective.

The 'new' theory of 'separatism' merely confirms that a French 'machine' stigmatises and marginalises its Muslim citizens by creating social ghettos, in its suburbs especially. On the edges of these ghettos, a counter-culture sometimes develops that argues for a more or less explicit break with and rejection of the national environment. With appalling irresponsibility, the limitation of this sweeping 'scholarship' is that it fails to question itself as to the *causes* of the assertion of this counter-culture. Much less does it seriously condemn these causes. Yet, primarily, these causes are none other than the enormous shortcomings and blatant discriminations that make up the matrix of this alleged 'separatism', and that Macron-the-head-of-state duly inventoried in his speech. As such, it would appear more realistic to dub it 'state' separatism. In July 2020 an especially exaggerated Senate report had provided initial political backing to the argument defended by Rougier and his co-authors (Kempf 2020). The tone set by the Senators was clear: it took aim at any visibility whatsoever for Islam in the public sphere:

> This religious renewal [of Islam] is, in some, tied to a desire to assert their belief in public space, in the workplace, in schools, and in having it acknowledged by institutions and public services, that clashes with the laws of the Republic and of *laïcité*. (Kempf 2020)

Even based on an especially fragile evidentiary basis, and before even the draft law was passed some time later, this offensive by the government of President Macron fuelled a highly paradoxical displacement of the Republican norm. This led to discrediting and criminalising, no longer merely a small and potentially sectarian militant fringe of French Muslims, but a great majority of practising Muslims. Official rhetoric no longer criminalised the jihadi adepts of militancy that it had for a time, and very legitimately, targeted. It now took aim at nothing less than the entire activist spectrum of the Muslim community. This included the Salafis, of course. But no less, it included the activists of humanitarian or civic non-governmental organisations (NGOs) (such as the *Bondy Blog*, a news website with deep roots in the social tissue of the so-called 'difficult' or 'sensitive' suburbs). It included the vast associative movement connected with the Muslim Brotherhood's legalist tradition, which is deeply involved in the management of prayer halls. It included, that is, almost all those whose only supposed flaw was that they had not abandoned the practice of their faith. And it included those who practised it within the strictest respect of the legal requirements of *laïcité*. Further, it included those who merely wished to take part, in the opposition in the alchemy of national political debate.

One of the very first repercussions of the aforementioned speech, referred to as the Les Mureaux speech, was the campaign that led to dissolving the Observatory of *Laïcité*, a quasi-governmental body whose activity was deemed too 'permissive' by the polemicists of the 'Republican Spring' and, at their side, Marlène Schiappa, secretary of state for Equality Between Women and Men. Equally grave were the subsequent dissolution, on an especially weak legal basis,[4] of two NGOs, Baraka City and the Collective Against Islamophobia in France (CCIF). The dissolution of the CCIF (Burgat, 2020), which was confirmed by the administrative court of appeal where it had been challenged, pushes the paradox of governmental policy very far indeed. The obvious contradiction of this radical turn is that it attacked the CCIF, an organisation that was described as one of the few NGOs in which French Muslims have a genuine trust (Doubre 2020). In reality, the CCIF was one of the rare institutional mechanisms that had the capacity – and the will – to limit the counter-productive setbacks of brutal governmental radicalisation. The worst of the new governmental strategy provided a 'precious' credibility to the old accusation of systematic hostility on France's part towards Muslims. It may even have benefited the mobilising capacity of the radical and sectarian rhetoric of ISIS. Founded in 2000 and long directed by Marwan Muhammad,[5] the CCIF had been created because, very significantly, the traditional anti-racist organisations – with the International League Against Racism and Antisemitism at their head – did not recognise the reality and the mechanisms of Islamophobia. In a certain sense, in the name of fighting terrorism, the French state ironically dissolved a rare institution that could provide legal avenues for redress to victims of anti-Muslim stigmatisation; an institution that could potentially turn vulnerable individuals away from more radical modes of contestation.

The tensions inherent to the problematic of the 'defence of *laïcité*' were long restricted to only certain sections of French society: the far-right and the right, then, more recently, as mentioned above, a considerable part of the left, including the Socialist Party. From 2 October 2020, this spectrum expanded to make up a genuine 'State Islamophobia'.

On the heels of the highly symbolic campaign against the CCIF came the closing of several mosques – again on a startlingly weak legal basis.[6] The direction provided by the Les Mureaux speech was made explicit a few weeks later through the loud controversy of the 'invention' of 'Islamo-Leftism' – and then of its criminalisation. As its name suggests, the purported phenomenon of 'Islamo-Leftism' is tightly correlated to the (real or fantasised) support of a part of the non-Muslim intellectual class vis-à-vis the aspirations of French Muslims. On 14 February 2021, on the set of the far-right television channel CNews, and in the wake of an op-ed signed in *Le Monde* newspaper by a hundred or so academics,[7] the minister for Higher Education and Scientific Research, Frédérique Vidal, announced that she planned to ask the National Centre for Scientific Research (CNRS) to launch an inquiry into this purported phenomenon of 'Islamo-Leftism'. She had not first taken the time to define the contours of this phenomenon. (Somewhat curiously, Vidal associated 'Islamo-Leftism' with Trump's rioting voters who had just stormed the US Capitol!) Without waiting for the results of the inquiry that she meant to request of the CNRS, she nonetheless felt that she could assert that 'Islamo-Leftism' 'gangrenes society as a whole' – and therefore also 'the university' as part of this society.

The common features of the unstoppable ebb of colonial history

The supposed 'separatism' created through 'Islamo-Leftism' that is thus condemned was partly created by those responsible for state policies – and was in part invented for their electioneering needs. At the root of this reactionary positioning that has recently amplified in France, a more general opprobrium is cast on 'Decolonial Studies'. Regardless of their religious or non-religious backgrounds and persuasions, the scholars of this approach find themselves tarred with the accusation of 'Islamo-Leftism'. Between Islamophobia and the condemnation of 'Islamo-Leftism', the common features, or the common causal matrix, are clear. Neither the debate on 'Islamo-Leftism', nor that on Muslim 'separatism' in France is truly grounded in intellectual and scientific fields. This tensing-up on the part of society, that the government seeks to exploit to electioneering ends, has a single common origin: French society is going through a period in which, in the interstices of the discriminations that still exist today, some part at least of the descendants of the colonised have by now acquired the intellectual, social, and political resources that enable them to do what their parents were largely forbidden to do: that is, to take part in the writing of their history, and to demand the rights that – even while in theory they exist by virtue of citizenship – have for so long been denied them.[8]

When these demands originate in groups of individuals coming from Muslim cultures, these claims are (sometimes) expressed through that culture's vocabulary, which has been lastingly marginalised, if not 'Otherised', since the period of the West's colonial, then imperial, hegemony. Consequently, these demands are discredited inasmuch as they are branded 'Islamist'. When, however, they originate in sub-Saharan or more broadly non-Muslim populations, and when they express themselves without having recourse to this specific discursive resource, these claims and their authors are denounced as 'racialists'. In both cases, faced with 'Islamist' or 'racialist' claims, the

West's dominant reaction is thus united: denial, discrediting, and contempt – if not criminalisation.

As argued above, the foreign, regional, or even 'international' discourse on Islam has very directly influenced and impacted on French perceptions of Muslims and Islam. These perceptions have been influenced over a trajectory of historical moments, which will be discussed in the following section.

From the Iranian Revolution to the Emirati counter-revolution: the growing affinity between Arab authoritarianisms and Western Islamophobia

The first trends from abroad to interfere with the representations of Muslims in France were the echo of revolutionary dynamics in the Middle East, and the unstoppable self-assertion of the Islamist trends that were their corollary. The revolutionary self-assertion of the Islamist trends as first-rank political actors was very swiftly associated with their reactions to the various neo-colonial and imperial interventions by France or its Western partners, first within, then exterior to the Muslim world. In passing, these reactions were both predictable and, often, logical. These two tightly correlated dynamics gradually came to present the narrative on the Muslim presence in France through a 'security' dialectic. By serving as a pretext for the dynamics of suspicion and segregation towards Muslims in France, they led to worsening of the treatment and conditions of French Muslims.

Firstly, in 1979 it was the Iranian 'Islamic Revolution' that laid the foundations for the spectre of 'political Islam', by putting an end to a regime that was as authoritarian as it was idolised by its Western partners. Geographically and in human terms, Iran remained relatively distant. Lebanon, as Hezbollah's power increased, then the Algeria of the Islamic Salvation Front (FIS) in 1990, were much less so. In 1991, the military junta's repressive push against the FIS's election victory – a repression to which the French government closely associated itself (Rivoire and Aggoun, 2005)[9] – spilled over onto French territory. This lastingly inscribed in the French imaginary the correlation between 'Islam' and 'terrorism'.

The first World Congress Against Terrorism, which met in the seaside resort of Sharm Al-Sheikh on 14 March 1996, made explicit and, in part, institutionalised a 'global' alliance under the banner of the struggle against terrorism. In reality, this global alliance was turned against the political generation of Islamism.

This Sharm Al-Sheikh summit anticipated the Gulf States' later treaties with Israel. In many ways, it marked a turn in the history of Mediterranean inter-state relations – and even, given US and Russian participation, in global international relations. A repressive consensus took shape between the governments of the region: North, South, and Israel together. It largely prevails to this day, making explicit that it consisted in discrediting through ideology the various oppositions and resistances of all kinds that each category of leaders confronted, whether domestically or abroad. Alongside European leaders, Israel was now faced with the 'Islamic' Palestinian resistance led by Hamas. With unrestrained violence, Russia was then crushing the nationalist Chechen rebellion. From North Africa to Egypt, the Arab autocrats stuffed their prisons with one hand, and their ballot boxes with the other. They provided themselves with a common enemy. This enemy was not the legitimate will of those whom they oppressed to untie the fetters of their respective authoritarianisms. Rather, it was the 'Islamic fundamentalism' of the rising generation. And it was at that moment – overcoming their most ancient divisions – that this alliance of authoritarianisms decided to collaborate to fight this 'Islamic fundamentalism'. Khalida Messaoudi, alias Nadia Toumi, a self-proclaimed opponent of the Algerian military junta (she was later to become the junta's immovable minister of culture) then paid a surprising visit to Tel Aviv. This precursor step has since been expanded by the current treaties with Tel Aviv of several Gulf regimes, including the 2020 so-called 'Abraham Accords'. It symbolised and made explicit the historical moment at which the alliance of Mediterranean authoritarianisms was sealed, at the expense of the most legitimate political – and the most legalist – demands of their fellow citizens.

The Muslim Brotherhood

Next, the attacks of 11 September 2001 and the subsequent War on Terror very logically accelerated this process of defensive international cooperation on the part of the various authoritarianisms. 'You have Ben Laden, we have Yasser Arafat', the Israeli general–prime minister Ariel Sharon insinuated, in order to exploit the new world fear of a 'terrorism' that would from here on be almost exclusively portrayed as 'Islamic'. Fifteen years later came the murderous terrorist incursions by al Qaeda and the Islamic State in Iraq and Syria on French soil, which culminated with the assassination of the members of editorial team of the weekly *Charlie Hebdo* and, more so still, with the Bataclan massacre. These terrorist attacks spilled over from both the never-ending conflict in Syria and the exacerbation of the controversy over the cartoons of the Prophet Mohammed. Unstoppably, they provided the pretext for a major turn in how 'French Islam' was managed. From here on, the emotional tension generated by the self-assertion of French Muslims became quite systematically correlated with the most radical fringe armed sectarian activism.

In the early 2010s, the wave of 'Arab Spring' protests launched in Tunisia and Egypt brought a new dimension to this dynamic. The election successes of, first, Tunisian, then, Egyptian Islamists crowned the determination of Arab leaders to focus their repression not on the armed fringes of the Islamist spectrum but quite the opposite: against the most legalist majoritarian trend of their Islamist opposition. Not only in North Africa, as was already the case, but also in the Gulf: the Emirates, Saudi Arabia, and Bahrain, swiftly joined by Egypt's counter-revolution. Growing European Islamophobia is now encouraged and instrumentalised not only by Israel's powerful communicators but by the new Arab allies of Israel's diplomacy. Their interests converge: to discredit ideologically those who risk threatening their interests or their hegemony; far more than the threat posed by this opposition is their interpretation of the Muslim religion. Yet it so happens that that part of the Arab political spectrum that most naturally produces opposition movements and resistance to hegemonic power is the self-same part that French elites aim to criminalise, by labelling it 'separatist', or 'political Islam' – and by correlating it to the terrorist attacks that targeted France. The criminalisation of Islamist currents in France thus followed a relatively similar trajectory to the one followed in the Arab world. It now encompasses the entire spectrum of associative expression of religious practice. They are no longer the '*Gemaat musalaha*' (armed groups) that Anwar Sadat did battle with. Nor are they the Salafi school that the rhetoric of the Emiratis and their allies of the Arab counter-revolution criminalised. Rather, it is the entire spectrum of an undefined political Islam, and first and foremost the Muslim Brotherhood and their close derivations: the most legalist expression of political Islam, and the one that demonstrated its ability to mobilise electoral majorities. The Saudi secretary-general of the World Muslim League is a former minister of justice, responsible for 400 executions of political dissidents and for imprisoning – among others – the reformist Cheikh Salman Al Awdah. Highly significantly, on a visit to Paris in September 2019, he urged President Macron to do battle 'against political Islam'. A few months later, the authoritarian ruler of Egypt, Abdelfattah Sissi, made a third state visit to Paris, during which the 'Great Cross of the Legion of Honour', the French Republic's highest state decoration, was bestowed upon him.

Conclusion

French Islamophobia is deeply rooted in France's religious, revolutionary, and colonial history. It now boasts a powerful international milieu. 'Liberty, Equality, Fraternity'; of the three ambitions asserted by France's Republic, the last – fraternity – is likely today the most abused. Unlike the first two, mere legal assertions are far less sufficient to ensure it. The majority are sorely lacking in fraternity. Furthermore, it also requires an effort on the part of the minority. More so than even liberty, the coexistence promoted by fraternity is an endeavour that must enable a rethinking of responsibility: responsibility towards the marginalised – and the responsibility of each citizen when faced with the requirement of social, economic, and cultural integration and not of assimilation (Hanafi, 2020).

In France's plural society, fraternity is today, then, sorely lacking – not only on one side, but, unsurprisingly, on both sides of the border that separates the cultural majority from the cultural minority.

Notes

1 This is an allusion to the popular French song: 'He's one of us, he's downed his glass (of alcohol) like the others.'
2 One may mention here, beyond Imam Hassen Chalghoumi, the former *Charlie Hebdo* journalist Zineb Al Rhazoui, and Zohra Bittan.
3 The speech announced a series of education and social measures designed to 'ensure a Republican presence at the foot of each towerblock, at the foot of every high-rise'. In particular, it promised to 'double classes for 300,000 pupils, open 80 Educational Cities, label 530 "France Services" institutes […] extend library opening hours in over 600 towns and cities [and] create around a hundred digital museums'.
4 The administrative appeals court is currently examining these cases.
5 Two intellectuals in France share this name: one, of Yemeni origin, is a researcher at the National Centre for Scientific Research and the author (with Julien Talpin) of *Communautarisme* (Presses universitaires de France, 2013); the other was the CCIF's second director.
6 The latest being a mosque in Noisy-Le-Grand, a closure that was confirmed by the administrative court on the mere basis of statements by its imam (regarding certain summer clothing deemed indecent) that were judged to be 'contrary to equality between men and women'.
7 Six hundred academics signed a call for higher education minister Frédérique Vidal to resign. This was later taken up by 28,000 of their colleagues. The Conference of University Presidents very swiftly distanced itself from the minister's initiative. As for the CNRS, it refused to proceed with it. See Various Authors (2020), by some 100, later 158, academics.
8 Alongside the aspirations of the descendants of the colonised, those of other social 'minorities' that had for a time been denied access to public debate – women in general, and sexual minorities in particular – are regularly lumped into the field of 'Islamo-Leftism' by the rhetoric that condemns it – and that cares little for precision with respect to facts.
9 In particular, it was established that the most emblematic terrorist attack committed on French soil (the attack of the Saint Michel commuter-train station on 25 July

1995) was perpetrated by a group that was tightly manipulated by the Algerian intelligence services.

Bibliography

Bougarel, X. and Diallo, P. (1991). Les travailleurs musulmans à Renault-Billancourt: le repli, *Revue Européenne des Migrations Internationales*, 7(3): 77–90.

Burgat, F. (2020). France's state-sanctioned Islamophobia is the biggest threat to the republic, *Middle East Eye*, www.middleeasteye.net/opinion/banning-frances-collective-against-islamophobia-will-endanger-rule-law (accessed 5 November 2021).

Confluences Méditerranée (2006). L'affaire du voile: repères, www.cairn.info/revue-confluences-mediterranee-2006-4-page-31.htm (accessed 10 March 2020).

Doubre, O. (2020). Darmanin: Amalgame et stigmatisation; En voulant dissoudre le CCIF, le ministre de l'Intérieur sabote les liens déjà difficiles entre l'État français et les musulmans, *Politis*, www.politis.fr/articles/2020/10/darmanin-amalgame-et-stigmatisation-42419/ (accessed 8 November 2021).

Esmili, H. (2020). Les nouveaux faussaires: le maitre, l'établi et l'aspirant, *Contretemps*, www.academia.edu/43281093/Les_nouveaux_faussaires_Le_Ma%C3%AEtre_l_%C3%89tabli_et_lAspirant (accessed 3 December 2021).

Esmili, H. and Les invités de Médiapart (2021). Islam: reconquérir les territoires de la raison, *Les blogs de Médiapart*, https://blogs.mediapart.fr/les-invites-de-mediapart/blog/190220/islam-reconquerir-les-territoires-de-la-raison (accessed 6 January 2022).

Gabon, A. (2020). Rougier, Kepel et les territoires perdus de la raison universitaire, *Middle East Eye*, 26 May, www.middleeasteye.net/fr/opinion-fr/france-rougier-kepel-territoires-conquis-islamisme-musulmans (accessed 22 March 2021).

Hanafi, S. (2020). Renouer les fils rompus entre la sociologie et la philosophie morale dans un cadre post-séculier, *La Revue du Mauss*, https://sites.aub.edu.lb/sarihanafi/2020_connecting-moral_philo_fr/ (accessed 22 March 2021).

Kempf, R. (2020). Séparatisme: mettre au pas l'Islam et les musulmans de France, https://orientxxi.info/magazine/separatisme-mettre-au-pas-l-islam-et-les-musulmans-de-france,4173?fbclid=IwAR0rTNFzefRkguxHO1SfCE2Dsu6d-aVS_bAIMeg4Ko-htEEvDmhY20X9TvI (accessed 17 May 2021).

Rivoire, J-B. and Aggoun L. (2005). *Françalgérie, crimes et mensonges d'États. Histoire secrète, de la guerre d'indépendance à la 'troisième guerre' d'Algérie*, Paris: La Découverte.

Roy, O. (2019). *L'Europe est-elle chrétienne?* Paris: Seuil.

Various Authors (2020). Sur l'Islamisme, ce qui nous menace, c'est la permanence du déni, *Le Monde*, 31 October, www.lemonde.fr/idees/article/2020/10/31/une-centaine-d-universitaires-alertent-sur-l-islamisme-ce-qui-nous-menace-c-est-la-persistance-du-deni_6057989_3232.html (accessed 12 April 2021).

Various Authors (2021). 'Islamo-gauchisme': 'Nous, universitaires et chercheurs, demandons avec force la démission de Frédérique Vidal', *Le Monde*, 20 February, www.lemonde.fr/idees/article/2021/02/20/islamo-gauchisme-nous-universitaires-et-chercheurs-demandons-avec-force-la-demission-de-frederique-vidal_6070663_3232.html (accessed 5 January 2022).

Part III

Islamophobia in formerly colonised states
from the global South

Chapter 8

The framing of Muslims as threatening 'Others' in the tri-border region of Brazil–Argentina–Paraguay

Silvia Montenegro

Introduction

The association between Islam and violence in the general portrayal of Muslims by Western media, is equally, if not more, present in other geographical areas, and adopts specific tropes. Regions with a visible presence of Muslim immigrants are likely to be interpreted from the perspective of this narrative, as has been described by Said in his important work *Covering Islam* (1981). Based on fieldwork of Muslim communities in the tri-border or Triple Frontier (TF) region of Brazil–Argentina–Paraguay, as well as analysis of news stories published in United States (US) media that have had devastating impacts on Muslims in the region, this chapter attempts to shed light on the micro level at which Islamophobia operates, depicting firmly established Muslim immigrant communities as 'terrorists'. In the early 2000s, inhabitants, local media, and political authorities in the TF had knowledge of the international media portrayal of the region as a supposed hub of terrorist activities. In the local public arena, the spreading of the negative image was viewed with concern, especially with regard to the potential impact on the tourism sector, one of the region's most important sources of formal and informal employment.

The dissemination of this stigmatising view led to the response of various local actors, amid a wider political mobilisation aimed at claiming South American territorial sovereignty. While many studies have shown how mainstream media spread negative, stereotyped images of Islam and Muslims, presenting them as dangerous and threatening, and how this view has grown stronger after 9/11 (Saeed 2019; Maira 2011; Poole and Richardson 2006; Alsultany 2012), there is limited research focusing on the reception of these views among Muslims living in Latin America, as well as on the activism that emerged in order to oppose these globally defined portrayals at local levels.

The TF region between Paraguay, Brazil and Argentina is the host society of an important Muslim community, composed mainly of Lebanese immigrants and their Brazil- and Paraguay-born descendants. Arab Muslim pioneers arrived in the border region in the 1950s from Lebanon, and to a lesser extent from Palestine, but also from elsewhere in Brazil and Paraguay.[1] The most significant flow of Lebanese immigrants occurred from the second half of the 1980s, predominantly from the regions in conflict in South Lebanon,[2] most of them coming from their homeland or after living for a while in other countries. The community comprises 20,000 people (approximately 60 per cent living in Foz do Iguaçu, Brazil, and 40 per cent in Ciudad del Este, Paraguay), the vast majority of whom are from Lebanon or of Lebanese decent. There is a small Palestinian community made up of nearly fifty families, located in Foz do Iguaçu, and a small number of Egyptians and Jordanians living in both cities. Some immigrants of other descents – Bengalis, Pakistanis, and Indians – interact with Arab communities as members of the same religion.

In the late 1970s, Sunni Muslims, accounting for about 50 per cent of the community, created the Foz do Iguaçu Muslim Charity. In 1983, the same group founded the Omar Ibn Al-Khattab mosque. In 1986, Shi'ites founded the Islamic Association of Foz do Iguaçu, and by the early 1990s they completed the building of the Imam Al-Khomeini mosque. On the Paraguayan side of the frontier, in 1994, Shi'ite Muslims opened the Prophet Muhammad mosque. Also in Ciudad del Este, the Ibrahim mosque was founded by Sunni Muslims. In April 2012, Sunnis organised around the Paraguayan Islamic Arab Centre in Ciudad del Este and laid the foundation for building the Alkhaulafa Al-Rashdeen mosque, a more than 3,500-square-metre cultural complex whose completion took place in 2015.[3]

The TF emerges at the intersection of three neighbouring cities interconnected by bridges. Foz do Iguaçu, on the Brazilian side, is the most densely populated, with greater infrastructure and tourist activity due to the Cataratas do Iguaçu national park. Ciudad del Este, on the Paraguayan side, is a commercial zone. The Argentine city of Puerto Iguazú is the smallest one, its activity being also connected with tourism, as it has the Argentine-side access to the national park. While the Paraguayan and Brazilian sides form a continuum of movement and commercial activity, the Argentine side does not participate in such dynamics, and customs and documentation controls of people in transit are stricter on this side of the border (Giménez Béliveau and Montenegro 2006).

These immigrants share, at different stratification levels, the occupational niche of wholesale, retail, and import trade, given Ciudad del Este's free-port dynamics. Many immigrants have established a dual residence pattern: they set up business in Ciudad del Este (Paraguay), spending their working day on that side of the border and returning to the Brazilian side after work. Others both work and live in the same city, either Foz do Iguaçu or Ciudad del Este.[4]

The visible presence of the Arab Muslim community has nurtured imaginaries that have monopolised the view of the region since the 1990s. These discourses mark the way in which Muslims have been portrayed globally rather than locally. From the 1990s, but more intensely since 9/11, the region started appearing in the international press as a space associated with 'Islamic terrorism'. The name 'Tri-Border Area' (TBA) arose as the region began to be construed as newsworthy in the international press. For almost three decades, the area was portrayed as a singular place, some of the metaphors used including: a lawless land, a space out of state control, a grey area and a dangerous territory, and a sanctuary of terrorism. This portrayal and such discourses warned of the need to reinforce regional security agendas in the fight against global terrorism. The TF was also featured in reports by the US Department of State, as well as by governmental agencies of Argentina, Paraguay, and Brazil.

After 9/11 the Arab Muslim community organised itself through a series of movements supported by local civil society in order to repudiate these stigmatising campaigns. Local Muslim communities became the object of an Islamophobic discourse played out as an external phenomenon, without any echo among the area's inhabitants, which eventually triggered a widespread reaction. Other actors also started questioning the view of the press and of some local and American governmental agencies. Environmental organisations, alternative news agencies, social associations, religious leaders, and regional social forums participated in an ideological constellation that started to define the TF as a target of the greed of foreign countries' interests for natural resources. For such actors, the TF became a metaphor for a space of resistance, not against terrorism but against other threats: the militarisation of the region, the ravaging of biodiversity as a global public good, and the risks involved in increased social control – topics making up an anti-imperialist and strongly Latin Americanist discourse.

From neighbours to 'terrorists': the Triple Frontier as news, Muslims as a threat

By the 1990s, Muslim immigrants were already integrated into the TF cultural landscape, interacting with the locals as neighbours in social and work spaces. Any visitor in that decade would notice that mosques, shops selling Lebanese items – often decorated with religious symbols – Arab food restaurants, and women wearing the hijab were part of daily life in the area. Chinese immigrants, Indigenous people, and citizens of the three countries have also come together in a diverse, multicultural territory, where job opportunities have lured migrant populations. It was in that decade that the notion that those neighbours might also be terrorists slowly began to spread. These ideas started to become crystallised through media representations of Muslims by the international press after the commencement of War on Terror. The politics of interpretation of the Muslim presence in the region disseminated by the international press became part of the anti-Muslim bias of the post-9/11 US political discourse.

Shortly after 9/11, published news reports warned that Arab Muslims living in the area might be involved in the attacks perpetrated on the Israeli embassy in Buenos Aires in 1992 and on the headquarters of the Israelite Mutual Association of Argentina in 1994, but these allegations were never proven during the investigation. The erratic path followed in the attempt to clear up those attacks and the various 'clues' that emerged in the media – the so-called 'Iranian clue', the 'Syrian clue', the 'Hezbollah clue' – besides the growing conflict with which the legal case was imbued, diluted the issue until after 2001, when the region once again became the subject of intense media coverage.

The reports after 2001 were published in newspapers such as the *Washington Post*, the *Washington Times*, the *New York Times*, and also on television networks such as CNN and the BBC. Other accounts concerning the area were disseminated in journals specialising in the analysis of American military strategies, such as *Military Review*, and in others specifically devoted to reporting on the status of conflicts in the Middle East and their relationship with the US, such as *The Middle East*. Later, there were statements about the TF in official reports issued by the US Department of State. While reports became rarer in the subsequent decades, the picture constructed about the region stigmatised not only Muslim immigrants and their descendants but also the region itself. The TF was characterised as a 'lawless land' or as a 'remote, alien region' over which the three countries in whose intersection it is located have not wanted or have not been able to establish any order whatsoever. Since 2001 the media have tried to draw connections between the attacks on the World Trade Center, the high concentration of Muslim immigrants, and the problems of state control in Latin American borders, and the TF has consistently been given prominence in the news media. For example, drawing a panorama of the region, Hudson argues:

> Several free-trade Latin American areas with large Middle Eastern populations allow Islamic terrorist groups, organized crime mafias, and corrupt officials

to thrive in a mutually beneficial, symbiotic relationship ... The TBA, with already more than half a million inhabitants, soon became a lawless jungle corner of Argentina, Brazil, and Paraguay. (Hudson 2003: 4)

According to the same journalist, citing other reports, the region lacks national controls:

Despite this joint force, efforts by the TBA governments to counter organized crime and terrorist groups in the TBA have been hindered by institutional problems of corruption, inadequate funding and investigative capabilities, poor training, lack of motivation, inadequate penal codes, and so forth. These factors ... help to explain how organized crime and terrorist groups have operated so profitably in the TBA. (Hudson 2003: 60)

In late September 2001, Brazil's ambassador in the US wrote a letter to the *New York Times* in reply to a leading article about the TF published that month, 'Terrorists are sought in Latin smugglers' haven' (Rohter 2001). It was a response to the emphasis placed by this article on the lack of state controls in the region. The ambassador stated:

The Brazilian government is closely monitoring the situation in the Triple Frontier region, where Brazil, Argentina and Paraguay share a common border. To further ensure security, the ministers of justice of the three countries met on Thursday to study the issue and take appropriate enforcement measures.

The official denied that it was an area without control and claimed that there was no evidence of 'terrorist' activities: 'Police and security agencies of the three countries are jointly monitoring that border. The Brazilian government has no concrete evidence so far that either suspected terrorist groups or individual terrorists are in the area' (Barbosa, 2001).

However, the same newspaper insisted one year later, on a description of the area and of Muslims as a source of threat. The journalist specialising in Latin American issues for the *New York Times*, Larry Rohter, then described the TF as a highly conflict-affected South American region, trying to show that all kinds of illegal activities favoured the presence of so-called terrorists: 'The Triple Frontier has long been South America's busiest contraband and smuggling center, a corrupt, chaotic place where just about anything from drugs and arms to pirated software and bootleg whisky are available' (Rohter 2002: 35).

Due to the area's alleged reputation, the article stressed that it has been 'under close surveillance by the police and foreign intelligence services for decades', and that after 9/11 'the Triple Frontier has been transformed into a sort of Casablanca, a center of intrigue scrutinised more intensely than ever for its suspected links to Islamic terrorists'.[5] The sources cited by the journalist were American officials who had allegedly described the area, 'with its large Arab immigrant population, as teeming with Islamic extremists and their sympathisers, and they say those businesses have raised or laundered more than $50 million in recent years for terrorist groups'.

Just one week later, another article in the *New York Times* referred to the responses the US had in fact implemented against the threat represented by the Muslim population in the TF, claiming that the Bush administration had grown increasingly concerned about the 'activities of Islamic militants in the Triple Frontier region, and that it was stepping up efforts to staunch what it says is the flow of funds from the largely unregulated area to terrorist groups in the Middle East' (Dao 2002: 12).

The *Washington Times* also started to publish similar reports in 2001, highlighting the high concentration of Muslim Arabs and describing the area as 'housing a large market of illegal goods' in the hands of immigrant mafias. The stories took for granted that the region should be included in so-called anti-terrorist actions, and that 'Paraguayan authorities tried to regain control of the area and police swept through and arrested 14 Arab immigrants on immigration charges and began examining 46 bank accounts' (Ceaser 2002: 15).

It is interesting to note that very often, in the same journalistic report, Muslims would be characterised as terrorists and it would be suggested that their presence represented a threat, while some paragraphs below it was admitted that 'No ties to the terrorist attacks have been found'. In the *Washington Times* article, Mike Ceaser admits that Paraguayan police officers, whom he quoted, stated: 'the great majority of this area's considerable Lebanese immigrant community is made up of hard-working business owners'. Even so, the report concludes that the TF – which is itself porous to corruption and to the black market economy – could be a convenient hub from which 'terrorist' activities might be planned or financed.

The following year, an article in the same newspaper ventured even further with its hypotheses. A report focused on surmising about bin Laden's whereabouts and his possible physical and political death argued that 'he may live some more years in the hide-outs of the tribal zone in Pakistan, just as some Nazi fugitives survived in the remote areas of Argentina and Paraguay' (Pruden 2002a: 4). Some months later, another article, also in the *Washington Times*, authored by the same journalist, insisted again on highlighting the large number of Muslim Arabs in the region, mentioning between 25,000 and 30,000 Lebanese, Palestinians, and Syrians, as proof of their connections with terrorist organisations. The journalist reported the existence of a Hezbollah operations centre in the area: 'Terrorist training camps operated by Hezbollah continue to flourish in a remote and lawless area along the shared borders of Brazil, Argentina and Paraguay, according to law-enforcement officials and a recent report by anti-terrorism authorities'

(Pruden 2002b: 6). This time, the source cited was the Virginia-based Terrorism Research Center, where it had been concluded that the TF was an area intent on 'kill[ing] Americans and Jews'. The director of this entity, Walter Purdy, had claimed that the 'military leader' of terrorism in the region was a 'powerful business owner in Ciudad del Este' and that the area, lacking any control by the governments, had become an 'appropriate atmosphere for terrorist operations' and a place where 'al Qaeda terrorists move at large'. All these reports and hypotheses had very little, if any, proof or substance.

The various images conveyed about the region and Muslims were combined and articulated around the notion of threat, attributed both to the place and to the people living there, in this case communities taking or capable of taking advantage of the context to plan and carry out militant actions. The concept of 'sleeper cells', which emerged in international media to define the terrorist potential of Muslims in the region, clearly illustrates the idea of a violent essence that might 'awaken' all of a sudden. Discussing the scope of the notion of Islamophobia, Tyrer argues that Islam as a religion is not the fundamental problem, but, rather, that it is Muslims that are the subject matter of those fantasies. Thus, Islamophobia would consist in those practices by which Muslims are constituted and essentialised as a bounded group in order to manage the relationship between the idea of the West and its 'Others' or its outsiders (Tyrer 2013: 70). However, the notion of 'Islamic extremism' present in the reports seems to be a category existing before Muslims themselves, a potential capability of Arabs and Muslims, since, in the media discourse, ethnic and religious belongings appear as interchangeable categories. For our case, as Green (2015: 28) points out, it is evident that race, culture, ethnicity, and religion are often conflated in Western discourse about Islam, and hostility based on religious differences is difficult to extricate from bigotry based on cultural and ethnic differences. The homogeneity in the American media discourse was also present in the language used by US Department of State spokespeople when the TF was officially included as a global terrorism hub.[6]

The Triple Frontier on the official agenda against global terrorism

Throughout 2002, the content of the reports published by the *New York Times* and the *Washington Times* was perfectly in line with the view conveyed about the region by the US Department of State. It is worth mentioning that in late 2001 this agency's coordinator for counter-terrorism, Francis Taylor, had personally travelled to Paraguay, where he held a seminar on 'Preventing International Terrorism and Organised Crime in the Tri-Border

Area'. Giving a speech before the president of Paraguay and many guests from neighbouring countries, Taylor stated:

> It is no secret that you have, living in this area, more than 15,000 persons from the Middle East. Some of these people are from, or are descendants of persons from, countries such as Lebanon, Palestine and Syria. I applaud the cultural diversity that has been allowed to flourish here.

His following words showed the official position of the Department of State:

> What is not a wonderful thing – and this is based on information shared with me by law enforcement and intelligence officials from your governments – is our shared concern that Islamic extremist organisations such as Hezbollah, Hamas, Al Gama'a Al Islamiyya and others are using this vibrant area as a base from which to support terrorism. At a minimum, there is evidence that elements of the tri-border population are engaging in various types of organised criminal practices. We know, from close cooperation with your law enforcement officials, that Hezbollah members in the tri-border engage in document forgery, money laundering, contraband smuggling. (US Embassy, Argentina 2001)

In the year following this visit, the TF was mentioned in the US Department of State report *Patterns of Global Terrorism*. The publication outlined the potential terrorist threats in each country around the world, with Paraguay, Argentina, and Brazil appearing under the heading 'Tri-Border Area' (US Department of State 2002: 48–50). The pages devoted to the region summarised the threat attributed to the TF: trafficking in arms, drugs, smuggling, forgery of documents, money laundering and piracy, a large Muslim population, strategic significance after 9/11, and a ground for Hezbollah's and Hamas's logistical and financial activities. The report quoted US media as a source, explaining that there was no evidence of the above from official intelligence agencies.

With regard to the actions to be taken, the report suggested that, in principle, the three countries had agreed to cooperate with the US in the fight against terrorism, evidenced by the following: the arrest of twenty-three suspects in Paraguay, the raid on shops in Ciudad del Este, the discovery of clandestine call shops by Brazil from which phone calls were made to the Middle East, as well as the commitment by all three countries to participate in regional meetings.

The purpose of the report was to suggest that the area should be placed under steady control, deeming it necessary to implement specific criminal laws against terrorist activities. The urge for the implementation of amendments to the existing laws in the three countries was put forward in the report as an official concern of American entities to ensure the efficacy of the fight against global terrorism. The report openly claimed that, without new legislation, it would be necessary to keep using contrivances such as 'criminal association, tax evasion, money laundering or possession of forged documents' in order to capture suspects (US Department of State 2002: 50).

Military Review articles warned of the connection between Chinese mafias and Islamic terrorists, since there has also been Chinese immigration into the area since the 1980s. This tenuous claim drew baseless conclusions that the Egyptian terrorist group Al Gama'a Al Islamiyya had built a financial network in the region in association with Chinese families, using electronics shops as cover-ups (Bartolomé 2002). The criminalisation of ethnic diversity was evident in the news discourse, terms such as 'ethnic mafias' being used to describe the immigrant population living in the South American border area.

In these documents, the TF was classified under the 'grey area' category, a name given to some of the conflict areas included in the global counter-terrorism agenda. This classification referred to certain portions of a territory falling into the hands of partly criminal, partly political organisations, eroding the legitimacy of governments. Grey areas are described as regions within which the boundaries between internal or external security issues are blurred – they are 'no-law zones, serving as refuge and sanctuary for (often interconnected) terrorist and criminal organisations that thrive in the place with total impunity, getting support from part of the local population' (Bartolomé 2002: 69).

This definition was extended in other newspapers and journals during 2003. For example, *The Middle East* denounced the existence of a large number of Muslim Arab militants in the area, also arguing that Islam was the fastest-growing religion in Latin America and that terrorists from the Middle East were taking refuge in Brazilian 'jungles'. The situation, labelled as serious, had allegedly led to the continued presence of intelligence agencies from several countries, 'including Argentina's SIDE, Israel's Mossad, the US CIA, DEA and FBI, the secret services of Germany, Spain, China and their Brazilian and Paraguayan counterparts, among others' (Blanche 2003).

By the middle of that year, the reports on the TF were condensed into an extensive document drafted by the US Library of Congress Federal Research Division (Hudson 2003). The report was based on articles from newspapers, journals such as *Military Review*, and others devoted to the Middle East. The report, which intended to serve as information basis for investigators and officials, presented a detailed description of everything that had been recorded about the TF from 1999 to 2003. It enclosed photographs of 'suspected Arab residents' or individuals who had been arrested throughout the period, as well as a brief biography of each of them, specifying the organisation they were supposedly connected to – in all cases Hezbollah and Al Gama'a Al Islamiyya. The report confirmed a hypothesis considered novel, and central to the politics of interpretation of the Muslim presence in the TF, where there are Sunni and Shi'ite Muslims. According to this hypothesis, unlike other places around the world, in this region Sunnis and Shi'ites would cooperate: 'while it may be conventionally believed that the Sunni organisation al Qaeda and the Shi'ite Hezbollah do not cooperate, since they belong to two different branches of Islam, their mutual cooperation and alliance are emblematic in the region', and both might operate by carrying out terrorist attacks.

Over the following years, many articles in American media interpreted the Muslim presence in light of the global dangers that had worsened after 9/11, considering Latin America as made up of weak democracies exposed to new domestic and external threats. An increasingly central issue became the idea of the local governments' limited capacity to control an area seen as practically independent, a 'grey area', a 'stateless' and 'lawless place' that was convenient for 'ethnic mafias' and 'terrorism'.

Citing sources is key in journalism, and the articles discussed here almost without exception mentioned official sources to give credibility to their claims. A review of them shows a limited number repeating themselves throughout the stories, including different governmental authorities (US authorities, the US Department of State, Paraguayan and Brazilian officials, the interior ministers of the three countries, US embassy spokespeople, law-enforcement officers). In addition, sources connected with security forces and intelligence services are mentioned (Brazil's Federal Police, Argentina's intelligence service, the Argentine counter-terrorism agency, Western and Latin American intelligence services, the FBI, and the CIA). Finally, other sources refer to the credibility attributed to experts in various fields (investigators from Argentina and the US, international terrorism experts and analysts). Some of the sources mentioned are significantly vague and are quoted just for the purpose of providing a framework for specific details of events for which it is later made clear that there is no evidence. At the same time, the articles from *Military Review*, as well as the report on the TF written by the US Federal Research Division, cited the press as a source, in a feedback that homogenised the narratives. Undoubtedly, the TF entered the crosshairs of a journalistic agenda informed by 9/11. In this sense, it can be stated that the articles were addressed to the typical readers of those newspapers, probably in the wider context of the 'patriotic momentum', followed by some media to support the strategic discourses that US official agencies were implementing as part of their global counter-terrorism agenda (Zelizer and Stuart 2003).

As an object of representation, the TF contained the key element allowing it to be rendered 'newsworthy' – a high concentration of Muslims. While the TF could have been destined to disappear as news, following the specific logic of the journalistic field (aiming, as Pierre Bourdieu said, at the production of such a highly short-lived item as news), the region has continued to be a long-lasting news subject matter to this day. The homogeneity of the view on the region could partly be explained by the characteristics of the mechanisms inherent in journalism, where competition for clients tends to take the shape of competition for priority. The assessment of a piece of information based on its topicality forces the media to keep mutual watch on publications concerning the same issue. The paradoxical effect of this is that competition, rather than leading to originality and diversity, tends to promote uniformity of offer (Bourdieu 1994: 5). To mention but one example, the idea of a 'lawless land' to refer to the TF emerged in one of the 2001 reports and has consistently been repeated thereafter in other years and in other newspapers. Many articles repeated the idea of a legal loophole in the region, with slight variations. Most of them also mentioned the arrest of Muslim citizens of Arab descent, using the same data in different contexts, to refer to the alleged presence of al Qaeda, to the existence of 'terrorist training camps', or to denounce money laundering and associations of ethnic mafias. All these claims are unsubstantiated, as no evidence to support these claims has been presented.

Although the area of focus was new, the manner of performing the journalistic coverage of the topic was based on traditional patterns: crystallised representations that act as frameworks for interpreting the threat posed by the new 'civilisational enemies'. The articles on the TF spread by American newspapers were written for both domestic and international audiences, as part of the upsurge of reporting on the dangers to which the US was said to be subject after 9/11. Once in circulation, this stigmatising view invigorated other discourses that tried to denounce what some activists called 'the true American interest in the region'.

From terrorists to neighbours: counter-discourses of resistance from an 'anti-imperialist' viewpoint

A counter-discourse with an anti-colonial and anti-imperialist flavour emerged strongly between 2001 and 2006 and was expressed in the organisation of social forums and events interpreting the stigmatisation of Muslim immigrants as a means for ensuring the economic and political dominance of an area with access to valuable natural resources. While reports warning against the Muslims in the region kept appearing in international media, alternative media were engaged in publishing articles that responded to those arguments. In the case of Brazil, the position of the government and of the Foreign Office on the view of the TF disseminated by American media led to the emergence of critical discourses in some traditional print media. In September 2001, Brazilian newspapers published statements by President Fernando

Henrique Cardoso challenging claims of the presence of terrorist cells in the TF. On a visit to the US, Cardoso had stated that 'The TF was safer than Washington' (*O Globo* 2001a). These statements became publicly known when he engaged in a dispute with a Federal Bureau of Investigation member who, in an interview given to another newspaper, had described the area as a 'den of terrorists'. Cardoso then gave an interview to CNN that was covered by various media, arguing that Brazilian intelligence services had never detected anything of this nature, even on the Paraguayan side. He then argued that 'there are many Arabs and Muslims here in Brazil, but this should in no way lead us to think that they are involved in terrorism', and he added that he was concerned about the reprisals the Muslim community in the area might face from these biased representations. Furthermore, the statements made by a Brazilian Intelligence Agency official, about the pressure exerted by the US on Brazil, became public for the purpose of insisting on proving something (i.e. Muslim militancy) that did not actually exist (*O Globo* 2001b). In 2002, other Brazilian government officials made similar declarations. The minister of defence for the Cardoso administration, Geraldo Magela da Cruz Quintão, in his speech at the Defence Ministerial of the Americas, said:

> I express my concern for certain recurrent news about the hypothetical presence of people connected with terrorist activities in the so-called Triple Frontier. As President Fernando Henrique Cardoso said, there is at present no proof whatsoever of activities in this region linked with terrorist actions. This multi-ethnic region houses communities of Arab descent with many Palestinians and many Muslim faithful, all living together in peace and harmony; any hasty, groundless attitude certainly amounts to discrimination. Brazil, in line with one of its constitutional goals, namely promoting the common good, with no discrimination, permanently condemns harmful attitudes against those communities. (Quintao 2002)

Of course, this official position was echoed in some local media that chose to publish articles denying international suspicions, while others kept on repeating the description provided by American media.

In the TF, the reaction against the stigmatising campaign was immediate. After 9/11 a movement called 'Peace Without Borders' was created, coordinated by a committee made up of Brazilian, Paraguayan, and Argentine Arabs and backed up by local media, non-governmental organisations (NGOs), and governmental agencies. The movement had the purpose of reversing the negative image of the region and the propaganda against the local Muslim communities. The perpetuation of these negative views damaged commercial and tourist activities, as well as the reputation of the border, for which over several decades local municipalities had endeavoured to build an image that exemplified multicultural integration and coexistence.

Recruiting volunteers, the movement started handing out pamphlets bearing the message that 'the tri-national region is being unjustly offended and disparaged, and so are its communities' (*Folha de Londrina*, 2001). Movement leaders gave interviews to local media saying that they were planning a huge mobilisation to prove that 'neither is there terrorism in the TF, nor is it exported', and that an invitation to participate in the event had been sent to US President George Bush himself and to the presidents of Argentina, Brazil, and Paraguay (*Diario do Grande ABC* 2001). The movement held an ecumenical rally with a massive attendance to show disapproval of the accusations of terrorism, inviting the representatives of all the religions and ethnic groups present in the region. The event gathered 45,000 people on 11 November 2001, playing a role in publicly expressing the local response to the stigmatisation of the region. Local media not only covered and promoted the rally, but also took part in a humorous campaign to repel the rumours, which was based on satirising bin Laden's alleged presence in and visit to the TF, which was hinted at in a CNN report. However, as argued by Karam (2011), the impact of the ecumenical rally had a regional scope, and the international mass media covered the event only late and partially.

What ensued was the construction of a growing consensus on the need to continue rejecting the international representations. In early 2002, local media including alternative news agencies, independent media centres, websites of environmental and socialist organisations, and social forums from the region started presenting counter-narratives about the image of the TF spread by American media. The online journal *Perspectiva Mundial* published a series of articles about the TF. In January 2002, the socialist journal covered the development of the São Paulo Forum, which since 1990 has brought together several organisations connected with left-wing parties and entities. According to *Perspectiva Mundial*, one of the key issues brought up in the forum was the denunciation of the US anti-terror fight vis-à-vis Latin America, which was being used as a smokescreen for militarising the region, particularly in the case of the TF (Koppel and Water 2002). From this viewpoint, the implications of a 'terrorist' presence in the TF were a neo-imperialistic tactic, since 'American imperialism seeks to impose a broad, vague definition of terrorism, mixed up with narcotics trafficking, with the struggle for national liberation, with social protest and with migration flow'. A later article published by the same journal announced as a triumph the defeat of the attempt by the Paraguayan government to pass an anti-terrorism Act (Koppel and Green 2002). According to the article, the new Act purported to be based on the USA PATRIOT Act adopted by the US and the intention was to use it 'against workers, peasants, social activists and politicians', hence allowing the government to arrest individuals under 'vague charges'.

Several alternative media started denouncing an anti-Muslim campaign in the TF. Online media warned of immigrants' arrest without evidence. Some of the headlines showed the viewpoint on the issue: 'USA put forward terror threat to appropriate aquifers' (Glenza 2004a); 'The Triple Frontier, key to American strategy' (Ducrot 2002); 'The axis of evil in the Triple Frontier' (Pereyra Mele 2006); 'Triple Frontier: terrorism or commerce' (Acosta 2005); 'Iraq ends in the Triple Frontier' (Kollman 2003); 'The Guarani aquifer and the hoax of the terrorist danger in the Triple Border' (Bruzzone 2003); 'Control of the Guarani aquifer: the terrorist threat is foundering' (Glenza 2004b). The news about the TF in those media coexisted with slogans about the power of civil society, the democratisation of mass media, and the call for 'alter-globalisation'. This discursive universe and the views about the region that were manufactured were later expressed in the Triple Frontier Social Forum, held during 2004, where the rejection of an alleged militarisation of the TF under the pretext that it housed terrorists was one of the key discussion topics for several social organisations (Setton 2010). The Forum organisers relied on previous examples that had shown strong participation by the local audience, supporting the struggle against the negative view of the region. In 2003, the Brazilian city in the TF, Foz do Iguaçu, had hosted the First International Festival of Graphic Humour, an event sponsored by the municipalities and the secretariat of tourism involving many comedians from various countries. Among the themes included in the call for comedians competing in the event were the expropriation of natural resources in the region, primarily water, and criticisms of accusations of terrorist presence in the region. The festival became known as a comedy event against the accusations of terrorism.

In turn, some Muslim entities in the TF, supported by local municipalities, engaged in clarifying the five pillars, the values and basic norms of Islamic practice, and opening the mosques to visitors. For this purpose, they made a video that was later distributed to primary schools, they printed leaflets, and they gave interviews to local media, thereby trying to put in the spotlight their own self-portrayal, which favoured the religious over the ethnic or national ascription. The activism denouncing the stigmatisation process enabled the confluence of different actors who managed to play out a counter-discourse which tried to shed light on the grounds and possible consequences of the region and its population's involvement in global securitisation agendas.

Conclusion

The analysis of Islamophobic practices in mass media becomes more complex as we examine the local responses that Muslim communities succeed in building, and how these responses are connected with wider resistance movements through discursive universes that, in the case of the TF, converge on the criticism of the historical American hegemony. The significance of examining the impact of media and political discourse on the micro-level interaction strategies that Muslims deploy to prevent, circumvent, and challenge also implies noting how actors manage problematised identities (Khan and Mythen 2019: 316). When Muslim communities in the TF began to organise in order to challenge the stigmatisation campaign of the region, they devised three strategies. The first was the creation of the local movement 'Peace Without Borders', a broad-based combination of individuals and groups aiming to preserve the reputation of the TF. The second was to attend rallies, demonstrations, or public events in support of local activists and NGOs denouncing American interests in securing hegemony over the region. Finally, Muslims attempted to explain to a wider population the basis of Islamic belief, using videos and educational pamphlets.

In spaces where communities are institutionally organised and build bonds with the local civil society, the prevalence of stigmatising discourses can be challenged. In the case of the TF region of Latin America, this was accomplished by creating opportunities to reaffirm the image of local integration, as well as opposing the global 'Otherising' trend that targets Muslim communities locally and internationally in the War on Terror.

Notes

1 Argentina, Brazil, and Paraguay had a previous Arab immigration, from the late nineteenth and the early twentieth centuries, within which Muslims were a minority.

2 The civil war (1975–90) and the occupation of South Lebanon territories by Israel (1982–2000) were determining factors for these migrations.

3 Palestinian immigrants and their descendants belong to the Sunni branch of Islam, live on the Brazilian side and attend the Omar Ibn Al-Khattab mosque. Bangladeshis have their own prayer room on the Paraguayan side and gather around a shaykh of their own nationality.

4 For an analysis of identity narratives among the various Muslim generations in the region and among the institutions established by immigrants and their descendants, see Montenegro (2018a; 2018b).

5 Referring to the city of Casablanca, as portrayed in the homonymous film (*Casablanca*, 1942) directed by Michael Curtiz.

6 From 1995 to 2005, over 400 news stories were published about the TF in US and Argentine newspapers; to name but a few: 'Jungle hub for world's outlaws', *Los Angeles Times* (24 August 1998), 10; 'Terror cell on rise in South America', *Washington Times* (18 December 2002), 6; 'Al Qaeda South', *Washington Times* (23 August 2002), 11; 'The terror threat in the Southern Cone', *Washington*

Times (16 August 2004), 18; 'Focus on terror funding', *Washington Times* (23 August 2004), 18; 'Teams to target financial crimes; lawless region feeds terrorism', *Washington Times*, (24 March 2006), 13; 'Tri-border organized crime stirs concern; money laundering by Arab groups suspected', *Washington Times* (25 April 2006), 12.

Bibliography

Acosta, S. (2005). Triple Frontera: terrorismo o comercio, *Aporrea.org*, 4 April, www.aporrea.org/tecno/a13080.html (accessed 8 July 2021).

Alsultany, E. (2012). *Arabs and Muslims in the media: race and representation after 9/11*, New York: New York University Press.

Barbosa, R. (2001). States of readiness: do new threats loom? Stopping terror, *New York Times*, 1 October, 22.

Bartolomé, M. (2002). La Triple Frontera: principal foco de inseguridad en el Cono Sur americano', *Military Review*, 83(2): 61–74.

Blanche, E. (2003). 'The Latin American connection: the lawless tri-border region between Brazil, Argentina and Paraguay is under new scrutiny as a haven for Arab extremists, *The Middle East*, (334): 28–32.

Bourdieu, P. (1994). L'emprise du journalisme, *Actes de la Recherche en Sciences Sociales*, 101–2: 3–9.

Bruzzone, E. (2003). El Acuífero Guaraní y la patraña del peligro terrorista en la Triple Frontera (The Guarani aquifer and the hoax of the terrorist danger in the Triple Border), 22 May, https://opsur.org.ar/2010/02/10/la-patrana-del-peligro-terrorista-en-la-triple-frontera/ 2003 (accessed 8 May 2021).

Ceaser, M. (2002). Border town's Hezbollah link spurs concern', *Washington Times*, 26 October, 15.

Dao, J. (2002). Threats and responses: South America; US expanding effort to block terrorist funds in Latin region', *New York Times*, 21 December, 12.

Ducrot, V. (2002). The Triple Frontier, key to American strategy, *Peacelink*, 4 October, https://lists.peacelink.it/latina/2002/10/msg00178.html (accessed 5 May 2021).

Diario do Grande ABC (2001) FHC é convidado para marcha da paz em Itaipu, 10 November 2001, www.dgabc.com.br/2017/Noticia/116535/fhc-e-convidado-para-marcha-da-paz-em-itaipu (accessed 25 March 2022).

Folha de Londrina (2001). Paz sem Fronterias espera reunir 40 mil en Foz, 3 November, 2.

Giménez Béliveau, V. and Montenegro, S. (2006). *La Triple Frontera: globalización y construcción social del espacio*, Buenos Aires: Miño & Dávila.

Glenza, F. (2004a). Estados Unidos esgrime el peligro terrorista como excusa para apropiarse de los acuíferos de Argentina, Brasil y Uruguay, *Revista Koeyu Latinoamericano*, 3(2): 4.

Glenza, F. (2004b). Control del acuifero guarani: el peligro terrorista en la TF hace agua, *Rebelion Internacional*, 5 May, https://rebelion.org/autor/fernando-glenza/ (accessed 5 May 2019).

Green, T. (2015). *The fear of Islam. An introduction to Islamophobia in the West,* Minneapolis, MN: Fortress Press.

Hudson, R. (2003). *Terrorist and organized crime groups in the Three Border Area (TBA) of South America,* Federal Research Division, Washington: Library of Congress.

Karam, J. (2011). Atravesando las Américas: la guerra contra el terror, los árabes y las movilizaciones transfronterizas en Foz do Iguaçu y Ciudad del Este. In: V. Giménez Béliveau and S. Montenegro (eds), *La Triple Frontera. Dinámicas culturales y procesos globales,* Buenos Aires: Espacio Editorial, 119–51.

Khan, F. and Mythen, G. (2019). Micro-level management of Islamophobia. Negotiation, deflection and resistance. In: I. Zempi and I. Awan (eds), *Routledge International Handbook of Islamophobia,* New York: Routledge, 313–24.

Kollman, M. (2003). Irak termina en la Triple Frontera, *Página 12,* 23 March, 14.

Koppel, M. and Green, R. (2002). 'Derrotada ley antiterrorista', 'Campaña anti-musulmana', 'Crece presencia militar EE.UU', *Perspectiva Mundial,* 26(8): 7.

Koppel, M. and Water, M. (2002). Se reúne Foro de São Paulo en Cuba, *Perspectiva Mundial,* 26(1): 4.

Maira, S. (2011). Islamophobia and the war on terror: youth, citizenship, and dissent. In: J. Esposito and I. Kalin (eds), *Islamophobia: the challenge of pluralism in the 21st century,* Oxford: Oxford University Press, 109–25.

Montenegro, S. (2018a). Sense of community among Muslims in the Brazil–Paraguay border: narratives of belonging and generational differences, *Journal of Contemporary Religion,* 33(3): 509–26.

Montenegro, S. (2018b). Écoles arabo-musulmanes à la frontière du Brésil et du Paraguay: reproduction culturelle et différences générationnelles, *Brésil(s),* 14, https://journals.openedition.org/bresils/3554 (accessed 25 March 2022).

O Globo (2001a) Fernando Henrique Cardoso diz nos EUA que Tríplice Fronteira é segura, 9 October, 27.

O Globo (2001b). O presidente responde a CNN e pede provas, 9 October, 26.

Pereyra, M. (2006). El eje del mal en la Triple Frontera, *America Latina en Movimiento,* 18 July, www.alainet.org/es/active/12434?language=es (accessed 1 September 2020).

Poole, E. and Richardson, E. (2006). *Muslims and the news media,* London and New York: I.B. Tauris.

Pruden, W. (2002a). A corpse or not, his time is gone, *Washington Times,* 23 July, 4.

Pruden, W. (2002b). Terror cell on rise in South America, *Washington Times,* 18 December, 6.

Quintao, C. (2002). Speech at the plenary meeting of the 5th Defence Ministerial of the Americas, Santiago de Chile, November, www.gov.br/mre/en.

Rohter, L. (2001).Terrorists are sought in Latin smugglers' haven, *New York Times,* 27 September, www.nytimes.com/2001/09/27/world/terrorists-are-sought-in-latin-smugglers-haven.html (accessed 25 March 2022).

Rohter, L. (2002). South America region under watch for signs of terrorists, *New York Times,* 15 December, 32.

Saeed, A. (2019). 'Race, racism, Islamophobia in the media. Journalists' perceptions and Muslim responses'. In: I. Zempi and I. Awan (eds), *Routledge international handbook of Islamophobia,* New York: Routledge, 325–39.

Said, E. (1981). *Covering Islam. How the media and the experts determine how we see the rest of the world*, London: Routledge and Kegan Paul.

Setton, D. (2010). 'La construcción de la Triple Frontera a través de los encuentros sociales de la alter-globalización'. In: V. Giménez Béliveau and S. Montenegro (eds), *La Triple Frontera. Dinámicas culturales y procesos globales*, Buenos Aires: Espacio Editorial, 75–98.

Tyrer, D. (2013). *The politics of Islamophobia: race, power and fantasy*, London: Pluto Press.

US Department of State (2002). *Patterns of global terrorism 2001*, www.hsdl.org/?view&did=1012 (accessed 25 March 2022).

US Embassy, Argentina (2001). Responses to terrorism. Press release, 20 December.

Zelizer, B. and Stuart, A. (2003). *Journalism after September 11*, New York: Routledge.

Chapter 9

Think-tanks and the news media's contribution in the construction of Islamophobia in South Africa

Mohamed Natheem Hendricks

Introduction

In a recent publication sponsored by an American think-tank, the American Enterprise Institute, Emily Estelle and Jessica Trisko Darden (2021) portray Africa as a scary and insecure continent. They write that the 'rapid growth of an Islamic State affiliate in northern Mozambique is the latest iteration of a frightening trend. Salafi-jihadi insurgencies, led by groups affiliated with al Qaeda and the Islamic State, are maturing across much of Africa' (Estelle and Darden 2021: 3). They continue with their alarming security assessment and infer that the threat is not limited to Mozambique. Instead, according to them, a number of African countries are vulnerable to this so-called 'Salafi-jihadi threat' (Estelle and Darden 2021: 3). In a similar vein, a South African news broadcasting company, Carte Blanche, current affairs documentary, *Kenyan Attack*, which was broadcast on 29 September 2013, refers to the supposed attackers of the Westgate Mall in Kenya as 'terrorists' who aim to establish an 'Islamic State':

> The deadly four-day siege was claimed by al Qaeda linked terrorist group, al Shabaab. Al Shabaab is an Islamic militant group who is fighting to overthrow the Somali government and establish an Islamic State. On Saturday the group of attackers stormed the [...] Westgate Mall [...]. (Carte Blanche 2013a, Part1, 1:28)

The above descriptions of security in Africa are not unique, nor value free. Quite the reverse. The continuous vilification of Islam and Muslims by associating them with terrorism, jihad, and violence is a persistent feature and, at times, manifestation of Islamophobia.

This chapter argues that Islamophobia in South Africa should not be understood as a natural negative reaction to an unfamiliar, foreign, or strange group of people. On the contrary, this chapter demonstrates that South African-based security research institutes (think-tanks) and popular media are key actors in the construction of Islamophobia. Indeed, these actors are often complicit in the representation of African and South African Muslims and Islam as sources of terror and terrorism. Furthermore, this chapter confirms that security think-tanks systematically manufacture terrorism knowledge and expertise in support of the so-called global War on Terror in a way that mimics Western discourses on Islamophobia. Here it will be shown how think-tanks and the media construct Islam and Muslims, in support of a hegemonic discourse that define Muslims as a 'scapegoat – real or invented – and excluding this scapegoat from the resources/rights/definition of a constructed "we"'. This is Islamophobia that 'operates by constructing a static "Muslim" identity, which is attributed in negative terms and generalised for all Muslims' (Hafez 2018: 218). Moreover, the chapter asserts that the technologies of securitisation are often employed towards creating a climate of widespread fear of Muslims that has the potential to justify anti-Muslim racism or anti-Islamic prejudice, and Islamophobia.

The chapter starts with an interrogation of securitisation theory (Buzan, Wæver, de Wilde 1998; Wæver 2003) that serves as the theoretical lens through which the chapter exposes how think-tanks and the press construct Muslims and Islam as a security threat. Then, the entities 'think-tanks' are problematised. Thereafter, a discussion follows of how the news media and think-tank experts have securitised Muslims and Islam and have contributed to an atmosphere in South Africa that sustains Islamophobia.

Securitisation theory

Securitisation theory provides insight into the processes that make it possible to construct Muslims and Islam as an existential security threat and/or concern. Introducing the technologies associated with securitisation does not negate nor justify the racist and anti-Black thought at the origins of this theory (Howell and Richter-Montpetit 2020). Securitisation is based on the assumption that identifying an issue as a 'security' concern is not necessarily based on objective factors. Instead, a threat comes into existence through a 'speech act' (Wæver 2003: 10), an utterance, that an issue is a security concern which 'creates a new social order' (Balzacq 2005: 171): Ole Wæver explains that 'by labelling something a security issue, it becomes one' (2004, quoted in Taureck 2006: 55). This move justifies the introduction of emergency measures and state actions in order to annihilate the threat.

To re-emphasise the intellectual underpinnings of securitisation: 'the utterance *itself* is the act' (Wæver 1995: 55, emphasis in original). Theoretically, at least, it can be argued that any actor has the capacity to securitise any issue. However, securitisation actors, as theorised by its original architects, are limited to those with the appropriate power and capability as well as the means to construct a threat socially and politically (Taureck 2006: 55). This authority, according to Wæver (1995: 55), is the preserve or domain of state representatives with the institutional power to claim a 'special right to use whatever means necessary to block' the constructed threat.

Having stated the above, scholars have pointed out that functional actors such as academics, the media, and think-tanks, while not having the power to introduce extreme measures to stop a constructed threat, do have the capacity to influence and draw attention to an issue as a security concern (Hendricks 2020; Eroukhmanoff 2017; Vuori 2008). These functional actors, 'help frame storylines about the existentially threatening nature of the issue, often creating divides between "us" and "them" – and often implicated in "othering" processes' (Eroukhmanoff 2017: 107–8). Concurring with this perspective, Huha Vuori (2008: 76–7) claims that these functional groups do have 'sufficient social capital' to achieve political aims such as ensuring that the issues they have framed are included on the security agenda of state bureaucrats (Vuori 2008). Having described the notion of securitisation, the chapter now turns to describe actors which are actively involved in processes that operationalise securitisation, namely, public policy research institutes, which the chapter refers to as think-tanks.

Think-tanks as political actors

While the origins of the term 'think-tank' will not be recounted here, due to space limitations, it is proper to recognise that the current meaning of the term can be traced to the RAND Corporation, with civilian researchers, which was established in the 1950s to advise the US military on national security, social, and economic policy matters (Hounshell 1997: 240). The RAND Corporation, as the prototype think-tank, has not limited its research to technical and/or scientific matters. On the contrary, its social science research was ideologically guided by the imperative that the strategic interests of the United States (US) should at all times be defended (Hounshell 1997: 244). Consistent with such a strategic requirement, the RAND social scientists would explore different ways by which populations, whether these are the US's enemies, its allies, and even its own citizens, can be manipulated as part of the US's 'secret psychological warfare' (Brodie 2011: 655). Presenting this detail about RAND's research is to suggest that think-tanks often relinquish their scholarly independence in the presence of political power.

Following this legacy, public policy research institutions are currently referred to as 'think-tanks'. However, scholars have not as yet defined the term precisely. Some conceive of them as research institutes which conduct contract research to 'solve complex problems or predict or plan future developments' (Versi 2016: 54), while others define them as autonomous policy research institutions, established as non-profit organisations, that are active in the policy-making process (Stone 2000). Yet others argue that political think-tanks are public policy research institutes that primarily aim to influence the policy process with their ideas. Andrew Rich, for pragmatic reasons, defines think-tanks as '*independent, non-interest-based, non-profit organizations that produce and principally rely on expertise and ideas to obtain support and to influence the policymaking process*' (Rich 2004: 11, italics in original). Despite an inability to reach a common agreement over a definition of the term, scholars seem to concur that think-tanks do aim to influence policy-making processes through the proposal of ideas and suggestions.

This introduces the question of whose interests are being served by their policy advice. Policy makers and journalists, expected to respond to complex political and social environments, do rely on expert advice on offer by think-tanks, who do make an effort to translate their research into relevant and practical ideas for public policy. However, this expertise has been questioned, both for the undue influence think-tanks have on political decision making and, at times, for advocating partial and/or incorrect propositions (Schröder 2006). Furthermore, some have asserted that funders are also beneficiaries of think-tanks, as research institutes allow them to 'achieve indirect societal impact on public opinion and policy agenda' (Stone 2007: 344). The relationship of funders from the global North with their benefactors in Africa is no different.

Julia Hearn (2007) found that development aid in Africa is used by foreign donors to entice institutions such as think-tanks to facilitate and promote the policies that support their goals in Africa. This should come as no surprise, as foreign funding is integral to the ways in which a country's foreign relationships are conducted (Parmar 2002). It is thus no secret that USAID, a US funding organisation, utilised foreign aid to maintain and construct US hegemony, globally (Parmar 2002). Condoleezza Rice, the former US secretary of state, drew a link between foreign aid and the US's 'security interests', its 'development goals', and its 'democratic ideals' by stating that these are all interrelated (quoted in Howell and Lind 2009: 1285). For this reason, she announced, USAID 'would be required to work more closely with the [US] State Department' (Hills 2006: 629).

In a study that investigates Northern funding of non-governmental organisations (NGOs) in Africa, Julia Hearn equates the role played by missionaries during the colonial period and contemporary NGOs such as think-tanks in Africa and concludes that think-tanks/NGOs 'represent a continuity of the work of their precursors, the missionaries and voluntary organisations that co-operated in Europe's colonization and control of Africa' (Hearn 2007: 1100). As a concluding remark to this section, it is important to note that think-tanks are not benign, nor is their policy advice value free, as they have specific material interests. Instead, think-tanks 'can reflect, reinforce and amplify division in society and exaggerate societal tensions' (Stone 2000: 169). Scholars have shown the intertwined relationship between think-tanks, neo-conservative funders and the promotion of Islamophobia in the US, and in Europe (Griffin et al. 2015; Griffin, Miller, Mills 2017; Aked 2015). Also, Jemal Muhamed (2019), in an article on the 'Securitisation of Islam in contemporary Ethiopia', notes a link between academics, think-tanks, and the spread of Islamophobia. The next section examines manifestations of Islamophobia which became popularised by media and think-tanks in South Africa.

Islamophobia in the media

The South African media, both television and print, have supported a discourse that constructs Islam and Muslims as a threat to Western civilisation. In the contexts of the so-called War on Terror, the media has performed the ideological work by portraying the motives of the West as noble saviours while, conversely, presenting those of Muslims as dishonourable and threatening, thus perpetuating Islamophobic discourse.

As a powerful institution in society, the media has the ability to regulate public debate and opinion through its 'agenda setting' capacity and capabilities. This is done by privileging certain perspectives while being silent on others. Generally, as agents of socialisation, the media has promoted and popularised the worldviews of the political and economic elites in society (Bates 1975: 352). In this role, the media has manufactured 'consent' and legitimised the reproduction of cultural life (Heywood 1994: 101).

Muslim portrayals in a South African television documentary

We start by analysing selected events in a television documentary, *Kenyan Attack*, broadcast on 29 September 2013 and hosted by Carte Blanche (2013a; 2013b). The documentary sets out to confirm the alleged South African links to the military attacks on the Westgate Mall in Nairobi, Kenya, on 21 September 2013. In recounting the events, the documentary introduces viewers to a woman called Samantha Lewthwaite. This woman was suspected as the leader and/or a perpetrator of the attacks which were carried out, allegedly, in support of the Somalian armed group al Shabaab. However, other than speculation, no evidence was provided to confirm Lewthwaite's involvement in the attack – a point vaguely alluded to in the documentary itself when the narrator stated that 'there [was] no absolute confirmation of Samantha's involvement in the Mall shooting' (Carte Blanche 2013b, Part 2, 2:33–7). Despite this uncertainty, Carte Blanche continued to inform its viewers that Lewthwaite was a British convert to Islam and was married to Germain Lindsay, 'one of the four bombers of the July 2005 terror attacks in London' which killed fifty-two people and injured 'hundreds'.

The theme that associated Islam with terrorism ran throughout the documentary, in the form of Muslims being involved in terrorism, or as potential terrorists, or as protectors of terrorists. To establish that Lewthwaite was indeed Muslim, the interviewer asked a South African neighbour where she allegedly lived and 'how was she usually dressed?' In responding to this question, the neighbour stated: 'With a Muslim outfit' (Carte Blanche 2013b, Part 2, 3:40). Establishing that Lewthwaite was Muslim allowed Carte Blanche to associate Muslims and terrorism. From this point, the documentary attempted to suggest that if one dressed like a Muslim, one must be a terrorist. This association was further developed when the local mosque became a central landmark during interviews with Muslims who lived in the neighbourhood where Lewthwaite resided. The centrality of the mosque became more prominent during interviews with its caretaker and a Muslim scholar, associated with the University of Johannesburg, whose interviews were conducted at and inside the mosque, respectively. The prominence of the mosque during these interviews might have served the ideological function of associating a community and a religion with terrorism.

An examination of this narrative, which limits Lewthwaite's identity to being a Muslim convert while ignoring all other social, political, and emotional influences to her identity, as well as associating the religious community she allegedly adopted with terrorism, suggests that the Carte Blanche documentary was promoting Islamophobic tropes. Not only did the Carte Blanche narrative construct Muslims as a 'suspect community' (Hillyard 1973: 7), it also served as 'evidence' that this community was dangerous, as it committed acts of terror, which had the potential to cause death to the innocent. Furthermore, associating Muslims with the notion 'terrorism' continues to perpetuate the prejudiced idea that Muslims are inclined to acts of random violence.

In Part 1 of the documentary the singing of a Christian hymn is played to symbolise the grief of Kenyans. The grief was confirmed by the narrator's words that the Kenyans were in mourning and 'devastated, shattered, grief stricken, by the terrorist attack ...; but as a nation they [were] not broken' (Carte Blanche 2013a, Part 1, 00:07). Continuing, the narrator states that 'the situation on the ground' is tense, with 'scores still unaccounted for'. Despite the grieving, an anonymous voice then appeals for people not to point 'fingers at any religion', since '(w)e are one ... we Kenyans. Let us love each other, let us protect each other' (00: 35). In contrast to the victims who were promoting reconciliation, the 'attackers' were introduced as 'terrorists' who aimed to establish an 'Islamic state':

> The deadly four-day siege was claimed by al Qaeda-linked terrorist group, al Shabab. Al Shabab is an Islamist militant group who is fighting to overthrow the Somali government and establish an Islamic state. (Carte Blanche 2013a, Part 1, 1:28)

The point here is not to show an essentialisation of Muslims as an imminent threat. Instead, the contrasting representations above have been used to indicate that the Carte Blanche documentary applied Huntington's (1996) 'Clash of Civilisations' thesis to serve as its conceptual framework. In this thesis, Huntington argued that 'relations between states and groups from different civilizations will be ... antagonistic' and that Islam and the West would be two of the primary conflicting civilisations in [the] future (Huntington 1996: 183).

The Carte Blanche documentary counterposed Western and Islamic civilisations. Western civilisation was presented as good through the depiction of Christian hymns and the anonymous voice calling for reconciliation and love. In contrast, Islamic civilisation was demonised as it celebrated death and destruction and wanting to establish 'the Islamic state' (*Carte Blanche* 2013a, Part 1, 1:28). Completely absent from this documentary were Muslim reconciliatory voices. Rather, the only Muslim representations were of violence and terrorism, crystallising Huntington's mythology surrounding Muslims and Islam. Having analysed anti-Muslim representations in television media, we now turn our focus to the South African print media and its role in promoting Islamophobia.

Muslim portrayals in the South African print media

In addition to drawing on Huntington's thesis to frame articles related to Muslims, South Africa's newspapers used numerous strategies to construct an atmosphere that promoted Islamophobia. These strategies included dehumanisation, orientalisation, and associating Muslims with terrorism.

In a newspaper article, a journalist for the *Saturday Star* (2006) reported on an interview with a documentary producer whose work focused on 'fundamentalist' content in Middle Eastern television programmes. The article reported that the documentary producer was disturbed by the material that appeared on an Abu Dhabi television channel, as the content showed how Muslim children were 'indoctrinated by radical Islamic rhetoric to feel hatred' towards the West:

> On Abu Dhabi Television, a sweet-faced girl from Bahrain says unemotionally: 'I hope Bush dies in flames, and I want to go to Ariel Sharon and kill him with a gun and stab him with a sword [...]'. (*Saturday Star* 2006)

This narrative suggests that Muslims have normalised hatred and the killing of opponents through the indoctrination of their young. This construction is also meant to confirm that 'fundamentalist' Muslims lack humanity. The *Saturday Star* (2006) article cited above is an illustrative example of the dehumanisation of Muslims in the press, as it represents Middle Eastern Muslims as if they lack any trace of moral conscience. This representation of Muslims usurps the authority and power to name those who are excluded from a humanity 'we' subscribe to. In this instance, Muslims are represented in negative terms by the construction of a 'static "Muslim" identity, which is attributed in negative terms and generalized for all Muslims' (Hafez 2018: 218). The article then went on to discuss how producing the documentary involved using translated works.

The *Saturday Star* (2006) reported that the original content for the documentary was sourced from two Israeli organisations that monitored and translated 'hundreds of hours' of Arab television. The translated transcripts were then made 'available on the internet', freely. While translation services are not necessarily ideologically neutral, the matter of translations is introduced not to challenge the accuracy of the quotation above; rather, it is raised as an illustration about the validity of sources which the local print media draw on. As already suggested, the Arabic translations sourced from the internet and used in the documentary might be accurate; however, it remains important to treat translations with caution, because translations can 'mystify', 'mislead', and/or distort (Baker 2010: 347). It is well known that translation services delivered by the Middle East Media Research Institute (MEMRI), established in February 1998, have a strong ideological slant (Baker, 2010). This is because the translation programmes of MEMRI, a pro-Israeli think-tank with a direct association with the Israeli intelligence service (Bonney 2008: 104), are 'heavily funded' (Baker 2010: 348) to ensure that their translations are available at no financial cost. Furthermore, Hilary Aked (2015) draws a link between pro-Israeli advocacy groups and their attempts at sustaining Islamophobia. Here they suggest that the 'embrace of anti-Muslim racism by many other pro-Israel actors' is strategic in that 'pro-Israel advocates believe Islamophobia encourages sympathy for Israel'

(Aked 2015: 4). MEMRI's translated works, like those discussed in the documentary, have the potential of promoting Islamophobia in a strategic manner with the purpose of encouraging sympathy for Israel, especially in Western countries. In addition to Islamophobic narratives, there are also Orientalist tropes which are perpetuated through South African print media.

Edward Said (1979: 188) defined Orientalism as the Western discourse of othering Easterners. Through this construction, Muslims, and more generally 'Arabs', are represented as exotic, mysterious, dangerous, inherently 'barbaric', and fanatical. We will now identify instances where orientalisation has been used in South African media to describe Muslims and Islam.

In a *Saturday Star* (2006) article, the religion of Islam is associated with barbarism: 'Islam is spread through the sword. How do you spread through the sword? Submit or die. The ultimate sword is to bring the world to its knees or die' (*Saturday Star* 2006). This representation of Islam is clearly an instance of anti-Muslim racism. In deconstructing the above, it becomes clear that the purpose of representing Islam negatively was to associate it with negative attributes such as barbarism and senseless violence while suggesting that 'we' are better. Iman Attia (2007, cited in Hafez 2018: 217) argues that such anti-Muslim racism serves to stabilise hegemonic power. For Attia, anti-Muslim racism is conceived as a 'form of cultural racism, in which "religion is ... culturalized and transformed into the essential components of the cultural conceptions of the self and other"' (Hafez 2018: 217). These associations with violence and barbarism, naturally, create opportunities to frame Muslims as perpetrators of terrorism.

Another strategy employed by the South African newspapers that has had the potential to increase Islamophobia in the country has been to associate Muslims and Islam with terrorism. In doing this, the print media promoted the idea that terror activities in and/or from a country risk potential negative catastrophic consequences for South Africa and its population. Associating Muslims with terrorism was integral to the media's attempt to construct South Africa as a partner in the US's declared global War on Terror. In this war, al Qaeda was constructed as the primary enemy, as not only was it responsible for providing logistical infrastructure, financial, and technical support for terrorist activities in the name of Islam, but it also provided the ideological leadership to these activities. Suggesting and/or speculating that South Africa has become a safe haven for international Islamic extremist groups like al Qaeda was one of the ways that newspapers associated Muslims with terror. The newspaper articles referred to below that were used as illustrative examples of how South African Muslims were associated with terrorism all appeared during a period when South Africa was urged to actively support the so-call global War on Terror (Hendricks 2020).

In one article by the *Saturday Weekend Argus* (2004) a headline read: 'Al Qaeda leaders "hiding in SA": top militants may be operating "from Cape Town to Durban; from Eastern Cape to Gauteng"'. This publication further claimed, based on 'intelligence reports', that al Qaeda operatives were foreign and these operatives were assisted by local and immigrant Muslims. These claims, though, were never validated or substantiated. In another article unrelated to this incident, Hussein Solomon, a former director of a South African-based security think-tank, was asked to confirm that terror organisations were using South Africa as a place of safety (*Die Beeld* 2011). In responding in the affirmative to *Die Beeld*'s question, Solomon warned that not only has the country become a convenient sanctuary for terror groups, but it also has become a pivotal location from where these groups planned international terror activities. It is important to note here that if any of these claims held any weight or substance, the South African police or its intelligence services would have intervened and would have attempted to arrest those involved. However, no such actions have occurred to substantiate these claims.

We do know that associating terrorism with a group or an individual is not an innocent practice, as the term 'terrorism' is pejorative and is invoked only when referring to the action of the enemy (Stampnitzky 2013). Despite its popular usage, terrorism, as a social problem, does not have an objective meaning, nor are policy makers, experts, and scholars in agreement on the meaning and/or a definition of this concept (Staun 2010). Due to its inherent instability as a concept, Jørgen Staun (2010: 403–4) proposes that instead of determining what terrorism is, as a concept, scholars should instead describe 'which political actors are involved in defining terrorism, how they frame the threat and when and why they do so'. As previously discussed, securitisation (Wæver 2003) is the process of constructing an action, or a group, as a threat that requires emergency action to annihilate it. Drawing on speech-act theory (Austin, 1962), Wæver (1995: 55) emphasises that 'the utterance *itself* is the act'. Thus, stating that 'Al Qaeda leaders [are] "hiding in SA"' and that these '[terrorist] operatives were assisted by local and immigrant Muslims' (*Saturday Weekend Argus* 2004), or warning that South Africa has become a convenient sanctuary for terror groups and that it is a pivotal location from where these groups planned international terror activities, has severe consequences for the local and immigrant Muslim community.

This section of the chapter has shown how local media has manufactured an atmosphere for increased Islamophobia. It has argued that Muslims were framed as violent, dangerous, suicidal, irrational, and barbaric. Moreover, Muslims were singularly associated with terrorism. The section has also shown that Huntington's (1996) thesis has been used as a framework to construct narratives about Muslims and Islam. Here, Western civilisation has been presented as 'good' and Christian in contrast to the Islamic civilisation, which was presented as 'bad' and without humanity. The media reports discussed above drew extensively from the assumed 'expertise' of local South African think-tanks. Media outlets regularly rely on think-tanks' expertise to construct their stories or to substantiate the claims they are making. But this relationship is symbiotic, as think-tanks, for their part, use the media to propagate their ideas and perspectives in the public sphere. We accordingly now turn to focus on the role of think-tanks in promoting Islamophobia in South Africa.

Islamophobia and the role of think-tanks

The selected South African think-tanks discussed in this section are the South African Institute of International Affairs, the Institute of Security Studies (ISS), the Brenthurst Foundation, and the Centre for International Policy Studies (CiPS). The origins and history of these think-tanks will not be repeated, as they have been adequately covered by the author in an earlier publication (Hendricks 2020). However, a point worth mentioning is that the origins of these think-tanks can be traced back to their association with apartheid and/or British colonialism. It is also prudent to confirm that these think-tanks are primarily funded by Western governments such as the US, Britain, Canada, the Netherlands, and Germany, as well as philanthropic foundations associated with Western interests such as USAID, the Gorbachev Foundation, the Swedish International Development Agency, the Ford Foundation, the Geneva Centre for Security Policy, the Gesellschaft für Internationale Zusammenarbeit, and the Open Society Foundation for South Africa (Hendricks 2020).

This section sets out to demonstrate that South African security experts within think-tanks are pivotal actors who constitute the voices of 'authority' and 'expertise' and who transport and shape terrorism knowledge that securitises Muslims. In other words, think-tank experts have constructed Muslims as an existential threat to society. This section also confirms that local think-tanks are not neutral in their assessment of the security environment. Instead, they unquestionably transmit the security agenda that promotes Western interests in the South African security discourse.

A key strategy used by South African-based think-tanks to securitise Muslims was to associate them with terrorism. Here, my argument is that their stance on terrorism gave them access to funds available from the US through the global War on Terror (Hills 2006). Also, the act of labelling or associating Muslims with terrorism is pejorative, precisely because it is a term with negative connotations reserved for the 'enemy' in the so-called War on Terror. Ignoring the negative implication and consequences of associating a group with terrorism, it will be shown that local think-tanks have repeatedly constructed Muslims as inherently violent, dangerous, and associated with terrorism.

It was the founding director of the (South African) Institute for Security Studies (ISS), Jakkie Cilliers, who in 2003 located the roots of African terrorism in the Afghanistan Mujahideen, the group secretly funded by the US Central Intelligence Agency and credited with expelling the Soviet Union from Afghanistan during the 1980s. Cilliers (2003: 94) theorised that these Muslim 'liberators' 'became the 'terrorists', while training for a new international guerrilla brotherhood. He warned that Islamic terrorism in Africa targets the 'United States, Israel and [...] their allies', without explaining why these countries have become the targets of African terrorism. Moreover, Cilliers draws a direct link between the 'battle-hardened Algerian nationals' who allegedly formed the core of the African 'terrorism movement' and 'terrorist attacks in South Africa in the late 1990s (through PAGAD [People Against Gangsterism and Drugs]) and a series of attacks in East Africa' (Cilliers 2003: 94). Earlier, when we examined the media's role in promoting Islamophobia, terrorism as a concept, as well as its linguistic usage, was problematised. It is prudent to repeat that associating terrorism with Muslims and Islam is a highly political act that carries significant negative consequences. Cilliers's (2003) theorisation of terrorism in Africa is influential and privileged, as other local think-tank experts have repeated his assertions that African 'terrorism' can be traced back to the Afghanistan Mujahideen and that US and Israeli interests are the primary targets of terrorism committed by Africa. Yet, Cilliers (2003) and his followers have failed to present credible evidence that support their assertions.

PAGAD, established in 1995, is an organisation Cilliers connects with Islamic terrorism in Africa. However, PAGAD is not a Muslim organisation. According to Hendricks (2020: 52), PAGAD was initially 'not an exclusive Muslim network'. However, since it started off in residential areas with significant Muslim populations,

> Muslims became predominant in its public marches and the drawing on selected Islamic symbols – such as referring to leaders as *amir* and inviting their activists to *iftaar* – led voices, especially in the popular media, to associate PAGAD with Islam and eventually with the international Islamic threat. (Hendricks 2020: 52)

After the establishment of PAGAD, Muslim representations in Africa became more associated with terror and extremism (Hough 2000), which escalated following Cape Town's Planet Hollywood restaurant bombing incident in

August 1998. In writing about this, Mike Hough (2000: 68) argued that the Planet Hollywood incident, as well as the prior 'wave of bombings [in the Western Cape], seemed initially part of an international terrorist campaign'. Other 'experts', members of the South African ISS, echoed this sentiment by stating, without any credible evidence, that the Planet Hollywood bombing was a retaliatory response to the American bombings in Sudan and Afghanistan in August 1998 (Boshoff, Botha, Schönteich 2001: 37). Hough (2000: 69) went a step further and suggested that the 'pipe bomb is the Islamic signature in the Western Cape'. The above examples highlight how think-tank mouthpieces are actively engaged in a securitising process of Muslims through tenuous affiliations with PAGAD. Assessing these constructions, Hendricks (2020: 52) concludes: 'Apart from generalising wildly, the assertions of these "experts" securitised PAGAD and, by implication, called for extreme measures to stop the threat posed by it.' We will now shift our attention to another incident which was highlighted by another South African think-tank expert.

After reporting that Tuareg nationalists in Mali militarily conquered the country's national army in January 2012, Hussein Solomon, a former CiPS director, stated that the nationalists' effort 'was quickly overtaken by Islamist elements' who allowed northern Mali to be transformed into a 'terrorist enclave as it attracted thousands of jihadists from other countries' (Solomon 2013: 428). Solomon (2013: 428) accordingly warned that this Malian 'terrorist enclave' was a threat to the rest of Africa that must urgently be stopped. Here, Solomon (2013) disparagingly classifies the Tuareg nationalists as 'Islamist elements' and proposes that under their leadership Mali will degenerate into a 'terrorist enclave'. This threat is amplified by him stating that Mali will become a sanctuary for 'thousands of jihadists'. Solomon orientalises supporters of the Tuareg cause by constructing them as war-loving 'Islamists' and uses a foreign label, 'jihadists', to signal that they are 'Other'. In another instance, think-tanks promote Islamophobia in Africa by associating terrorism with Islam purely based on the substantial population of Muslims in Africa.

After having established that the Muslim population in Africa was approximately 40 per cent of the total population, the director of the Brenthurst Foundation, Greg Mills applied zoomorphism to speculate that Africa had the 'potential to become a breeding ground for new terrorist threats', as it was a 'cancer growing in the middle of nowhere' (2004: 158–9). In the same speculative manner, Mills, together with a collaborator, exaggerated the enormity of an assumed Muslim threat by noting that '40 per cent of Africa's 700 million people are Muslim, [which highlights] the danger posed by the pathology of violent, fundamentalist Islam to Western interest(s)' (Herbst and Mills 2003: 13). In this example, Herbst and Mills securitised 'fundamentalist Islam' by their utterance that Islam posed a threat to Western interests. They emphasised this danger by declaring a speech-act, claiming that '[t]here [was] no doubt that alienated and radicalized, Africa's 250 million Muslims could make the continent ungovernable' (Herbst and Mills 2003: 14). These utterances were strengthened by the claim that Africa's Muslim population gave 'rise to domestic [African] terror' (Mills 2004: 161), as Islamic groups had the potential to recruit 'angry, marginalized and anti-American [Muslim] youth from Somalia to Senegal, ... Cape Town to Casablanca' for terrorist activities (Mills and Herbst 2007: 41).

The structure of the utterances of Cilliers (2003), Solomon (2013), and Mills (2004) suggests that African Muslims are being securitised. In other words, they are being constructed as a security threat which, if it is not urgently stopped, there may not be another opportunity to do so. All three use speech-acts in securitising African Muslims. In the case of Cilliers (2003), he pronounced that the Algerian veterans who fought against the Soviet Union to liberate Afghanistan had turned around to form the core of the African terrorist movement that targets the US, Israel, and their allies. If these terrorists are not urgently annihilated, there will be no US, Israel, or their allies, at least not in Africa. Cilliers continues, claiming that this terrorist group already has had links to terrorism acts in South Africa and East Africa. Identifying South Africa as an actual target of terrorists surely suggests that South Africa should become a partner under the leadership of the US in the global War on Terror.

Solomon's (2013) utterances in the first instance draw on orientalist symbolism to securitise. He uses terms that have some association with Islam and the Arab world but have been reinterpreted to have a special meaning in the War on Terror. Just being associated with the rebranded concepts that have their origins in Arabic, such as 'jihadist', which the Merriam-Webster dictionary defines as a 'Muslim who advocates or participates in a jihad' and 'Islamist', suggests a backwardness to some extent. The term jihadist, as used by Solomon (2013), is an ideologically driven term, which is a corrupted form of the Arabic word 'jihadi', which means the one who exerts. Yet, jihadi came to be equated, in an ideological battle of ideas, with the notion of being predisposed or inclined to war. As by the definition above, 'jihadist' is exclusively reserved for Muslims. The term 'Islamist' is similarly a constructed concept to perform an ideological function.

This section has focused on South African-based think-tanks and argued that they have securitised Muslims and Islam in Africa. The instances presented were all manifestations of Islamophobia, in that Muslims were represented negatively using strategies such as speculation and without providing substantiating evidence for the negative claims and associations with terrorism.

Conclusion

This chapter has discussed how South African-based security research institutes (think-tanks) and popular media are key actors in the promotion of Islamophobia in the nation and the African continent. Indeed, these actors were often complicit in the representation of African and South African Muslims and Islam as sources of terror and terrorism. The local media, in particular, manufactured an atmosphere for increased Islamophobia by representing Muslims as violent, dangerous, suicidal, irrational, barbaric, and prone to commit acts of terrorism. Huntington's (1996) thesis, which argued that Islam and the West are destined to be future enemies, has been used as the ideological framework to construct narratives about Muslims and Islam.

Furthermore, this chapter has confirmed that security think-tanks systematically manufactured terrorism knowledge and expertise in support of the so-called global War on Terror in a way that mimicked Western Islamophobic discourses. Moreover, it has confirmed that the technologies of securitisation were evident as a way of creating a climate of widespread fear of Muslims. Here, associating Muslims with terrorism became a pivotal weapon. This chapter has demonstrated that Islamophobia in Africa is a continuation of coloniality on this continent by the South African media and think-tanks whose practices have the effect of promoting and protecting material and strategic imperialist interests.

Bibliography

Aked, H. (2015). The undeniable overlap: right-wing Zionism and Islamophobia. Discussion paper series: September, London: Centre for Research on Migration, Refugees and Belonging.

Austin, J.L. (1962). *How to do things with words*, Oxford: Oxford University Press.

Baker, M. (2010). Narratives of terrorism and security: 'accurate' translations, suspicious frames, *Critical Studies on Terrorism*, 3(3): 347–64.

Balzacq, T. (2005). The three faces of securitization: political agency, audience and context, *European Journal of International Relations*, 11(2): 171–201.

Bates, T.R. (1975). Gramsci and the theory of hegemony, *Journal of the History of Ideas*, 36(2): 351–66.

Beres, L.R. (1991). The permissibility of state-sponsored assassination during peace and war, *Temple International and Comparative Law Journal*, 5(2): 231–50.

Bonney, R. (2008). *False prophets: the 'clash of civilisations' and the global war on terror*, Oxfordshire, UK: Peter Lang Ltd.

Boshoff, H., Botha, A., and Schönteich, M. (2001). *Fear in the city, urban terrorism in South Africa*, Institute for Security Studies, www.iss.co.za/pubs/Monograph/No63/ (accessed 1 May 2006).

Bravo López, F. (2011). Towards a definition of Islamophobia: approximations of the early twentieth century, *Ethnic and Racial Studies*, 34(4): 556–73, https://doi.org/10.1080/01419870.2010.528440 (accessed 15 June 2021).

Brodie, J.E. (2011). Learning secrecy in the early Cold War, *Diplomatic History*, 35(4): 643–70.

Buzan, B., Wæver, O., and de Wilde, J. (1998). *Security: a new framework for analysis*, London: Lynne Rienner Publishers.

Buzan, B., Kelstrup, M., Lemaitre, P., Tromer, E., and Wæver, O. (1990). *The European security order recast: scenarios for the post-Cold War era*, London: Pinter Publishers.

Carte Blanche (2013a). *Kenyan Attack (Part 1)*, M-Net, Carteblanche.dstv/player/361064/ (accessed 20 May 2014).

Carte Blanche (2013b). *Kenyan Attack (Part 2)*, M-Net, Carteblanche.dstv/player/361114/ (accessed 20 May 2014).

Cilliers, J. (2003). Terrorism and Africa, *African Review*, 12(4): 91–103.

Cilliers, J. (n.d.). Jakkie Cilliers *LinkedIn* profile, www.linkedin.com/pub/jakkie-cilliers/25a9b/a74, (accessed 15 September 2017).

Citizen (2003). Muslims 'a bigger threat', 17 February.

Conway, G. (1997). *Islamophobia: a challenge for us all*, Report of the Runnymede Trust Commission on British Muslims and Islamophobia, www.runnymedetrust.org/publications/islamophobia-a-challenge-for-us-all (accessed 27 January 2021).

Die Beeld (2011). SA nie immuun teen terreur, waarsku kenner, 26 January.

Ernst, C.W. (2013). Introduction: the problem of Islamophobia. In: C.W. Ernst (ed.), *Islamophobia in America: the anatomy of intolerance*, New York: Palgrave Macmillan, 1–20.

Eroukhmanoff, C. (2017). Securitisation theory. In: S. McGlinchey, R. Walters, and C. Scheinpflug (eds), *International relations theory*, E-International Relations Publishing, www.e-ir.info/publications/ (accessed 15 January 2021).

Hough, M. (2000). Urban terror in South Africa: a new wave? *Terrorism and Violence*, 12(2): 67–75.

Estelle, E. and Darden, J.T. (2021). *Combating the Islamic State's spread in Africa: assessment and recommendations for Mozambique*, American Enterprise Institute, Research Report, www.jstor.org/stable/resrep30196 (accessed 15 May 2021).

Ghanea Bassiri, K. (2013). Islamophobia and American history: religious stereotyping and out-grouping of Muslims in the United States. In: C.W. Ernst (ed.), *Islamophobia in America: the anatomy of intolerance*, New York: Palgrave Macmillan, chapter 2.

Gottschalk, P. and Greenberg, G. (2013). Common heritage, uncommon fear: Islamophobia in the United States and British India, 1687–1947. In: C.W. Ernst (ed.), *Islamophobia in America: the anatomy of intolerance*, New York: Palgrave Macmillan, chapter 1.

Griffin, T., Miller, D., and Mills, T. (2017). The neoconservative movement: think tanks as elite elements of social movements from above. In: N. Massoumi, T. Mills, and D. Miller (eds), *What is Islamophobia? Racism, social movements and the state*, London: Pluto Press, 215–33.

Griffin, T., Aked, H., Miller, D., and Marusek, S. (2015). The Henry Jackson Society and the degeneration of British neoconservatism: liberal interventionism,

Islamophobia and the 'War on Terror', Glasgow: Public Interest Investigations, https://researchportal.bath.ac.uk/en/publications/the-henry-jackson-society-and-the-degeneration-of-british-neocons (accessed 27 February 2017).

Hafez, F. (2018). Schools of thought in Islamophobia studies: prejudice, racism, and decoloniality, *Islamophobia Studies Journal*, 4(2): 210–25.

Hassan, I. and Azmi, M.N.L. (2021). Islamophobia in non-Western media: a content analysis of online newspapers, *Newspaper Research Journal*, 42(1): 29–47.

Hearn, J. (2007). Africa NGOs: new compradors? *Development and Change*, 38(6): 1095–110.

Hendricks, M.N. (2020). *Manufacturing terrorism in Africa: the securitisation of South African Muslims*, Gateway East: Palgrave MacMillan.

Herbst, J. and Mills, G. (2003). Africa and the war on terror, *The RUSI Journal*, 148(5): 12–17.

Heywood, A. (1994). *Political ideas and concepts: an introduction*, London: Macmillan.

Hills, A. (2006). Trojan horses? USAID, counter-terrorism and Africa's police, *Third World Quarterly*, 27(4): 629–43.

Hillyard, P. (1973). *Suspect community: people's experiences of the Prevention of Terrorism Act in Britain*, London: Pluto Press.

Howell, A. and Richter-Montpetit, M. (2020). Is securitization theory racist? Civilizationism, methodological whiteness, and antiblack thought in the Copenhagen School, *Security Dialogue*, 51(1), https://journals.sagepub.com/doi/full/10.1177/0967010619862921 (accessed 25 March 2022).

Howell, J. and Lind, J. (2009). Changing donor policy and practice in civil society in the post-9/11 aid context, *Third World Quarterly*, 30(7): 1279–96.

Hounshell, D. (1997). The Cold War, RAND and the generation of knowledge, 1946–1962, *Historical Studies in Physical and Biological Sciences*, 27(2): 237–67.

Huntington, S.P. (1996). *The clash of civilisations and the remaking of world order*, New York: Simon and Schuster.

Mamdani, M. (2005). Good Muslim, bad Muslim: America, the Cold War and the origins of terror, *India International Centre Quarterly*, 32(1): 1–10.

Merriam-Webster (n.d.). www.merriam-webster.com/dictionary/jihadist (accessed 17 October 2021)

Mills, G. (2004). Africa's new strategic significance, *The Washington Quarterly*, 27(4): 157–69.

Mills, G. and Herbst, J. (2007). Africa, terrorism and AFRICOM, *RUSI Journal*, 152(2): 40–4.

Muhamed, J. (2019). Securitization of Islam in contemporary Ethiopia. In: E. Bayrakh and F. Hafez (eds), *Islamophobia in Muslim majority countries*, New York: Routledge.

Parmar, I. (2002). *Think tanks and power in foreign policy: a comparative study of the role and influence of the Council on Foreign Relations and the Royal Institute of International Affairs, 1939–1945*, New York: Palgrave Macmillan.

Rich, A. (2004). *Think tanks, public policy, and the politics of expertise*, New York: Cambridge University Press.

Said, E.W. (1979). *Orientalism*, New York: Vintage Books.

Saturday Star (2006). Islamic fundamentalism gets REEL, 2 December.

Saturday Weekend Argus (2004). Al Qaeda leaders 'hiding in SA', 3 October.

Schönteich, M. (2003). The White Right: a threat to South Africa's internal security? *SA Crime Quarterly*, 3(March): 1–4.

Schröder, U.C. (2006). Security expertise in the European Union: the challenge of comprehensiveness and accountability, *European Security*, 15(4): 471–90.

Solomon, H. (2013). The African state and the failure of US counter-terrorism initiative in Africa: the cases of Nigeria and Mali, *South African Journal of International Affairs*, 20(3): 427–45, https://doi.org/10.1080/1022046 (accessed 27 March 2016).

Stampnitzky, L. (2013). *Disciplining terror: how experts invented 'terrorism'*, Cambridge UK: Cambridge University Press.

Staun, J. (2010). When, how and why elites frame terrorists: a Wittgensteinian analysis of terror and radicalisation, *Critical Studies on Terrorism*, 3(3): 403–20.

Stone, D. (2000). Think tanks, transnationalisation and non-profit analysis, advice and advocacy, *Global Society*, 14(2): 153–72.

Stone, D. (2001). Think tanks, global lesson-drawing and networking social policy ideas, *Global Social Policy*, 1(3): 338–60.

Stone, D. (2007). Recycling bins, garbage cans or think tanks? Three myths regarding policy analysis institutes, *Public Administration*, 85(2): 259–78.

Sunday Tribune (2008). Academic under fire, 31 August.

Taureck, R. (2006). Securitization theory and securitization studies, *Journal of International Relations and Development*, 9(1): 53–61.

Versi, A. (2016). Time for leaner fitter, think tanks, *New African*, Supplement, THINK-TANKS: 52–5.

Vuori, J.A. (2008). Illocutionary logic and strands of securitization: applying the theory of securitization to the study of non-democratic political orders, *European Journal of International Relations*, 14(1): 65–99.

Wæver, O (1995). Securitization and desecuritization. In: R.D. Lipschutz (ed.), *On security*, Columbia International Affairs Online, Columbia University Press, www.ciaonet.org/book/lipschutz/lipschutz13.html (accessed 18 January 2006).

Wæver, O. (2003). Securitisation: taking stock of a research programme in Security Studies, draft, http://zope.polforsk1.dk/securitytheory/oletext/ (accessed 18 January 2006).

Weekend Post (2006). Pope needs to be forgiven, agree: East Cape Muslims, 23 September.

Part IV

Islamophobia at the 'breaking point'

Chapter 10

India, Islamophobia, and the Hindutva playbook

Farhan Mujahid Chak

Introduction

Among the most disingenuous and carefully orchestrated playbook strategies of the Hindutva fascist movement in India, of which the current Narendra Modi-led Bharatiya Janata Party (BJP) government is part and parcel, is the manner in which it pursues its Islamophobic agenda. Arguably, there are few other spaces where Islamophobia is as dangerously manifest as it is in India today (Bazian et al. 2019: 3–10). This is not just because of the frequency of Islamophic attacks – a daily occurrence now – or the depth of depravity of the demonising language, or even the level of violence perpetrated against Muslims. Beyond that, the seriousness of Islamophobia in India is two-fold: (1) institutional support for Islamophobia from the highest political office in the country; (2) no recourse for Indian Muslims to appeal to the police or other legal authorities for meaningful protection. Today, it is open season on Muslims in India. Worse, there is not even any pretence of abiding by the rule of law or acknowledging the rights of minorities (Yeung 2020). It is a rabid, unadulterated hate-mongering that manifests in the most obscene of ways. This includes well-documented, blatant prejudice and discrimination against Muslims and other minorities that has stripped citizenship from millions of people, demagoguery that threatens to rape dead Muslim women, and lynching of Muslims in broad daylight – with police looking on (Goradia 2020). Even worse, in a twisted way, there seems to be a sense of amusement, even glee, at the rising levels of hate speech and violence directed towards Muslims, Christians, Dalits, Sikhs, and other minorities (Sharma 2011: 1–5). All this makes the unabashed nature of Islamophobia in India abhorrent.

To understand the origins of Islamophobia in India, and the depths of its depravity, this chapter looks at three intersecting variables. First and foremost, the rise of Islamophobia in India is directly linked to the Hindutva social imaginary. That poisonous social imaginary paints a misleading image of India and then positions Muslims as its nemesis in order to create a sense of victimisation among the majority community (Truschke 2020: 2–4). It is there, in the demonising discourse, that the roots of Islamophobia are located. Second, this chapter will explore how those myths of Hindutva precisely contribute to an overall demonising narrative against Islam and Muslims, and its relationship to Pakistan. Third, this chapter will delineate how Hindutva myths are weaponised to justify acts of criminality, such as: (1) Cow Vigilantism, also known as *Gau Rakshak*; (2) Ghar Wapsi – forced conversion; (3) Love Jihad – hatred against Muslim males marrying Hindu females; and (4) Bahu Lao, Beti Bachao, which translates as 'save your daughter and bring a (Muslim) daughter-in-law'. All in all, there is a carefully orchestrated strategy to demonise Islam and Muslims in order to rationalise crimes against them in both India and Kashmir. However, due to the nature of India's occupation of the disputed territory of Kashmir, and Kashmir's not being a part of India, it will be only briefly mentioned in this analysis.

The Hindutva social imaginary

To begin, Taylor describes a social imaginary as 'the ways people imagine their social existence, how they fit together with others, how things go on between them and their fellows, the expectations that are normally met, and the deeper normative notions and images that underlie these expectations' (Taylor 2004: 23). It is, for all intents and purposes, a binding creed that makes existence intelligible for social actors. For that purpose, this section considers it important to make a close examination of what exactly the 'Hindutva' social imaginary is, and to do so it closely scrutinises and outlines two interrelated variables: (1) the meaning of social imaginaries; and (2) the origins, growth, development, and eventual widespread usage of Hindutva imagery, symbols, and ideology to manufacture an Indian identity. This process of Hindutva myth making really began in the mid-1920s as a reaction to British dismissals of claims that a monolithic India existed. In response, the founding fathers of the Hindutva movement played a critical part in the invention of identity in India, which both their own propagandists and Congress leaders utilised in order to manufacture the myth of a monolithic India (Baghavan 2008: 39).

Taking a step back, Taylor describes a social imaginary, as distinct from social theory, on the basis of three conditions: (1) the emphasis is on ordinary people and the manner in which they 'imagine' their surroundings – especially by way of images, stories, and legends; (2) social imaginaries are shared by large groups of people, if not the whole society; and (3) a social imaginary leads to shared practices, and a widely shared sense of legitimacy. Of course, in practical terms, a social imaginary is complex and complicated. It is the collective expression of norms – the way things should be done – that are often unspoken but have great resonance. In this way, Taylor goes on to describe a social imaginary as 'the very nature of what contemporary philosophers have described as the "background"' (Taylor 2004: 25). It is in fact that largely unstructured and often unarticulated understanding of our lived experience, within which particular features of our world show up for us in the sense they have (Taylor 2004: 25–6). Importantly, none of this need be rational or factual.

Another essential component of social imaginaries is referred to as 'repertory', or the collective actions at the disposal of a given group in society. Essentially, a by-product of a social imaginary is that it creates a repertory, which is defined as the behavioural and attitudinal norms understood by participants in a given culture/social setting. It is the 'common actions that they know how to undertake, all the way from a general election, involving the whole of society, to knowing how to strike up a polite but uninvolved conversation with a casual group in a reception hall' (Taylor 2004: 26). Importantly, the relationship between actions, the conceptualisation of those actions, and the 'background' is not unidirectional. An understanding carries a particular action forward, and it is also true that the action imparts an understanding on another, and vice versa. In this way, a unique dialogical relationship carries both the act and its consequence back and forth towards heightened levels of shared reality for those involved. Likewise, the more actions are a manifestation of those ideas, the more deeply they become embedded.

Looking closely, the Hindutva social imaginary clearly demonstrates the way ordinary people imagine their surroundings – the past, present, and future (Snehi 2003: 10). It uses symbols, stories and legends to invent a past, rationalises the problematic present, and champions a potential bright future. It does this by invoking certain emotions, ideas, and reactions. By doing so, it creates – as Taylor described, a repertory that attempts to concretise something in the minds of those it aims to engage with. Moreover, this repertory of shared beliefs and practices is then widely disseminated and propagated through film, print, music, and social media; in fact, in every conceivable way possible, other than rigorous academic work. This is how the entire edifice of Hindutva began.

To further explain, the word Hindutva was first coined by Chandranath Basu in his 1892 Bengali work entitled *Hindutva – Hindur Prakrita Itihas*

(Hindutva – An Authentic History) (Sampath 2019b: 472). Yet, it was not until the imprisoned Vinayak Damodar Savarkar wrote his *The Essentials of Hindutva* in 1923 that the term was popularised in ideological/political ways, and based on sloppy history and hyperbole (Savarkar 1923). Moreover, it was explicitly connected to 'Otherisation', and Savarkar wrote extensively against all minorities, but especially Muslims for wanting to divide India (Sharma 2011: 6–12). Interestingly enough, this work outlined the reasons for Hindutva and was written while Savarkar was in prison in the Andaman Islands. During his incarceration he had written several mercy petitions to the British Crown, even writing that he would renounce all his former beliefs and remain a loyal British subject (Islam 2016: 30). For that reason, many of his detractors call him out as a charlatan. On the other hand, rather incredulously, his supporters point out that his pleas were a tactic employed only to escape the hardships of prison life (Islam 2016: 31–4). Aside from that, it is indicative of the duplicitous and inconsistent nature of Hindutva messaging, which demonises minorities and then uses a rhetoric of peace and harmony through plurality. It was this work that was fundamentally critical in creating that written repertory of duplicity, shared ideas, and beliefs – without being inconvenienced by fact and evidence. Basically, it was a fictional account of the origins of Indians that encouraged Hindus to develop a sense of pride and self-dignity on the basis of an aggressive demonisation and 'Othering' of Muslims and other minorities (Waikar 2018: 162).

Furthermore, what is important to mention about the Hindutva social imaginary is that its reactionary self-projection focuses not only on 'Othering', but also against perceived slights that taunt their historic irrelevancy. At its heart, it is insecure and ashamed. It is that shame that has propelled the use of myth and falsehood to encourage bravado. As already mentioned, the British undermined the formation of any type of resistance to their authority. They did so by denying that 'India' existed as a single, unified socio-cultural unit and by stating there was no such thing as a place called 'India'. A consequence of such assertions was the rise of *Savarkar's Hindutva*. He was frustrated at the accusation that there was no 'India' and no such thing as a Hindu. Why is this so important? Because it provides the backdrop from which the term Hindutva originates, and explains why it was conceived and how it was used to create a sense of what it means to be '*Indian*' – a sense that was directly linked to a living land. This would play a very important psychological role in developing antagonism against the so-called 'partition', and against Muslims in particular for dividing Mother India and creating their own homeland. The resentment at Muslims not accepting the Indian narrative of 'oneness' is what led to their vilification. This, even though the British Raj (British Empire in South Asia) was home to dozens of languages, peoples, and nations and it would seem ludicrous to insist that all should accept one identity. But Hindutva had both irredentist and hegemonic ambitions.

Commenting on Savarkar's treatise on Hindutva, Bakhle (2010) characterises it as:

> the politics of naming, the poetics of the list, the enchantment of territory, and the management and evocation of affect. Through these strategies he names into being a mythic Hindu community, identifies the magical territory it inhabits, and invokes through his enchantment of territory a militant affect of love. Savarkar uses a number of registers in Hindutva, from the theoretical and declamatory to the polemical, but the one he deploys most often is the poetic (Bakhle 2010: 156).

Essentially, Savarkar's militant and magical imaginative conceptualisation of the Hindu *Rashtra* (nation), is neither scholarly nor rational, but imaginary. Ratan describes Hindutva as a cultural community 'bound together by a common religion (Hinduism) and veneration for a piece of territory that was both the *Pitrubhumi* (fatherland) and the *Punyabhumi* (holy land). Muslims and Christians were suspect in this view because of their "foreign origin"' (Ratan 1998: 203). But not just because of that. From this perspective, since the land was holy, almost living, even the thought of '*partition*' was seen as the unholiest of unholy. Most Indian intelligentsia, whether Congress or Hindutva, accepted this narrative. As Ambedkar acknowledges, this explanation was needed to counter those who denied that 'India' existed and, therefore, did not have a right to self-determination (Ambedkar 2015). Be that as it may, a by-product of forging this identity was a visceral hatred towards Muslims.

The myths of Hindutva

The mythologies associated with the Hindutva ideology are closely linked to Islam and Muslims – hence the animus towards 'partition' – and this directly links it to delegitimising Pakistan and denying Kashmiri agency and identity. An important consideration when exploring the question of Kashmir and India–Pakistan tensions is, does land have a religion? While seemingly preposterous, this question is important because of the Hindutva conceptualisation of land as holy and 'Muslims' wishing to take Hindu land (Bakhle 2010: 152–6). For instance, Muslims taking Indian land to create Pakistan, and trying to do so again with Kashmir. Of course, this also belies the heterogeneity, cultural complexities, and historiography of the region that clearly reveal that the areas that would become Pakistan had major cultural and religious differences with larger India. Still, this is not about facts, culture, or religion. It is politics. According to Savarkar:

> Hindutva is not identical with what is vaguely indicated by the term Hinduism. By any 'ism' it is generally meant a theory or a code more or less based on spiritual or religious dogma or system. But when we attempt to investigate the essential significance of Hindutva we do not primarily – and certainly not mainly – concern ourselves with any particular theocratic or religious dogma or creed ... (Savarkar 1999: 2–3)

Rather, understanding Hindutva is to investigate its social imaginary, or, as Kuruvachira puts it, the 'myths of Hindutva' that are political (Kuruvachira 2005: 121). Those myths can be broadly categorised into three thematic areas: (1) the myth of a Vedic Golden Age; (2) the myth of eternal Hinduness; and (3) the myth of Aryans as the original Indians. All three are intricately linked to Pakistan, Kashmir, and Muslims, and have had an undeniable impact on the Indian psyche.

The first of these myths is that Hindutva proponents eulogise an imaginary Vedic Golden Age. As Sampath suggests, Savarkar appealed to a *fictionalised* Hindu past – 'one that was imagined and defined by a monolithic Hindu identity, linked geo-culturally to a mythical and ageless Hindu nation' (Sampath 2019b: 472). For Savarkar, the Hindu *Rashtra* or nation existed beyond the fluctuations, changes, and transformations of antiquity and political power. For that reason, his treatise on Hindutva begins: 'when the first Aryans "settled down" in different parts on the banks of the Indus river ...' (Sampath 2019b: 472). Describing this, Thapar says that Hindutva proponents project this Vedic Golden Age theory as one of the cornerstones of their ideology, occurring in the period 1200–600 BCE (Thapar 2015: 133). A 'golden age', she further articulates, is designed to be at once 'distant and mythical – enough that no one could question the historicity of the era or the values the historian wished to propagate' (Thapar 2015: 176). Arguably, that explains why Savarkar chose to speak of this 'magnificent' Hindu past that was violently disrupted by marauding Muslim warriors – even though in the seventh century the majority of the inhabitants of 'Sindh', in present-day Pakistan, were Buddhist, not Hindu (Proser 2011). Yet, Hindutva mouthpieces ignore facts for superficial, easy-to-believe theories, playing on the popular imagination and stereotypes of Muslim power and authority. By using an undeniable, obvious reality – that of historic Muslim rulership in the Sindh and other regions – they are at once nurturing a sense of resentment and censuring Muslims as the cause of all their current sufferings. That is precisely why Hindutva propagandists promote absurd assertions of 'oneness', intertwined with visceral hate. This imaginary is carefully constructed to mix fact with fiction, in ways that are not readily disprovable. Using superficial explanations, ignoring archaeological evidence, and disregarding historio-graphical authenticity, Hindutva propagandists propagate their false history and fear-mongering (Truschke 2020: 2–6).

Understandably, using a mythical past to reinvigorate community is a time-tested stratagem that nations use to facilitate identity construction and promote nativism. This has immense emotive power, especially in a society ridden with class, ethnic, religious, and all other kinds of disparities. Using this type of invented history is a method intended to unite India's diversity onto a Hindu majoritarian platform in the hope to re-establish a purported 'greatness' (Pathak 2015). For this reason, BJP fascists openly say that Sikhs, Jains, and Buddhists are Hindu – a sort of absurd hybridity in which other faiths are subsumed under Hinduness. This is not altogether different from other populist or nativist movements that utilise this approach to energise, motivate, and inspire their targeted communities (Chatterji 2019: 2). This tactic, in and of itself, is not the point of contention. After all, it is reasonable for all societies, and communities, to develop some type of camaraderie, and this is quite well understood in the scholarly work on nation building and state building. However, it is in the cultural appropriation of others, denial of another's right to participate in this exercise of identity construc-tion, or by viciously usurping others and demonisation that this becomes gravely offensive. In denying others those inalienable rights, and vilifying minorities, violence occurs. And this is precisely what the Hindutva ideology explicitly demands; an ideology that was largely embraced by Congress leaders as well, even though a Hindutva militant was responsible for the murder of one of the most important figures in Indian history, Gandhi (Islam 2016: 23–9).

More specifically, as Kuruvachira writes, Vedic culture was an amalgama-tion of many influences, especially those from the Indus Valley civilisation and the Indo-European immigrants, who some say originated from Central Asia and migrated to parts of Northern India (Kuruvachira 2005: 122). Interestingly enough, the earliest of the Vedic texts, the Rig Veda, does not resonate with what is contemporaneously projected as Hindu culture. Instead, it reflects a pastoral and cattle-keeping people. Moreover, the Vedic gods, like Varuna and Indra, are largely absent in the unlimited pantheon of the Hindu deities. Actually, major festivals of the Hindu calendar are based on the grand exploits of Rama and Krishna (Kuruvachira 2005: 122). The significance of this cannot be overstated, since it contributes to verifying the ways and means that Hindutva propagandists are manufacturing a monolithic India. Furthermore, as Thapar notes, this assertion that links Vedic culture to Hindu culture was consciously appropriated to provide what was 'thought to be an unbroken, linear history for caste (Brahmin) Hindus' (Thapar 2015: 14). However, the discovery of the

Indus civilization and its city culture in the 1920s contradicted this theory of linear descent. The cities of the Indus civilization are of an earlier date than the composition of the Vedic corpus – the literature of the Indo-Aryan speaking people – and do not reflect an identity with this later culture. The insistence on a linear history for the Hindus is now the reason for some attempts to take the Vedic culture back in time and identify it with the Indus civilization. (Thapar 2015: 14–15)

Thus, to believe in a Vedic age is to take refuge in a myth that has no historical foundation (Kuruvachira 2005: 122). Again, it is important to highlight that the Indus civilisation is today in Pakistan, and has little linkage to present-day India. Still, the Hindutva propagandists are desperate to show that it is linked to India, even to the point of creating a fake seal to demonstrate this (Truschke 2020: 4).[1]

The second belief that Hindutva propagandists promote is the 'Myth of Eternal Hinduness'. This explains the Hindutva tendency to appropriate everything into the Hindu fold, even when it is as far-fetched and contradictory as drawing links from the Indus civilisation to Buddhism, which is typically against caste rules and hierarchy. As Ratan writes, the idea of a 'unified Hindu identity is troubling in so far as it ignores the fact that Indian archaeologists and historians have for years challenged the idea of Hinduism as a monolithic, Brahmin-dominated religion with a distinct philosophy, iconology and rituals' (Ratan 1998: 202). Initial Western researchers into Hinduism documented this peculiarity. Unlike the Abrahamic faiths of Islam, Christianity, or Judaism, what was called Hinduism 'did not profess to have a prophet, church, revealed book, and did not recognise the practice of conversion, but they made little attempt to understand the different sects and religious communities which co-existed within this "Hindu" fold' (Ratan 1998: 202). And this, in particular, is what is most important to uncover – without any core beliefs, structure, messenger, or book, what does it mean to be a 'Hindu'? This concern is what compelled Hindutva myth making. Unfortunately, that process of identity construction led, simultaneously, to wilful, deliberate cultural appropriation/hegemony. Also, Hindutva ideologues felt that the presence of other communities – at least, those asserting their own identity – was a threat to their imagined India.

Intricately connected with the belief in 'eternal Hinduness' is its natural association with demonisation and 'Othering' – particularly against Muslims, Christians, and Dalits (Bazian et al. 2019: 91). In actuality, the angry outbursts of Hindutva fanatics is really against anyone opposing their monolithic Hindutva identity. By having an alternate view of history, identity, and culture, Muslims, Christians, and Dalits are all on a direct collision course with Hindutva. But Hindutva zealots have a particular vehemence directed towards Muslims that includes demonising language, mob lynching, theft, and rioting (Bazian et al. 2019: 91–4). This hatred is rationalised as Muslims are accused of being disloyal to India, no matter whether indigenous or otherwise, and responsible for the so-called 'partition'. Also, when Muslims are accused of being non-Indigenous, they are belittled and ostracised as foreigners whose presence is an affront to the Hindutva fantasy of eternal Hinduness. In addition, authority is often resented, irrespective of where it is. And, as Muslims were, in fact, the authority figures of the Sindh and other regions for the preceding several hundred years in the history of South Asia, it is that awareness of Muslims as power and authority figures that makes the Hindutva ideologues want to target them.

At the heart of the matter is Hindutva uneasiness with diversity. Their propagandists describe Indian culture as 'Hindu culture', which is an assertion that utterly belies the construction of identity, along with the massive diversity and plurality of contemporary Indian society. In November 2019, the Indian consul general in New York outrageously described 'Kashmiri culture as Hindu culture', even though 95 per cent of the Kashmir Valley heartland is Muslim (Chak 2019). Still, they promote this absurd line of reasoning. By doing so, they culturally appropriate all others and trace their history to the Aryan invasions. Thapar describes this as a form of nationalist historiography which is political rather than scholarly (Thapar 2015: 57). She says that the 'who was here first' argument is put forth by those who claim to speak on behalf of Aryans, which is factually not doable. Not only are the 'claims to these identities as being historical and having an immense antiquity untenable, but the paucity of the required evidence to prove this makes it impossible to give answers with any certainty' (Thapar 2015: 57). Adding to this, Thorat writes that it 'will not be an exaggeration to say that the Bharatiya Janata Party (BJP) tried to appropriate Dr. B.R. Ambedkar, knowing completely that Ambedkar's views on many issues deviated considerably from the party's ideological position' (Thorat 2019: 217). This was particularly the case with Prime Minister Narendra Modi, who, allegedly, felt 'indebted' to Dr Ambedkar for inspiring him to push forward the cause of depressed castes (Thorat 2019: 217). This appropriation of Buddhist culture, the depressed classes, and all other communities – especially the Muslims, has been done to attempt to concretise the theory of eternal Hinduness, redirect grievances towards an imagined enemy (i.e. Muslims), and project a rhetoric that claims to target the wealthy classes, while being entirely in cahoots with them.

The third myth associated with the Hindutva social imaginary is that the origins of India begin with the Aryan migration. In other words, the Aryans were the first 'Indians'. Romila Thapar maintains that 'Indo-Aryan is in fact a language label, indicating a speech-group of the Indo-European family, and is not a racial term. To refer to the Aryans as a race is therefore inaccurate' (Thapar 2015: xxiii). Again, as previously highlighted, Hindutva ideology uses the 'Aryan' migration theory in a somewhat absurd political manner. By claiming that they are the descendants of the Aryans it directly contradicts their own animosity against Christians and Muslims – who, they claim, came from outside. In a way, the Hindutva belief in the Aryan migration theory ridicules their own claims of being authentic, indigenous Indians. For that reason, noted Dalit specialist Jyotiba Phule argues that the Sanskrit-speaking Brahmans, who originated from the Aryans, are alien to India. Upon arriving, they claimed rulership and essentially relegated the Indigenous peoples to lower castes – who were, actually, the rightful inheritors of the land (O'Hanlon 1985: 141–5). Phule persuasively argues that this is an explanation for caste hierarchy in India.

According to Sampath (2019a), Savarkar locates Hindutva as an all-embracing 'ideological phantasm of a Hindu identity', which was used 'to create a common rallying point'. It must be mentioned that contentious debates are still underway on the subject of the Aryan invasion theory. Many scholars have refuted the Hindutva Aryan theory, both through scientific and genetic studies, as well as through scriptural studies of the Rig Veda (Sampath 2019a). However, Savarkar seems to believe in the Aryan migration theory, which memorializes the moment Aryans arrived into the land of Sindh and saw the mighty Indus River. In the Hindutva social imaginary the Aryans immediately felt a deep sense of belonging. Then they began to call this land Sapta Sindhu, or the land watered by seven rivers and presided over by the Sindhu, or Indus, and another part of the land as Bharat-Varsha (Savarkar 1923). Yet again, here, looking closely, we realise another major inconsistency. The lands of Bharat-Varsha and Sapta Sindhu were not the same, nor were the peoples inhabiting the regions. In fact, they even to this day speak different languages and belong to different socio-cultural and ethnic groups.

Bringing this all together, how does this relate to the (ab)use of deepening Islamophobia in India? Recall that Hindutva myths largely revolve along the following themes: (1) the Vedic Golden Age that occurs in present-day Pakistan; for that, they must usurp Indus civilisation culture as their own, and call the people living there 'Indians', in order to create a linear cycle of Hindu identity; (2) the concept of 'eternal Hinduness' is also used to sweep/usurp everyone into the 'Hindu' fold and gives a mythical holiness to the land of India – which, to them, includes Pakistan and Kashmir, and their mere presence there is feeding Islamophobic tropes. Again, this coincides with describing Vedic culture as Hindu culture, even though archaeological evidence is overwhelming in describing the Indus civilisation as distinct from Vedic culture – unfortunately, Muslims are living in their 'cherished land'; and (3) Hindutva propagandists believe that the original 'Indians' were Aryans and this land has been violated by Muslim invasion in the seventh century – even though the majority population of Sindh was Buddhist. As Tanika Sarkar writes, this is all being done to showcase, and emphasise, Muslims as 'alien', and to promote this eternal Hindu–Muslim feud (Sarkar 2019: 151). Naturally, if history were taught and viewed as such, it would invite fury. Overall, the Hindutva ideology wishes to claim the areas of land that Muslims are inhabiting as their own; propagates false tales of massacres allegedly committed by Muslims when they arrived in Sindh, even though a majority of the people there were Buddhist; and bewails the dismemberment of their holy land during the so-called 'partition'. Here, it is important to cite Phule, who argues that Indo-Aryan-speaking peoples imposed the caste system on society to sanction their power and privilege, against the original inhabitants of what is now called India – the Dalits (O'Hanlon 1985).[2] The real reasons behind the Islamophobic discourse of the Hindutva ideologues follow a similar pattern of appropriation.

The weaponisation of Hindutva

This section will delineate how Islamophobic Hindutva myths are weaponised to justify acts of criminality occurring in India today. Christophe Jaffrelot clarifies that in India 'the strategy of stigmatisation and emulation of "threatening Others" is based on a feeling of vulnerability born of a largely imaginary threat posed by "aliens," principally Muslims and Christians' (Jaffrelot 1996: 552). However, 'within Hindu nationalist discourse, the "threatening Other" has historically been the Muslim community … [and] protecting the "Hindu nation" against conversion to Islam has, in turn, been of central concern to leading Hindu nationalist organisations' (Jaffrelot 1996: 552). Specifically, the act of 'protecting' the Hindu majority results in criminal acts that have been well documented and that take a grotesque Islamophobic turn. Those criminal acts include the following: (1) Cow Vigilantism, also known as *Gau Rakshak*; (2) Ghar Wapsi – forced conversion; (3) Love Jihad – hatred against Muslim males wedding Hindu females; and (4) Bahu Lao, Beti Bachao. All in all, there is a carefully orchestrated strategy, supported at the highest levels of government, to demonise Islam and Muslims in order to rationalise crimes against them.

First, since the political victory of the BJP in 2014, India has witnessed a new type of brutality in the name of cow protection or cow vigilante squads (Human Rights Watch 2019). Certainly, in the Hindu pantheon cows are considered sacred animals and even the animal's urine is understood to contain a healing factor. These cow vigilante squads, referred to as *Gau Rakshaks* – literally translated as cow protectors – roam the countryside searching for those who, they claim, are slaughtering cows without permission. Bazian et al. (2019) write that violence at the hands of self-described vigilantes (*Gau Rakshaks*) who take 'the law into their own hands in the name of "cow protection" is among the leading recorded sources of violence against Muslims in India. It has increased annually since Prime Minister Modi took office ...' (Bazian et al. 2019: 78). In reality, these gangs of Hindutva criminals are accusing Muslims of disrespecting the cow, or of unlawful slaughter and stealing their livestock, and then lynching them. Human Rights Watch (2019) and Amnesty International (2017) have both documented the atrocities well, and there have been hundreds of instances. Pehlu Khan and Junaid Khan are two such cases that received considerable media attention, as their lynching was uploaded onto social media for the world to see (Bazian et al. 2019: 74–84). Sadly, the perpetrators of the violence are often roaming free, and the victims' families remain terrified.

In 2017 a special investigative report by Reuters uncovered the murky world of Hindutva fanaticism and deliberate economic devastation of the Indian Muslim community. The report revealed how the cow-theft racket, under the guise of protecting cows, was a huge financial boon for the BJP Party (Siddiqui et al. 2017). The report outlines how almost every single instance of cow theft was from Muslims, and that it amounted to 190,000 cattle stolen since 2014 (Siddiqui et al. 2017). Once stolen, the cattle were given to BJP/Hindutva supporters in a clear instance of economic strangulation and coercive redistribution. Altogether, the report presented a factual and damning account of the reality behind the cow-protection racket, which is intricately tied to further disempowerment and marginalisation of the Muslim community in India.

Second, Hindutva propagandists have launched a sinister campaign that insists Muslims should return/reconvert to their ancestral Hindu religion. As previously mentioned, this is absurd, considering the Hindutva narrative of Muslims being foreigners. Nevertheless, this process of forced reconversion has become thoroughly institutionalised into the '*Ghar Vapasi*' – or 'return home' – movement in Hindutva India (Gupta 2018: 84). It is a large-scale spectacle, with massive political and grassroots support, often attended by tens of thousands of people witnessing the forced conversions of Muslims, Christians, and Adivasis to their allegedly Hindu roots and religion (Chatterji 2019: 413–17). With theatricality and pomp, these forced reconversions are happening with a fanfare bordering on the absurd. A Hindu priest performs a ceremony that is meant to purify and signify the return of the lost souls to their genuine roots, while onlooking mobs chant religious hymns.

Gupta explains that 'Ghar vāpasī' has been hyped as a sort of return to an individual's authentic Hindu roots. As such, 'it produces and enforces notions of a primordial religious identity, whereby all and everyone are declared Hindus' (Gupta 2018: 100). Likewise, this line of reasoning is explained by Hindutva propagandists, such as Praveen Togadia of the Vishwa Hindu Parishad (VHP – a radical Hindutva organisation), who claimed: 'At one point of time, the entire world was Hindu. There were 700 crore (seven billion) Hindus, and now there are just 100 crore (1 billion)' (Indian Express News 2014). The shift from the whole world to the Hindu nation is swift and all encompassing, as *ghar vāpasī* denationalises Islam and Christianity, facilitating their 'Othering' (Gupta 2018: 100). *Ghar vāpasī* not only has the consequence of encouraging Muslims, Christians, and other groups to become Hindu, but also involves strict laws to prevent Hindus from becoming Muslim or Christian. This is happening through a bizarre series of anti-conversion laws that penalise through imprisonment or fines someone seeking to convert to either Christianity or Islam. These laws have been passed by six legislatures: Chhattisgarh, Himachal Pradesh, Gujarat, Rajasthan, Madhya Pradesh, Arunachal Pradesh, and Odisha (Bazian et al. 2019: 92). The irony of these laws is that government officials are required to personally assess whether or not these conversions are valid or have been made by 'force' (Bazian et al. 2019: 92). It is in this ambiguity that Hindutva ideologues operate to prevent conversion away from Hinduism.

Third, among the most sinister narratives that Hindutva ideologues have launched in India is the preposterously named Love Jihad. Even the name has embedded in it a deep Islamophobic trope of Muslims waging war (i.e. the abuse of the concept of jihad), but doing so through romantic liaisons with Hindu women, instead of swords. The 'Love Jihad' campaign is almost too absurd to be believable; however, it is precisely in line with the demonising and Islamophobic narratives that Hindutva spreads throughout India (Gupta 2018: 85). Posters, film, social media, and music all push these messages of a threatening Muslim out to dupe Hindu women unawares. The gullible Hindu girl is attracted to the virile, masculine Muslim who has a ploy to snare the unwitting girl. Tropes such as this are then used to promote hypernationalism and Hindu machismo to save their women from the cunning, dangerous Muslim man. Gupta writes, 'in actual practice, "love jihad" was an emotive mythical campaign, a "delicious" political fantasy, a lethal mobilisation strategy, and a vicious crusade – a jihad against love – for political gains in election' for the BJP (Gupta 2018: 85–6).

Not only does this framing of Muslim men play on the Orientalist myths of Muslim licentiousness and lust, but in the context of India it is rebranded as trickery and romance. Gupta observes, that Love Jihad relies on 'a series of lies, whereby reckless and venomous generalisations have been made, without concrete proof, of abductions and conversions of Hindu women. Wild claims have been made that 30,000 to 300,000 women have been converted till now' (Gupta 2018: 97). There is absolutely no truth to these statements, but, as Audrey Truschke writes:

> Hindutva has a fact problem ... the vast majority of their claims about premodern India are incorrect. But their falsehoods about history – many of which center around an imagined Hindu golden age of scientific progress interrupted by Muslim invaders who sought to crush Hindu culture and peoples – serve clear political goals of projecting a modern Hindutva identity as an ancient bulwark of Indian culture and maligning Muslims as the ultimate Other. (Truschke 2020: 1–2)

Fourth, another Islamophobic campaign launched by the Hindutva brigade is the '*Beti Bachao, Bahu Lao*' campaign, which translates to 'save your daughter and bring a (Muslim) daughter-in-law'. Even more problematic, this crude campaign has the backing of the state and is openly propagated on news and social media. The campaign is closely linked to the concept of 'Love Jihad' but reversed. It encourages Hindu males to adopt the warlike, martial traditions according to which Muslims have been historically described, and not only save naive Hindu girls from Muslim paramours but also wed Muslim women to bring them into the Hindu fold (Mishra 2014). The ways and means of its propagation are bordering on encouraging rape and abduction of Muslim and other minority women. It is despicable, and occurring in the so-called largest democracy in the world, with little if any social resistance and criticism. The depth of global Islamophobia intersects with Islamophobia in India to create a veil of silence over the atrocities that are being committed every day. Anywhere else in the so-called civilised world, promotion of a campaign which encourages one religious community to forcibly wed women from other religious communities would be an outrage. However, in India, and with the pervasiveness of global Islamophobia, such audacious policies and practices can continue without censure or condemnation.

Conclusion

This chapter has aimed to deconstruct the deep reasoning behind Islamophobia in India, which is accelerating at an unprecedented pace. It has traced the roots of contemporary Islamophobia to the Hindutva social imaginary and certain myths that it promotes in the rewriting of history. The Hindutva social imaginary creates a 'repertory' of meaning that is then propagated throughout society. It includes writing a misleading, false image of historic India and then positioning Muslims as its nemesis, which creates a sense of victimisation among the majority community (Truschke 2020). It is there, in the disparaging discourse, that the roots of Islamophobia are located and then contribute to an overall demonising of Islam and Muslims. Naturally, if Muslims are described as licentious homebreakers, who have violated the sanctity of Mother India by 'partitioning' her, then it is understandable how people fed these fantasies would develop hatred towards Muslims. But in actuality, as Gupta (2018: 104) writes, the Hindutva zealots escape genuine questions on ethnic, religious, cultural, and caste differences in India by scapegoating Muslims.

This chapter has also explained how Hindutva myths were weaponised to justify acts of criminality against Muslims. Well-organised, Islamophobic campaigns of cow vigilantism, also known as *Gau Rakshak*; or of *Ghar Wapsi* – forced conversion; 'love jihad – hatred against Muslim males wedding Hindu females'; and the 'Beti Bachao, Bahu Lao' movement – save your daughter and bring a daughter-in-law (Muslim) – are instances of how the Hindutva social imaginary is weaponised. All in all, there is a carefully orchestrated strategy by the state to demonise Islam and Muslims in order to rationalise and legitimise crimes against them at the hands of the Hindu majoritarian masses.

To conclude, there is much insight and merit in Gupta (2018), Chatterji (2019), and several other scholars such as Truschke (2020), who explain that at the heart of Hindutva are feelings of deep shame, insecurity, and contrived aspirations to manliness. This includes feelings of resentment over parts of the land encapsulated within the Hindutva national imaginary being in Pakistan, as well as the monuments that the world knows of India being a product of Muslim rule and civilisation. Rather than take a sense of shared pride in this, it is seen as a source of humiliation, due to the demonising narratives that the Hindutva ideology has pushed for so long. Furthermore, as previously mentioned, much of the Islamophobic animus behind acts of criminality in India is used by Hindutva zealots to regain a lost sense of masculinity; a sense of masculinity that they have been falsely led to believe involves punishing, lynching, and intimidating minorities in their own country. It is a pity that they do not know, or care not to understand, that real strength does not target the weak, impoverished, or disenfranchised. Courage is speaking truth to power, and not engaging in callous actions that push mobs to attack the vulnerable in society. Therefore, at the heart of Hindutva fanaticism is not just insecurity and shame, but cowardice. A cowardice that is masked by pompous bravado.

Notes

1 Truschke describes how Indian propagandists desperate to show a connection between the Indus Valley civilisation and India claimed to have unearthed a seal which purportedly verified this link. However, it was found to be a fake.

2 Essentially, India's caste system is a complex and strict hierarchical and socially immobile societal structure that relegates hundreds of millions of people to perpetual servitude to higher-caste individuals. While in theory the practice is condemned, in reality it is still a strong part of India's social fabric.

Bibliography

Ambedkar, B.R. (2015). *Pakistan, or, the partition of India*, 3rd edn, www.columbia.edu/itc/mealac/pritchett/00ambedkar/ambedkar_partition/ (accessed 25 March 2022).

Amnesty International (2017). India: hate crimes against Muslims and rising Islamophobia must be condemned, 28 June, www.amnesty.org/en/latest/press-release/2017/06/india-hate-crimes-against-muslims-and-rising-islamophobia-must-be-condemned/ (accessed 7 April 2022).

Baghavan, M. (2008). The Hindutva underground: Hindu nationalism and the Indian National Congress in late colonial and early post-colonial India, *Economic and Political Weekly*, 43(37): 39–48.

Bakhle, J. (2010). Country first? Vinayak Damodar Savarkar (1883–1966) and the writing of *Essentials of Hindutva*, *Public Culture*, 22(1): 149–86. doi: https://doi.org/10.1215/08992363-2009-020 (accessed 8 April 2022).

Bazian, H., Itaoui, R., and Thompson, P. (2019). *Islamophobia in India: stoking bigotry*, Islamophobia Research and Documentation Project, Center for Race and Gender, Berkeley: University of California.

Chak, F.M. (2019). Kashmir and India's settler colonial project, *TRT World*, December, www.trtworld.com/opinion/india-s-settler-colonial-project-in-kashmir-should-force-the-world-to-act-31848 (accessed 5 November 2020).

Chatterji, A. (2019). Remaking the Hindu nation: terror and impunity in Utter Pradesh. In: A.P. Chatterji, T.B. Hansen, and C. Jaffrelot (eds), *Majoritarian state: how Hindu nationalism is changing India*, New York: Oxford University Press.

Chatterji, A.P., Hansen, T.B., and Jaffrelot, C. (eds) (2019). *Majoritarian state: how Hindu nationalism is changing India*, New York: Oxford University Press.

Express News Service (2014). VHP presses for anti-conversion laws, *Indian Express*, https://indianexpress.com/article/india/india-others/vhp-presses-for-anti-conversion-law-at-one-point-the-entire-world-was-hindu/ (accessed 15 December 2014).

Goradia, A. (2020). Palghar lynching: when police watches helplessly, where does one go for justice, asks wife of deceased, *Indian Express*, 21 April, https://indianexpress.com/article/india/palghar-lynching-when-police-watches-helplessly-where-does-one-go-for-justice-asks-wife-of-deceased-6371593/ (accessed 21 April 2020).

Gupta, C. (2018). Allegories of 'Love Jihad' and 'Ghar Wapsi': interlocking the socio-religious with the political. In: M. Rehman (ed.), *Rise of saffron power: reflections on Indian politics*, London: Routledge India, 85–110.

Human Rights Watch (2019) India: vigilante 'cow protection' groups attack minorities, 18 February, www.hrw.org/news/2019/02/19/india-vigilante-cow-protection-groups-attack-minorities (accessed 5 November 2020).

Islam, S. (2016). *Hindutva: Savarkar unmasked*, Delhi: Media House.

Jaffrelot, C. (1996). *The Hindu nationalist movement and Indian Politics: 1925 to the 1990s: strategies of identity-building, implantation and mobilisation*, Delhi: Viking Penguin in Association with C. Hurst & Co.

Kuruvachira, J. (2005). *The roots of Hindutva: a critical study of Hindu fundamentalism and nationalism*, Delhi: Media House.

Mishra, I. (2014). Hindu right-wing organization launches new campaign, *Times of India*, 29 December https://timesofindia.indiatimes.com/city/agra/Bajrang-Dal-to-launch-bahu-laao-beti-bachao-in-February/articleshow/45669704.cms? (accessed 25 March 2022).

O'Hanlon, R. (1985). *Caste, conflict and ideology: Mahatma Jotirao Phule and low-caste protest in nineteenth century western India*, Cambridge: Cambridge University Press.

Pathak, V. (2015). Bid to unite Indic religions, *The Hindu*, 15 September, www.thehindu.com/news/national/hindutva-outfit-in-attempt-to-unite-indiaborn-religions/article7675046.ece (accessed 15 May 2021).

Proser, A. (2011). *The Buddhist heritage of Pakistan: art of Gandhara*, New York: Asia Society.

Ratan, S. (1998). Hindutva – the shaping of a new Hindu identity, *Southeastern Political Review*, 26(1): 201–17.

Sampath, V. (2019a) The father of Hindutva believed Aryans MIGRATED to India, *Quartz India*, 20 August, https://qz.com/india/1691223/new-savarkar-biography-sheds-light-on-the-origins-of-hindutva/ (accessed 20 August 2019).

Sampath, V. (2019b). *Savarkar: Echoes from a forgotten past: 1883–1924*, New Delhi: India Viking.

Sarkar, T. (2019). How the Sangh Parivar writes and teaches history. In: A.P. Chatterji et al. (eds), *Majoritarian state: how Hindu nationalism is changing India*, New York: Oxford University Press, 151–76.

Savarkar, V. (1923) *Essentials of Hindutva: who is a Hindu?* http://savarkar.org/en/encyc/2017/5/23/2_12_12_04_essentials_of_hindutva.v001.pdf_1.pdf (accessed 7 April 2022).

Savarkar, V. (1999). *Hindutva*, Mumbai: Swatantryaveer Savarkar Rashtriya Smarak.

Sharma, J. (2011). *Hindutva: exploring the idea of Hindu nationalism*, New Delhi: Penguin Books India.

Siddiqui, Z., Das, K., Wilkes, T., and Lasseter, T. (2017). Emboldened by Modi's ascent, India's cow vigilantes deny Muslims their livelihood, Reuters, 6 November, https://www.reuters.com/investigates/special-report/india-politics-religion-cows/ (accessed 24 March 2022).

Snehi, Y. (2003). Hindutva as an ideology of cultural nationalism, *Social Change*, 33(4): 10–24.

Taylor, C. (2004). *Modern social imaginaries*, Durham, NC: Duke University Press.

Thapar, R. (2015). *The Penguin history of early India: from the origins to AD 1300*, London: Penguin Books Ltd).

Thorat, S. (2019). Dalits in post-2014 India: between promise and action. In: A.P. Chatterji et al. (eds), *Majoritarian state: how Hindu nationalism is changing India*, New York: Oxford University Press, 217–36.

Truschke, A. (2020). Hindutva's dangerous rewriting of history, *South Asia Multidisciplinary Academic Journal* [Online], 24/25, https://doi.org/10.4000/samaj.6636 (accessed 20 December 2020).

Waikar, P. (2018). Reading Islamophobia in Hindutva: an analysis of Narendra Modi's political discourse, *Islamophobia Studies Journal*, 4(2): 161–80.

Yeung, I. (2020). India burning, *Vice News*, www.youtube.com/watch?v=MCyBL8dBOEo (accessed 1 April 2020).

Chapter 11

Islamophobia and anti-Uyghur racism in China

Sean R. Roberts

Introduction

The United States (US) response to the 11 September 2001 terrorist attacks on New York City and Washington, DC ushered in a new era of Islamophobia globally. However, this new and potent Islamophobia should not be understood as a monolithic ideology. Rather, it has interacted around the world with pre-existing forms of racism and prejudice against Muslims that are grounded in local contexts. This is not to belittle the impact that this event had on anti-Muslim racism worldwide. The 9/11 attacks and the US-led response transformed existing forms of anti-Muslim racism, and racism against people who happen to be Muslim, into a much more violent and exclusionary ideology, the brutality and racially profiled nature of which was obscured by the rhetoric of national security. However, as an ideology that was transposed onto existing forms of racism, post-9/11 Islamophobia has also been articulated in significantly different ways in countries around the world.

To illustrate this phenomenon, this chapter provides a case study of how the US-led global War on Terror (GWOT) and its inherently Islamophobic underpinnings helped to justify the acceleration of existing anti-Uyghur sentiments in the People's Republic of China (PRC) to such an extent that it has facilitated genocidal actions. The widely publicised mass internment of Uyghurs and the campaign to destroy their solidarity, culture, and identity that has been underway since 2017 could not have transpired with so little international accountability without the conditions created by GWOT. While there is a long-standing anti-Uyghur racism in the PRC, which has little to do with Islam, that motivates these extreme actions, it is post-9/11 Islamophobia that has made them possible.

Overall, the Uyghur case demonstrates the peculiar ways in which post-9/11 Islamophobia has mutated around the world and has justified and bolstered various forms of state-sponsored racism that can be vocalised more openly in the name of protecting society from the alleged existential threat of Islamic 'extremism' and 'terrorism'. As such, it reveals the complex and locally diverse ways that the 9/11 attacks and the resulting GWOT have impacted Muslims globally since 2001.

Colonialism and the Uyghur 'Other'

I have argued elsewhere that the relationship between Uyghurs and modern China has always been a fundamentally colonial one (Roberts 2020: 21–7). It is a relationship that was born of imperial conquest and occupation and is grounded in the same social Darwinian understanding of inequality that is seen in other colonial contexts. As a result, Uyghurs and other Turkic Muslims have never been fully accepted as equals in modern Chinese society and have been subjected to stereotypes typical of the colonial experience, characterised as 'Others' who are alternatively, and sometimes simultaneously, viewed as 'backward', 'uncivilised', 'exotic', 'lazy', and 'dangerous', in contrast to the majority Han population. These are colonial tropes to which many non-Han peoples in the PRC are subjected and which have been part and parcel of producing a positive image of the Han as 'progressive' and the penultimate representatives of 'civilisation' and modernism (cf. Gladney 2004; Schein 2000). However, these tropes take on a more sinister character with regard to the peoples of the Uyghur region, Tibet, and, to a slightly lesser extent, Inner Mongolia – regions that have an uncomfortable relationship with the concept of a historically unified Chinese national domain and are viewed implicitly as a threat to that concept. All three of these peoples have a strong non-Han national consciousness that is linked to homelands that make up substantial portions of the PRC's territory.

David Tobin suggests that the PRC has come to view these regions' inhabitants as 'inside/outside' threats, simultaneously an inseparable part of China and non-Han 'Others' who are pawns in the hands of external imperial powers seeking to divide China (Tobin 2020). For Tobin, this dynamic has become part and parcel of the PRC's nation-building project. It must thoroughly colonise these regions and make them and their populations constituent parts of a unified national ideal that is threatened both by these regions' tenuous attachment to the state and by the will of external 'imperialists' seeking to divide the nation (Tobin 2020).

In the context of the erosion of communism around the world in the late 1980s and early 1990s, the anxiety of the PRC about its own demise led the state to launch numerous campaigns against a perceived threat of 'separatism' from these peoples. These campaigns were perhaps the most acute in the Uyghur region, which was furthest from Beijing and had a long history of cultural and political ties to the now independent former Soviet states of Central Asia. The aims of these campaigns were simultaneously to blunt any indications of rising calls for self-determination in the region and to encourage the territory's peoples to assimilate into a Han-dominant Chinese national culture.

For a variety of reasons, these 'anti-separatism' campaigns in the Uyghur region during the 1990s also targeted Islam among Uyghurs, and especially those Uyghurs deemed to be particularly pious. A general reason for this focus was that both the PRC and Uyghurs viewed Islam as a deterrence to assimilation. Additionally, one of the first major acts of resistance to the state among Uyghurs in the 1990s, the Baren disturbance of 1990, began as a protest by pious Uyghurs against state-mandated birth control policies (Millward 2007: 327–8). As a result, from their beginning these 'anti-separatism' campaigns targeted informal religious institutions and practices as indications of 'separatist' aspirations.

By the end of the 1990s, the PRC had largely succeeded in stifling dissent in the Uyghur region and had imprisoned hundreds, if not thousands, on charges of separatism and/or illegal religious practices (see Amnesty 1999). This state-led crackdown did result in sporadic acts of Uyghur-led violence against security forces and symbols of the state, but there was no evidence that it had fostered an organised Uyghur militant resistance that could threaten Beijing. In urban areas, especially in the capital city of Urumqi, the state had also successfully encouraged many Uyghurs to undertake incentivised assimilation measures via education in the Chinese language and work opportunities in China proper (Smith-Finley 2013: 235–93). However, the PRC had not erased all Uyghur discontent. During the 1990s many Uyghurs sought refuge from the repressive atmosphere in their homeland by fleeing China, and others embraced Islam more strongly to repel state efforts at assimilation (Smith-Finley 2013: 235). This was the situation in the region in 2001, on the eve of 9/11, before the PRC reframed its alleged 'separatist' threat from Uyghurs as a 'terrorist threat.'

Making Uyghurs into terrorists after 9/11

It is important to note that the PRC had been introduced to the concept of Islam-inspired 'terrorism' prior to 9/11 through its interactions with neighbouring states. In the later 1990s, the PRC had established more extensive security cooperation with neighbouring states, which were the first destinations of discontented Uyghurs fleeing China. This included securing guarantees from the Taliban by 1999 that exiled Uyghurs could not threaten China from Afghanistan; but the most important agreements were established with the former Soviet states of Central Asia and Pakistan (see Small 2015; Zhao 2004). It was in this process of establishing security cooperation across borders that the PRC first began engaging with the emergent global-threat discourse of Islamic 'extremism' and 'terrorism'.

The alliances that the PRC was building in the former Soviet Union were particularly instructive in this regard. Although the 'Shanghai Five' group, later to become the Shanghai Cooperation Organisation (SCO), was established to resolve all remaining border disputes between the PRC and the successor states of the USSR on which it bordered, at Beijing's urging it also discussed security cooperation (Iwashita 2004: 264). The PRC was primarily concerned with obtaining guarantees from the former Soviet states that they would not harbour alleged Uyghur 'separatists' on their territory, but the other states, particularly Russia, Uzbekistan, and Tajikistan, had already framed their domestic threats from Muslim citizens as 'Islamic extremism' and 'terrorism'.

In this context, at its inaugural meeting in June 2001, after transitioning from the 'Shanghai Five', the SCO adopted the 'Shanghai Convention on Combatting Terrorism, Separatism, and Extremism' (SCO Secretariat 2001). While the PRC remained mostly concerned with what it categorised as a Uyghur 'separatism' threat, the Convention drew little distinction between what would become the 'three evils' of 'separatism, terrorism, and extremism'. Furthermore, the Central Asian states, when cracking down on Uyghur activists or extraditing those requested by China, tended to employ a narrative of a 'terrorist threat' to explain their actions. As a result, PRC authorities were already primed to characterise the alleged Uyghur 'threat' as one of 'terrorism' and fuelled by 'Islamic extremism' three months before the attacks of 11 September took place. However, it was those attacks that made it clear to Beijing that doing so could come with numerous advantages.

After 9/11, PRC diplomats almost immediately began a concerted campaign to link what the PRC had to date characterised as a Uyghur 'separatist' threat to GWOT, which George W. Bush had declared in response to 9/11. Through meetings with other governments and the publication of a series of policy papers outlining what was now characterised as a 'Uyghur terrorist threat', PRC officials spent the remainder of 2001 and much of 2002 trying to convince the coalition being built around GWOT that Uyghurs should be viewed as among their enemies.[1] The policy papers were somewhat fantastical, claiming that over forty Uyghur diaspora groups across Europe, the US, Central Asia, and Turkey were part of an amorphous terrorist network that received support and financing from al Qaeda and the Taliban (PMPRCUN 2001; SCOIPRC 2002). They also claimed that this group had been responsible for over 200 attacks inside China throughout the 1990s resulting in 162 deaths and over 400 serious injuries; but many of the incidents they cited as 'terrorist attacks' clearly were not even premeditated political violence (SCOIPRC 2002).

As Richard Boucher, then US Deputy Assistant Secretary of State for South and Central Asian Affairs, recently stated about the pressure from China to recognise this alleged Uyghur 'terrorist threat' at the time, 'China had been asking us to do that for years and we'd say, "Who are these guys? We don't really see it, we don't see an organization, don't see the activity"' (Magnier 2021). However, something changed in US policy in the summer of 2002 as the Bush administration started planning its invasion of Iraq. On 19 August 2002, Deputy Secretary of State Richard Armitage drafted a document recognising one previously unknown group of Uyghurs in Afghanistan as an international terrorist organisation and a threat to the US (see Federal Register 2002). A week later, Armitage unveiled this recognition at a press conference while in Beijing (Pan 2002). The following month, on the first anniversary of the 9/11 attacks, the US State Department, together with the PRC and Kyrgyzstan, successfully requested that the United Nations (UN) Security Council also place this group of Uyghurs in Afghanistan, allegedly called the Eastern Turkistan Islamic Movement (ETIM), on the UN 'Consolidated List of Terrorist Groups' (Reeker 2002). In a press statement announcing this act, the US Treasury suggested that this group of Uyghurs had been responsible for over 200 terrorist attacks in China resulting in 162 deaths and over 400 serious injuries (US Department of the Treasury 2002). This echoed the statistics presented in PRC policy papers, but the US attributed all these alleged 'terrorist acts' to a single previously unknown organisation called ETIM instead of to a network of over forty different Uyghur groups as Beijing had done. In doing so, the US greatly inflated the threat of this group in ways that the PRC had not even done.

The international recognition of an alleged Uyghur 'terrorist threat' not only facilitated increased state crackdowns on the Uyghurs but also characterised the perceived threat from Uyghurs as a product of Islam and their character as Muslims. As such, it changed the course of history for Uyghurs in China over the following twenty years.

From 'separatists' to 'terrorists', 2002–8

The impact of this international recognition of Uyghurs as a part of the post-9/11 global 'terrorist threat' was not immediate inside China. For almost eight years following 9/11, the PRC's policies towards the Uyghurs remained only subtly different to those the state had pursued throughout the 1990s. The state continued to crack down on those who practised religion independent of state-approved institutions as well as those perceived as disloyal to the state, and it continued to incentivise Uyghur assimilation into Han-centric society through educational and work programmes. In public discourse, the label of 'separatist' was replaced with that of 'terrorist' and there was increased scrutiny of Uyghurs who appeared particularly pious, but these were merely subtle changes to the state 'anti-separatism' campaigns during the 1990s.

The major shift in state policy in the early 2000s had little to do with the GWOT and much more to do with the PRC's economic expansion. The PRC accelerated its state-led development efforts during the early 2000s throughout its western regions, including in the homeland of the Uyghurs. This effort was branded as the 'Open up the West' campaign and mostly focused on infrastructure investment, but in retrospect it was laying the foundations for more intensive development in the Uyghur region that would alter its character as the Uyghur homeland. While this development had nothing to do with a perceived 'terrorist threat', real or imaginary, the PRC often suggested that it would bring stability and contentment to the Uyghurs of the region. Furthermore, there were very few instances of violence inside the Uyghur region between 2002 and 2008, suggesting that no actual 'terrorist threat' existed (Hastings 2011: 893–912).

In this context, it is difficult to argue that there was an immediate proliferation of Islamophobia inside China directed towards the Uyghurs during the seven and a half years following 9/11. In its external communication with the international community, the PRC continued to push the narrative about the alleged Uyghur 'terrorist threat', issuing its own list of Uyghur 'terrorists' abroad who were placed on China's 'most wanted' lists of criminals and frequently on Interpol lists (Xinhua 2003). However, domestically, state demonisation of Uyghurs differed little from before 9/11. The PRC did use the 'terrorist' label to increase penal punishments via laws on 'terrorism', and these laws also increased limits on religious practice even more than in the 1990s, but among the citizens of China the idea of a 'terrorist threat' from Uyghurs remained an abstraction (Amnesty 2002).

If there was not a palatable Islamophobia dominating popular views of Uyghurs in China during this time, it did not mean that Uyghurs were not feeling more pressures in the country during the early years after 9/11. The reframing of 'anti-separatist' campaigns as 'counter-terrorism' had served to normalise political repression in the Uyghur region both locally and internationally. International criticism of PRC policies towards Uyghurs was not as pointed, as locally increased securitisation appeared to many external observers to be warranted as a 'counter-terrorism' measure. Perhaps more importantly, the situation in the Uyghur region was rapidly changing as development brought more Han migrants and put increased pressures on Uyghur communities to learn the Chinese language and adapt to Chinese cultural norms. These tensions would erupt near the end of the first decade of the twenty-first century.

From anti-Uyghur racism to Islamophobia, 2008–9

The first event that brought a fear of Uyghurs as a possible existential 'terrorist threat' into the Chinese popular consciousness was the 2008 Beijing summer Olympic Games. In the run-up to the Games, several videos surfaced on the internet showing shadowy Uyghur militants brandishing symbols of jihadist groups and threatening to attack the Olympics. The group did not call itself ETIM, but instead the Turkistan Islamic Party (TIP) (see TIP 2008a). My subsequent research into this group suggests that it was a small group of Uyghurs in Waziristan at the time, who were likely fighting alongside other foreign fighters with al Qaeda and the Pakistan Taliban against US and Pakistani forces in both Afghanistan and Pakistan, but it had no capacity to carry out violence inside China (see Roberts 2020: 97–129). Although the group would eventually claim to be carrying on the legacy of the Uyghurs identified as ETIM in Afghanistan during the late 1990s, there was little to connect them to that former group of Uyghur would-be militants (see Roberts 2020: 116–27).

Nonetheless, the appearance of these videos seemed to vindicate both the PRC and the US 'terrorism' analysts who had expressed concern about ETIM and the alleged Uyghur 'terrorist threat', and both the Chinese state and US terrorism experts proclaimed that this group was in fact the same as ETIM, which was already on international 'terrorism lists'. As a result, one of the largest international news stories surrounding the Beijing Olympics became the possibility of a 'terrorist act' disrupting the games (cf. Sy 2008; France24 2008; Deutsche Welle 2008; StratFor 2008). At the time, the PRC also mobilised security forces to ensure that this would not happen, beginning a racially profiled campaign against Uyghurs as potential 'terrorists' (Wong and Bradsher 2008). In the run-up to the games, Chinese state media reported that security forces had broken up a 'terrorist camp' and had foiled a planned 'terrorist attack', but many observers questioned the veracity of these claims (Yardley and Hooker 2008). The hype associated with these videos and the claims of state organs to have prevented 'terrorist attacks' served to make the alleged Uyghur 'terrorist threat' more than an abstraction for the people of China for the first time, and it subsequently fuelled a long-latent Islamophobia in the population that was also articulated through state policies that racially profiled Uyghurs.

While the videos created by this small group of Uyghurs in Waziristan fuelled fear in the run-up to and during the Olympics, there was no evidence that the group ever carried through with any of its threats. TIP did claim to have carried out two bus bombings in Kunming and Shanghai, respectively, during the run-up to the Olympics, but the Chinese government categorically denied that these bombings had anything to do with Uyghurs (cf. TIP 2008b; Reuters 2008). Then there were two disruptions in the Uyghur region around the time of the opening ceremonies, but these instances were shrouded in mystery and they did not appear to be acts of political violence carried out by a group abroad (Jacobs 2016; Watts 2008). In many ways, the attention paid to the alleged Uyghur 'terrorist threat' during the Olympics served first and foremost as a distraction from the mass protests happening in Tibet at the same time. The disruptions in Tibet were much more of a threat to the PRC's reputation, and impossible for the state to connect with global security concerns about 'Islamic terrorism' (Coca 2019).

While there were no actual 'terrorist attacks' associated with the threats to the Olympics, the state significantly stepped up its repression of Uyghurs over the next year in response to the videos created by TIP. After the Olympics, the PRC released a new list of 'Uyghur terrorists' that included eight people allegedly working with this shadowy group in Waziristan (Associated Press 2008). It also began searching for Uyghurs inside China who it believed were associated with these people. The head of the Communist Party in the Uyghur region characterised this security campaign as a 'life or death struggle' against 'terrorists' (Beck 2008). According to official sources, during the run-up to and in the aftermath of the Olympics in 2008, the state had arrested nearly 1,300 Uyghurs on crimes related to 'state security', including those classified as 'terrorism' (Wong 2009).

This campaign obviously increased tensions in the Uyghur region, but it also drew more public attention in China to the alleged 'terrorist threat' that the state claimed it faced from Uyghurs. For most Chinese citizens, the stereotypes of Uyghurs – as of all non-Han – to which they had long been subjected by state media were those of happy and exotic 'minorities' being helped by the state to embrace modern socialism (see Stroup 2021: 5). During and after the Olympics, Chinese citizens had been introduced to a new stereotype of Uyghurs as adherents to an irrational and 'extremist' ideology based in their religion and as the perpetrators of unannounced violence against civilians. While the Chinese citizenry as yet had no experience of being the target of such violence, the state's coverage of its 'counter-terrorism' efforts in the media suggested that it was a real threat, primarily embodied in Uyghurs.

This stereotype of Uyghurs would become more pronounced the following summer when ethnic riots broke out between Uyghurs and Han in the capital of the Uyghur region, Urumqi. This violence would have nothing to do with either Islam or 'terrorism', but it would cement an increasingly prevalent profile of Uyghurs as irrationally violent. Like most violent incidents that have taken place in the Uyghur region of China, the full details of what happened on 5 July 2009 in Urumqi are elusive, but one can piece together the general course of events.

We know that on this day numerous Uyghur students gathered in the city to hold a peaceful protest against racially profiled injustices to which Uyghurs had been subjected, but it was particularly spurred by an incident where two Uyghurs had been killed in a toy factory in Guangdong a week earlier. The incident in Guangdong was an inter-ethnic riot spurred by a false rumour that Uyghur men at the factory had raped Han women (Ryono and Galway 2015: 235–6). Han workers entered the dormitory of the Uyghur workers to address the alleged rape, and violence broke out between Han and Uyghurs, leading to the deaths of two of the Uyghur workers (Ryono and Galway 2015: 235–6). When videos appeared online of what appeared to be a Uyghur being beaten to death by Han workers, it motivated students to organise a mass protest (Human Rights Watch 2009: 11).

Videos of the protest in Urumqi that later circulated showed a scene that would not have been out of place elsewhere in the PRC, with the Uyghurs leading the protest march holding a banner in the Chinese language and waving PRC flags, but such peaceful public protest had long not been tolerated by authorities in the Uyghur region. Human Rights Watch notes that riot police began pushing the protestors back at around 6:30 pm, leading to violent clashes (Human Rights Watch 2009: 2). Subsequently, ethnic violence began breaking out between Uyghurs and Han and lasted the entire night, reportedly leaving 197 people dead, most of whom were Han (Human Rights Watch 2009). On 7 July, Han groups of vigilantes also roamed the streets looking to attack Uyghurs. While Uyghur diaspora groups claim that these vigilantes killed many Uyghurs and were tacitly assisted by police, regional authorities have denied these claims (UHRP 2010).

The violence that was unleashed during the three days in Urumqi was vicious and raw, leaving deep scars on both ethnic communities. For many in the Han community, the mass violence confirmed their worst fears about Uyghurs being 'terrorists', especially coming just a year after the hype about a 'terrorist threat' to the Olympics. As Thomas Cliff, who was conducting fieldwork among Han in the region at this time, suggests, the events fostered an extreme Islamophobia among Han in the region that could be compared to that in the US after 9/11 (Cliff 2012). This Islamophobia was also seen in the state's response to the riots. Beginning on 7 July and lasting almost a year, the regional government put the entire region on lockdown, cut it off from external communications, and began a mass search for Uyghurs to hold responsible for the violence, leading to thousands of arrests. Furthermore, in implementing unprecedented repression against Uyghurs during this time, the state focused primarily on religious Uyghurs in the Uyghur-majority rural regions of the south as those suspected of being to blame for the violence.

The targeting of religious Uyghurs from the south in its post-riot crackdown suggested that the state continued to view dissent or disloyalty as products of Islam, perhaps equating the religion with 'extremism' and 'terrorism'. However, the violence in Urumqi during the summer of 2009 had nothing to do with either religion or 'terrorism'. It was very obviously a spontaneous eruption of violence that was demonstrative of the overwhelming tension and frustration in the region. Elsewhere, I have suggested that the Urumqi riots of 2009 were first and foremost a product of the tensions created by state-led, top-down development in the region (Roberts 2016). As such, it makes sense that it would occur in Urumqi, the centre of economic activity and the destination for both Uyghur and Han migrants. Since 2000, the pressures of development, combined with the state's constant 'counter-terrorism' campaigns, had created intense frustration among many Uyghurs, and it is not surprising that this frustration would be articulated in unbridled violence. Despite this context, the state, and many Han, saw in the Urumqi riots what they imagined to be the violence of an alleged 'terrorist threat' fuelled by Islamic 'extremism', which they now connected to the Uyghurs as a people, not just to a small minority of them.

The self-fulfilling prophecy of terrorism and the resultant rise of Islamophobia, 2010–14

In the aftermath of the riots, the state announced a series of new campaigns that were meant to overcome the tensions that had caused the violence. However, the proposed solutions served only to exacerbate that tension by doubling down on the two policies that had precipitated the violence in the first place – rapid development and 'counter-terrorism'.

In response to the riots, the Party called for a programme of 'expedited development', especially targeting the Uyghur-majority south of the region and including numerous policies intended to integrate the Uyghurs and their homeland more into a Han-dominant society (Shan and Weng 2010). As these development efforts transformed the environment in which Uyghurs were living, the state also increased its securitisation of the region substantially. This was immediately noticeable in Urumqi, where the regional government installed 40,000 new surveillance cameras and established checkpoints around Uyghur neighbourhoods (Associated Press 2011; Hoja 2016). However, the security measures in the Uyghur-majority south, while less accessible to outside observers, were even more intense and more targeted at religiosity. Uyghur refugees who had fled the south of the region for Turkey in the years after the Urumqi riots told me in interviews that these measures drove them to leave their homes and families to seek refuge abroad. They recounted being put under virtual house arrest because they were targeted as 'religious Muslims', and public security officers regularly were sent to their homes to conduct searches for evidence of their possible 'radicalisation'. Additionally, they complained of their children being told at school not to practise religion and to report on the religious behaviour of their parents. These messages at schools were further reinforced by surveillance of those attending mosques, local bans on head coverings for women and beards or religious dress for men, attempts to forbid fasting during Ramadan, and restrictions on travel to Mecca for the Hajj pilgrimage (see UHRP 2013).

If this securitisation and anti-religious environment in the south of the Uyghur region drove many to flee the country, other Uyghurs responded by violently lashing out at the police and security organs. Starting during the crackdown after the Urumqi riots and gradually escalating over the next several years, the PRC reported numerous attacks by Uyghurs on police (see Roberts 2020: 154–9). The state characterised this violence as 'terrorism', but the scant details of the incidences generally suggest that they were more likely spontaneous clashes or revenge attacks after family members had been detained by law enforcement. While the small Uyghur jihadist group in Waziristan often issued videos applauding these attacks on the police, they did not claim credit for them, and there is no reason to believe they were planned by any organised militant group, if planned at all. Rather, I have characterised these clashes between Uyghurs and law enforcement as a self-perpetuating and escalating cycle of violent repression–resistance–repression (Roberts 2020: 158–9). As law enforcement violently tightened security and increased arrests and harassment of the pious in the region, it was inevitably met with violent resistance from the local population, leading to a further tightening of security and again more resistance with no clear end in sight.

By 2013, this cycle of violence had escalated to the point that it had spilled outside the Uyghur region to inner China and began to look more like 'terrorism' in its targeting of civilians. The first incident occurred on 29 October 2013 in Beijing's Tiananmen Square when a Uyghur family drove a sports utility vehicle into a crowd of people. The vehicle caught on fire, killing two tourists and the family in the car (Wan 2013). This spilling over of violence into inner China had a substantial impact on the average Chinese citizen's understanding of Uyghurs as a dangerous people, but it would be another incident a few months later, in Kunming on 1 March 2014, that appeared to translate the fear of Uyghurs into a fear of Islam itself among many in the country.

Like all violent incidents involving Uyghurs, the details of this event remain unclear, but it is known that eight Uyghurs entered the Kunming train station in China's Yunan province and indiscriminately killed civilians with long knives. Reports suggested that Uyghurs had killed 31 people and injured an additional 141 (Wong 2014). This methodical attack on civilians was the first violence carried out by Uyghurs that truly looked like a planned 'terrorist act', even if it took place twelve years after the PRC had received international recognition for its claims that it faced an existential 'terrorist threat' from Uyghurs. In a sense, this attack was a self-fulfilling prophecy that had been cultivated by over a decade of PRC 'counter-terrorism' policies.

If the Kunming attack can be classified as an act of 'terrorism', this did not mean that it was necessarily indicative of the presence of an organised 'terrorist group' of Uyghurs inside China. TIP from Waziristan again issued a video applauding those who carried out the attack, but they again did not claim credit (TIP 2014a). Both state officials and Uyghur journalists from Radio Free Asia noted that the people who had carried out the killings had earlier been stopped from leaving the country through South-East Asia, but they offered different rationale for that departure, with the state claiming that they were leaving to join the 'global jihad', and Uyghur journalists outside the country noting that they were fleeing repression (Voice of America 2014; Hoshur 2014a). Regardless of their goals for leaving the country, they were likely on the run from law enforcement, and the attack may have been undertaken in desperation to make a statement before being imprisoned or killed.

Recent research suggests that this was a turning point in the transition from anti-Uyghur racism to *Islamophobia* among Han in China. This Islamophobia was still mostly focused on Uyghurs, but there were more voices in the Chinese public blaming Islam for the Uyghurs' transgressions and lashing out at the religion itself. Following the attack, Chinese social media was awash with anti-Muslim sentiments, and online anti-Muslim groups were set up to bombard the internet with slurs against Muslims (Stroup 2021: 5). In his study of Islamophobic internet activity following the 2014 attack on the Kunming train station, David Stroup notes that the anti-Muslim discourse on Chinese social media at the time was both racialised, portraying Islam as inherently violent, and nativist, accusing Uyghurs of seeking to displace and erase Han identity (Stroup 2021: 7).

While the Chinese public was more wilfully engaged in Islamophobia after the 2014 attack, the state had already begun attacking Islam more vigorously in the Uyghur homeland prior to 2014. By 2013, policies in the

Uyghur homeland were increasingly seeking to negate Uyghurs' identity as Muslims. As part of its 'counter-terrorism' efforts, the PRC had increasingly become focused on preventing the practice of Islam as the ideological underpinnings of 'terrorism'. This was accomplished both by placing restrictions on clothing that was associated with Islam and by trying to prevent Uyghurs from partaking in Islamic practices and religious observance, even in their life-cycle rituals (i.e. births, circumcisions, marriages, and funerals) (Traywick 2013; Leibold 2020: 8). Although these policies were unevenly enforced, they were particularly pronounced in rural areas, where the state sent Han cadres to monitor the daily life of religious Uyghurs to identify signs of 'extremism' (Leibold 2020: 8). In retrospect, these localised efforts may have also served as test cases for more universal policies on the horizon.

The attack in Kunming also increased the attention paid to Uyghurs by the leadership of the Communist Party, especially given that it had occurred only one year into Xi Jinping's tenure as chairman of the Party. In response to the incident at the Kunming train station, Xi made his first trip to the Uyghur homeland the following month, stressing the need to wipe out the 'terrorist threat' that the state viewed as emanating from the region, noting that the efforts to do so should show 'absolutely no mercy' (Ramzy and Buckley 2019). As Xi was ending his trip to the region, which was intended to demonstrate the power of the state to suppress violence, another incident took place at the Urumqi train station that looked definitively to be another act of 'terrorism'. A Uyghur apparently set off an explosion in his luggage in a crowded area of the station, killing himself and one other person and injuring another seventy-nine (Li and Wan 2014). TIP issued another video from Waziristan applauding the action, but again not claiming credit. However, this video encouraged local Uyghurs to carry out more acts like the one in Urumqi by showing a re-enactment of how one makes a bomb to be detonated in a luggage bag (TIP 2014b). If the Urumqi train station bombing and the associated TIP video did not create the same stir among the Chinese populace as the Kunming train station knifings, they did represent a more direct affront to Xi Jinping and the authority of the Party.

The state's reaction was to tighten security and restrictions on religion in the region even more, particularly in the Uyghur-majority south, even though the incident had occurred in the regional capital of Urumqi. This was most vivid in the massive security sweeps, resulting in over 100 arrests, in Aksu in response to protests spawned by the arrest of women and schoolgirls for wearing head coverings (Hoshur 2014b). These aggressive actions of the state predictably resulted in more violent resistance from Uyghurs, and on the morning of 22 May 2014 a group of Uyghurs drove two sports utility vehicles into a crowded market of mostly Han in Urumqi, killing forty-three people (Denyer 2014). While details of the incident remained scant, this again appeared to be a 'terrorist' attack deliberately targeting civilians. Again, there was no evidence that this incident was connected to TIP in Waziristan or that it was the work of an organised group at all, but it was the third attack on civilians in three months. As a result, the state decided to dedicate even more resources to stopping the violence, which it was now even more convinced was related to Uyghurs' embrace of Islam.

The 'People's War on Terror' and cultural genocide, 2014–22

Almost immediately following the Urumqi market incident, the Party declared a new campaign known as the 'People's War on Terror', which was meant to once and for all eliminate what it viewed as a 'terrorist threat' from Uyghurs. Framed as an ideological struggle, this campaign would be particularly focused on eliminating religiosity among the population and erasing its impact on Uyghur culture (see Xinhua 2014). However, it would also pilot many policies that would be scaled up after 2017 in the state's efforts to eventually erase Uyghur identity as we know it (Roberts 2020: 201–4). Foreboding of this larger attack on Uyghur identity, the regional Communist Party chairman announcing this 'People's War' added that part of its ideological struggle required that 'efforts should be made to make all ethnic groups in Xinjiang identify with the great motherland, the Chinese nation, the Chinese culture and the socialist path with Chinese characteristics' (Xinhua 2014).

The implementation of the 'People's War on Terror' mostly involved an intensification of policies intended to suppress religion that had been ongoing in the region since 2009. The campaign to regulate dress and grooming to prevent public displays of religiosity was now extended everywhere and more strongly enforced, campaigns against fasting during Ramadan were bolstered, surveillance of those attending mosques increased, and scrutiny of Uyghur life-cycle rituals was escalated to ensure that they were not religiously based (Grieger 2014; Tharoor 2014; Demick 2014). However, the enforcement of these policies was also novel and included a system to encourage civilian reporting of signs of 'extremism' among others, often incentivised with cash awards (Tiezzi 2014; Wong 2014a). Locals were also trained in how to attack 'terrorists' they encountered with farm tools and were encouraged to join 'volunteer' militias to assist the police in weeding out alleged 'terrorists' (Tiezzi 2014; Demick 2014).

By most accounts, the 'People's War on Terror' appeared to be a full-out assault on Islam in the region (which the state had apparently equated with 'extremism'), with the motivation of countering 'terrorism'. However, it was also an attack on Uyghur identity writ large. Indicative of this, some local administrations incentivised inter-ethnic marriage among Uyghurs with cash awards (Wong 2014). Furthermore, the scrutiny of traditional Uyghur life-cycle rituals for Islamic elements was a direct assault on one of the most critical aspects of Uyghur community activities that form their group consciousness, and the request that Uyghurs should inform on each other further broke down any sense of social capital in communities. However, the clearest sign that state intentions went beyond targeting Islam, but also Uyghur group solidarity and culture, was the arrest and life-sentencing of renowned Uyghur economist Ilham Tohti in 2014.

Tohti had been the only prominent independent Uyghur voice seeking to influence state policy on the Uyghur region. He was not particularly focused on issues related to religion but, rather, articulated an alternative vision where Uyghurs would be more involved in determining and benefiting from the development undertaken in their region. Tohti had been arrested in January 2014, even before the Kunming train station incident, for his efforts to encourage an inter-ethnic and grassroots dialogue on policies towards Uyghurs through the internet platform Online Uyghur, but in September 2014 he was sentenced to life in prison as a result after the Kunming and Urumqi incidents, on charges of promoting 'separatism' (Wong 2014b). Tohti's sentencing during the 'People's War on Terror' demonstrated how seamlessly anti-Uyghur racism had blended with Islamophobia in the eyes of China's Communist Party. While internationally the Chinese state continued to justify its repressive policies targeting Uyghurs as 'counter-terrorism', domestically multiple discourses aligning with the 'three evils' were used to target Uyghurs. If a Uyghur transgression involved violence, it was 'terrorism'; if it involved religiosity, it was 'extremism'; if it involved calls for more agency, it was 'separatism'. However, the Communist Party in China did not distinguish between these types of transgressions, which they saw increasingly as embodied in the idea of Uyghurs as a separate people from the Han. As a result, the Party seemed to have decided that not only religion, but the Uyghur people, needed to be completely pacified, marginalised, and their group identity and solidarity ultimately destroyed.

This logic would become more apparent after 2017, when state policies were implemented that included mass arrests of Uyghur intellectuals, mass internment camps for Uyghurs and related Turkic Muslim peoples, pervasive electronic and human surveillance, 're-education' programmes bent on assimilation, coerced labour programmes displacing Uyghurs from their home towns and placing them in residential factories, and attempts to erase all aspects of their group solidarity and cultural distinctiveness, including language and religion. These policies have been well documented elsewhere, including in my own work (see Roberts 2020: 199–235), and they do not require a complete summary here. However, I will reiterate an argument I have made elsewhere, that these policies reflect a logic of cultural genocide (Roberts 2020: 199–201). The intent is to decimate a people, their cultural identity, and their attachment to a perceived homeland as a prelude to the state developing that land in a way that fits its purposes rather than that of those with whom it has historically been identified. In this sense, it is a logic that is pregnant with settler colonialism and perhaps is inherent in the way that the PRC imagines its power over all territory within its borders. In this context, one might ask whether China would be committing cultural genocide against the Uyghurs today even if it had never opportunistically embraced the Islamophobia of GWOT in 2002. While this is plausible, I argue that GWOT's inherent Islamophobia was critical to facilitating the PRC's leap from repressing those Uyghurs who challenged state policies to a belief that all Uyghurs presented a challenge to the state and society. Furthermore, it allowed the PRC to make this leap both more rapidly and with impunity from the international community. This is because the logic of the War on Terror is inherently culturalist and racist as well as dehumanising.

Conclusion

Since 2017, Chinese officials have been fond of using allegories of biological infection to justify their broad assault on the Uyghur people, their identity, and their culture. They suggest that Uyghur culture has been 'infected' by 'extremism' and must be cured or quarantined. However, I would argue that it is the PRC and China's Communist Party that has been infected with the Islamophobia of GWOT's 'counter-terrorism' ideology. When the PRC first sought to convince the international community that it faced a 'terrorist threat', it was undoubtedly acting opportunistically to align what it perceived as Uyghur calls for self-determination with a global security threat that had been embraced by the world. With time, the narrative associated with this alleged global threat overtook PRC policy, and likely many officials began to believe that Uyghurs in fact did pose an existential 'terrorist threat'. In fact, after a decade of combatting what was essentially a non-existent 'terrorist threat', the PRC had provoked some Uyghurs to start using 'terrorist' tactics that targeted civilians to express their dissatisfaction with state policies.

Furthermore, by locating the root cause of that threat in the religion of Islam, the PRC eventually viewed both Uyghur religion and Uyghur identity as a threat. This racial profiling of a people and their culture as a threat is pregnant with genocidal possibilities (see Roberts 2018, 2020). When the UN recognised the existence of a 'terrorist organisation' led by Uyghurs in 2002, the PRC still viewed this alleged threat as emanating from a small group of discontent Uyghurs. By 2008–9, the state policy began viewing this threat as being a cultural one, largely embodied in those Uyghurs who were particularly religious. However, by 2014, the state had decided by extension that the problem was the Uyghur people as a whole and their entire identity as Muslims, regardless of their personal religiosity. Today, that belief is translating into genocidal actions.

In conclusion, I believe the example of Uyghurs' experience inside China since 9/11 is demonstrative of the ways that GWOT's Islamophobia can be overlaid on existing racist sentiments to create a powerful and violent assault on a given cultural group. As such, like much of GWOT's employment elsewhere, such as its use to justify the invasion of Iraq, the Chinese state's narrative of 'counter-terrorism' is being used for purposes that have nothing to do with 'terrorism'. China's present mass atrocities against Uyghurs are primarily motivated by Chinese nation building and the settler colonisation of the Uyghur homeland. However, the assertion that it is being done to eliminate an existential threat that comes from violent 'extremists' helps to facilitate mass repression by dehumanising those being assaulted. Their human rights can be suspended because they are now no longer perceived as human.

Note

1 As evidence of the PRC's dedication to getting Uyghurs recognised as an international terrorist threat, the Ministry of Foreign Affairs website lists an impressive number of meetings and statements it made about international terrorism in the two months following 11 September 2001. See Ministry of Foreign Affairs of the PRC (MFAPRC) (2015)

Bibliography

Amnesty International (2002). *China's anti-terrorism legislation and repression in the Xinjiang Uyghur Autonomous Region*, New York, NY.

Amnesty International (1999). *People's Republic of China: gross human rights violations in the Xinjiang Uighur Autonomous Region*, New York, NY.

Associated Press (2008). China releases blacklist in Olympics terror plot, 22 October.

Associated Press (2011). China puts Urumqi under 'full surveillance', *The Guardian*, 25 January.

Beck, L. (2008). China warns of 'life or death' battle with terror, *Reuters*, 14 August.

Cliff, T. (2012). The partnership of stability in Xinjiang: state–society interactions following the July 2009 unrest, *The China Journal*, (68): 79–105.

Coca, N. (2019). Beijing's Olympics paved the way for Xinjiang's Camps, *Foreign Policy*, 8 February.

Demick, B. (2014). China imposes intrusive rules on Uighurs in Xinjiang, *Los Angeles Times*, 5 August.

Denyer, S. (2014). Terrorist attack on market in China's restive Xinjiang region kills more than 30, *Washington Post*, 22 May.

Deutsche Welle (2008). Experts split on threat of terrorism at Beijing Olympics, *Deutsche Welle*, 8 June.

Federal Register (2002). Determination Pursuant to Section 1(b) of Executive Order 13224 Relating to the Eastern Turkistan Islamic Movement (ETIM) [FR Doc. 02-22737], *Federal Register*, 63:173 (19 August), 57054.

France24 (2008). Terrorism cloud over Beijing Olympics, *France24*, 27 July.

Gladney, D. (2004). *Dislocating China: Muslims, minorities, and other subaltern subjects*, Chicago, IL: University of Chicago Press.

Grieger, G. (2014). China: assimilating or radicalising Uighurs? *European Parliament Research Service*.

Hastings, J. (2011). Charting the course of Uyghur unrest, *The China Quarterly*, 208: 893–912.

Hoja, G. (2016). Uyghurs 'fenced in' to neighborhoods in China's Xinjiang region, *Radio Free Asia*, 19 August.

Hoshur, S. (2014a). 'China train station attackers may have acted 'in desperation', *Radio Free Asia*, 3 March.

Hoshur, S. (2014b). 'Over 100 detained after Xinjiang police open fire on protesters, *Radio Free Asia*, 23 May.

Human Rights Watch (2009). 'We are afraid to even look for them': enforced disappearances in the wake of Xinjiang's protests, October.

Iwashita, A. (2004). The Shanghai Cooperation Organization and its implications for Eurasian security: a new dimension of 'partnership' after the post-Cold War period. In: A. Iwashita and Sh. Tabata (eds), *Slavic Eurasia's integration into the world economy and community*, Sapporo, Japan: Slavic Research Center, Hokkaido University, 259–81.

Jacobs, J.M. (2016). *Xinjiang and the modern Chinese state (Studies on ethnic groups in China)*. Seattle, WA: University of Washington Press.

Leibold, J. (2020). Surveillance in China's Xinjiang region: ethnic sorting, coercion, and inducement, *Journal of Contemporary China*, 29(121): 46–60.

Li, J. and Wan, A. (2014). Security tightened after three killed in bomb, knife attack at Urumqi train station, *South China Morning Post*, 1 May.

Magnier, M. (2021). 9/11, 20 years later: how China used the attacks to its strategic advantage, *South China Morning Post*, 2 September.

Millward, J. (2007). *Eurasian crossroads: a history of Xinjiang*, New York, NY: Columbia University Press.

Ministry of Foreign Affairs of the PRC (MFAPRC) (2015). China opposes terrorism, *MFAPRC website*, www.fmprc.gov.cn/mfa_eng/topics_665678/3712_665976/ (accessed 24 September 2021).

Pan, P. (2002). US warns of plot by group in W. China, *Washington Post*, 29 August.

Permanent Mission of the People's Republic of China to the United Nations (PMPRCUN) (2001). *Terrorist activities perpetrated by 'Eastern Turkistan' organizations and their links with Osama bin Laden and the Taliban*, 29 November.

US Department of the Treasury (2002). Press statement on the UN designation of the Eastern Turkistan Islamic Movement, 11 September

Ramzy, A. and Buckley, C. (2019). The Xinjiang papers: 'absolutely no mercy' – leaked files show how China organized mass detentions of Muslims, *New York Times* 16 November.

Reeker, P.T. (2002). Designation of the Eastern Turkistan Islamic Movement under UNSC Resolutions 1267 and 1390', *Homeland Security Digital Library*, 11 September.

Reuters (2008). China denies group's claims of role in bus bombings, *Reuters*, 26 July.

Roberts, S.R. (2016). Development with Chinese characteristics in Xinjiang: a solution to ethnic tension or part of the problem? In: M. Clarke and D. Smith (eds), *China's Frontier Regions: Ethnicity, Economic Integration and Foreign Relations*, London: I. B. Tauris.

Roberts, S.R. (2018). The biopolitics of China's 'war on terror' and the exclusion of the Uyghurs, *Critical Asian Studies*, 50(2): 232–58.

Roberts, S.R. (2020). *The war on the Uyghurs: China's internal campaign against a Muslim minority*, Princeton, NJ: Princeton University Press.

Rostow, W.W. (1960). *The stages of economic growth: a non-Communist manifesto*, Cambridge: Cambridge University Press.

Ryono, A. and Galway, M. (2015). Xinjiang under China: reflections on the multiple dimensions of the 2009 Urumqi uprising, *Asian Ethnicity*, 16(2): 235–55.

Schein, S. (2000). *Minority rules: the miao and the feminine in China's cultural politics*, Durham, NC: Duke University Press.

Shan, W. and Weng, C. (2010). China's new policy in Xinjiang and its challenges, *East Asian Policy*, 2(3): 61.

SCO Secretariat (Shanghai Cooperation Organization) (2001). *The Shanghai Convention on Combating Terrorism, Separatism and Extremism*, Shanghai: SCO Secretariat.

Small, A. (2015). China's man in the Taliban, *Foreign Policy*, 3 August.

Smith-Finley, J. (2013). *The art of symbolic resistance: Uyghur identities and Uyghur–Han relations in contemporary Xinjiang*, Leiden: Brill.

State Council Office of Information of the People's Republic of China (SCOIPRC) (2002). *'East Turkistan' terrorist forces cannot get away with impunity*, January.

StratFor (2008). China: a pre-Olympic attack in Xinjiang, StratFor website, 4 August, https://worldview.stratfor.com/article/china-pre-olympic-attack-xinjiang (accessed 7 April 2022).

Stroup, D. (2021). Good *Minzu*, bad Muslims: Islamophobia in China's state media, *Nations and Nationalism*, 22 January.

Sy, S. (2008). Terrorism and Beijing Olympics, *ABC News*, 10 May.

Tharoor, I. (2014). China's war on Ramadan sees Muslim students forced to break fast, *Washington Post*, 11 July.

Tiezzi, S. (2014). China's 'People's War' against terrorism, *The Diplomat*, 2 August.

Tobin, D. (2020). *Securing China's Northwest Frontier: identity and insecurity in Xinjiang*, Cambridge: Cambridge University Press.

Traywick, C. (2013). 'Chinese officials ask Muslim women to unveil in the name of beauty, *Foreign Policy*, 26 November.

TIP (Turkistan Islamic Party) (2008a). [Untitled] [Initial video threatening the Olympics].

TIP (2008b). *Yunandiki Mubarak Jihadimiz* [About our congratulations to our Jihad in Yunan].

TIP (2014a). *Kunmingdiki 2-Qetimliq Jihadi Amaliyat Munisivati Bilan: Khitaygha Ochuq Khat* [In connection with the second act of Jihad in Kunming: an open letter to China].

TIP (2014b). *Ürümchi Jänubi Vokzalda Elip Berilghan Pidaiyliq Ämäliyiti Toghrisida Bayanat* [Announcement about the martyrdom act taken at Urumqi's South Station], 1 May.

UHRP (Uyghur Human Rights Project) (2010). *Can anyone hear us? Voices from the 2009 unrest in Urumqi.*

UHRP (2013). *Sacred right defiled: China's iron-fisted repression of Uyghur religious freedom.*

Voice of America (VOA) (2014). Train station attackers were trying to leave China for Jihad: official, *VOA News*, 5 March.

Wan, W. (2013). Chinese police say Tiananmen Square crash was 'premeditated, violent, terrorist attack', *Washington Post*, 30 October.

Watts, J. (2008). China takes action against Olympic 'terrorists', *The Guardian*, 10 July, www.theguardian.com/world/2008/jul/10/china.terrorism (accessed 8 April 2022).

Wong, C.H. (2014). 'People's war' on terrorism in China turns lucrative with one million yuan rewards, *Wall Street Journal*, 11 September.

Wong, E. (2009). Nearly 1,300 arrested in Muslim region of China, *New York Times*, 5 January.

Wong, E. (2014a). To temper unrest in western China, officials offer money for intermarriage, *New York Times*, 2 September.

Wong, E. (2014b). China sentences Uighur scholar to life, *New York Times*, 24 September.

Wong, E. (2015). China executes 3 over deadly knife attack at train station in 2014, *The New York Times*, 15 March.

Wong, E. and Bradsher, K. (2008). Beijing orders highest alert for Olympics, *New York Times*, 4 August.

Xinhua (2003). China seeks cooperation worldwide to fight 'East Turkistan' terrorists, *Xinhua*, 15 December.

Xinhua (2014). 'Xinjiang's party chief wages 'people's war' against terrorism, *Xinhua*, 26 May.

Yardley, J. and Hooker, J. (2008). Recent incidents add to China's edginess about terror, *New York Times*, 9 March, www.nytimes.com/2008/03/09/world/asia/09iht-china.3.10843551.html (accessed 7 April 2022).

Zhao, H. (2004). Security building in Central Asia and the Shanghai Cooperation Organization. In: A. Iwashita and Sh. Tabata (eds), *Slavic Eurasia's integration into the world economy and community.* Sapporo, Japan: Slavic Research Center, Hokkaido University, 283–314.

Chapter 12

The Rohingya genocide through the prism of War on Terror logic

Naved Bakali

Introduction

Islamophobia has an enduring legacy as one of the many iterations of racism, which scholars have traced back to the earliest encounters between Muslim and non-Muslim cultures. Though the term Islamophobia is synonymous with Muslim experiences in the global North, increasingly, in the context of the War on Terror, the term is being used in other spaces where Muslims occupy a minority status across the global South (Grosfoguel 2012). This chapter explores the phenomenon of Islamophobia in Myanmar, which culminated in the Rohingya genocide in August 2017. The Rohingya are a predominantly Muslim minority group indigenous to a region on the western coast of Myanmar, historically called Arakan and presently referred to as Rakhine State (Bari 2018). The Rohingya genocide was an organised campaign by the Myanmar state military in conjunction with Buddhist extremist groups which resulted in the murder of approximately 24,000 Rohingya (Habib et al. 2018). According to a survey by Médecins Sans Frontières, approximately 9,400 Rohingya were killed in Rakhine State between 25 August and 24 September 2017, with 730 of the victims being children (Médecins Sans Frontières 2018). Thousands of the survivors of the genocide were traumatised through sexual violence, physical attacks, and the destruction of their homes (McPherson 2017). The term 'genocide' will be used throughout this analysis when describing the violence against the Rohingya. The term has been contested by the state of Myanmar; however, many UN officials, as well as a number of nations, have acknowledged military actions against the Rohingya as genocide.

In September 2018, Canada recognised the crimes committed against the Rohingya at the hands of the Myanmar military as constituting genocide (Harris 2018). A UN investigative report released in August 2018 stated that top military commanders in Myanmar should be investigated and prosecuted for the 'gravest' crimes against civilians under international law, including genocide (United Nations News 2018). In November 2019, the nation of the Gambia filed a lawsuit with the International Court of Justice (ICJ) in The Hague, accusing Myanmar of genocide (Simmons 2019). As a result, a panel of seventeen judges at the ICJ took the unprecedented step of unanimously ordering Myanmar to take all necessary measures to prevent genocide of the existing Rohingya population in Myanmar, including the prevention of causing serious bodily or mental harm and killing of the Rohingya. Furthermore, they were required to preserve evidence of possible genocide that might have already occurred (BBC News 2020).

This chapter will explore the co-dependent relationship between state organised forms of Islamophobia, as well as Islamophobia at the hands of private actors since military rule in Myanmar from the 1960s to the present. The co-dependent relationship between institutional and interpersonal Islamophobia in the absence of a robust and unified resistance facilitated a pathological trajectory, which resulted in the Rohingya genocide. Furthermore, current-day geopolitical realities have sanitised state-sanctioned violence against the Rohingya in Myanmar through what this chapter describes as 'War on Terror logic'.[1]

The War on Terror and Islamophobia

As described at the outset of this edited volume, Islamophobia is a historical phenomenon that has been influenced over the centuries by strains of thought and ideologies that viewed Muslims as 'Other'. Islamophobia exists, both institutionally and interpersonally, which reinforces explicit and implicit power relationships. Explicit forms of power manifest through political policies, legislation, and inflammatory political rhetoric, while implicit power relations entail encounters with private citizens attempting to maintain cultural dominance over a threatening Muslim 'Other'. Furthermore, as demonstrated throughout this edited volume, Islamophobia in the current climate is a global phenomenon intimately connected to the War on Terror.

One of the more prominent archetypal figures that has emerged globally from the War on Terror is that of the 'dangerous Muslim man' (Razack 2008). The dangerous Muslim man is a trope which frames Muslim men as being misogynistic threats, prone to engage in violence and terrorism.

As such, if a Muslim man is not already radicalised, the potential of becoming a violent radical continually exists. This has led to the creation of mass surveillance systems, targeted laws, and the proliferation of countering and preventing violent extremism programmes (Younis 2019). These policies and legislation have disproportionately affected Muslim men across the global North and South under the pretext of preserving national security (Kundnani 2014).

Beyond structural processes that have targeted and policed the supposed dangerous Muslim man, interpersonal forms of Islamophobia also disseminate the dangerous Muslim man myth. This is prevalent in media representations of Muslims in news coverage of terrorist attacks and foiled plots and in films about terrorism, as well as in media stories about Muslims entangled in domestic violence, which are framed as 'honor-based violence' (Alsultany 2012). The constant ensemble of legislation, state actions, and messaging from private actors that reinforce the notion of Muslim men being prone to violence, needing to be policed by the state, and threatening to non-Muslims and Muslims alike, creates an echo chamber, the underlying assumption being that certain forms of violence exist exclusively as a consequence of the dangerous Muslim man. Members of the majoritarian culture are exalted above these tendencies, actions, and qualities (Thobani 2007). Exceptions may exist, as exceptionalism is essential to the perpetuation of racism and racial supremacy (Alexander 2012). However, these are understood as aberrations and anomalies. This is a line of thinking referred to as 'exaltation' (Thobani 2007). Exaltation serves to protect a pure and sanitised national imaginary by casting out undesirable qualities such as terrorism, radicalisation, and particular forms of violent abuse into an obscure realm of 'Otherness' (Bakali 2019a). The union between the dangerous Muslim archetype and the notion of exaltation forms the basis for War on Terror logic (Bakali 2021). This contrarian viewpoint imagines terrorism and other forms of political violence as existing exclusively through Muslim 'Otherness', while simultaneously sanitising blatant manifestations of them emanating from within the nationalist space/subject as a requirement to police the dangerous Muslim. War on Terror logic has increasingly become normalised in contemporary public and political discourse surrounding Muslims, and, as will be demonstrated throughout the chapter, was central to the state of Myanmar's justifications for the Rohingya genocide.

In addition to the 'dangerous Muslim man' archetype and the notion of 'exaltation', another critical paradigm for understanding Islamophobia in Myanmar is 'dialectical Islamophobia' (Beydoun 2018). Dialectic Islamophobia describes the relationship between institutional and interpersonal Islamophobia. It can exist in a top-down or bottom-up, or through a symbiotic relationship. In the case of Myanmar, dialectic Islamophobia was the co-dependence between institutional and interpersonal Islamophobia. This involved the state emboldening private actors of Islamophobia. However, populist nativist groups in Myanmar, particularly Buddhist monks and groups from the Theravada Buddhist tradition, also empowered and legitimised the state, which ultimately contributed to a state-endorsed genocide. The chapter now turns to describe institutional and interpersonal Islamophobia in Myanmar.

Institutional and interpersonal Islamophobia in Myanmar

The Rohingya genocide did not occur in a vacuum or without warning. Like all genocides, it was systematic, procedural, and many years in the making. The roots of the tensions between Rohingya Muslims and the Burman Buddhist majority can be traced back to imperial rule over Burma (Crouch 2016). However, these tensions were aggravated during the period of military rule in the 1960s.

Institutional Islamophobia in Myanmar after military rule

In 1962, Burma came under the military rule of Ne Win in a *coup d'état*. The Rohingya were steadily losing their rights under Ne Win's ultranationalist military regime. Under Ne Win's government there was an urgency to find internal enemies to detract from growing economic crises in Myanmar. This was accomplished by targeting the Rohingya 'Other', as well as by promoting nativism through a Burman Buddhist national identity. The Rohingya were targeted by the state because they were perceived as an easy and safe target. They were an easy target because they differed ethnically, religiously, and linguistically from the Burman Buddhist majority (Ibrahim 2018). This situation was exacerbated by the state promoting a mythology that framed the Rohingya as interlopers who had been supporting an independent Muslim state since the time of British rule over Burma from 1824 to 1948 (Wade 2017). As such, a key component to the brutal crackdown on the Rohingya during military rule was unfounded fears of the Islamisation of the Burman state. Islamisation is a conspiratorial view, which asserts that Muslim populations are threatening to numerically and culturally submerge a nation (Liogier 2012). Unfounded fears and paranoia over the Islamisation of non-Muslim majority lands have also been a common trope used to promote Islamophobic discourse and rhetoric in North American and European societies (Kumar 2012). The Rohingya were a safe target because they were less militarised. In other words, there was a minimal and passive resistance from the Rohingya to state oppression and discrimination, as compared to other ethnic and religious groups in Rakhine (Wade 2017). Among the few organisations that did resist were the Rohingya Patriotic Front, founded in 1974, and its successor, the Rohingya Solidarity Organisation (RSO), established 1982. The RSO's primary aim was to secure the citizenship and political rights of the Rohingya. To this end, they carried out attacks on police and military outposts in northern Rakhine throughout the 1980s and 1990s. However, the RSO was defunct by the late 1990s. More recently, the Arakan Rohingya Salvation Army (ARSA) has engaged in similar tactics as the RSO by attacking police outposts. However, as Wade suggests, there was no 'evidence of a broad sympathy among Rohingya for armed warfare ... The population was too vulnerable, and any mobilisation would invite the full wrath of the military, as well as local Rakhine' (Wade 2017: 83). This became abundantly evident when ARSA attacked police outposts in August 2017, which precipitated the Rohingya genocide.

The first major institutional process implemented by the military government which significantly curtailed the rights and freedoms of the Rohingya was the Emergency Immigration Act in 1974. This law introduced ethnicity-based identity cards, which identified Burmese nationals. The Rohingya were issued Foreign Registration Cards, designating them non-nationals. Furthermore, Article 145 in the 1974 constitution states that persons born of parents both of whom are nationals of the Socialist Republic of the Union of Burma are citizens of the Union (Ibrahim 2018). Article 145, along with the Emergency Immigration Act, made the Rohingya stateless. They were designated as foreigners in lands that they had been indigenous to for centuries. These severe citizenship laws sought to unify national identity along Burman Buddhist lines, solidifying the 'Otherness' of the Muslim Rohingya population through institutional processes. In addition to this, Ne Win instituted a pogrom in 1978 named Operation Nagamin (King Dragon). This pogrom involved military and immigration officials scrutinising those living in border regions of Myanmar to determine 'real' citizens and 'foreigners', with the aim of rooting out the Rohingya (Human Rights Watch 1996). At the commencement of this operation, word began to spread that the troops doing this census were raping and murdering Rohingya in their villages. This situation eventually led to 200,000 Rohingya fleeing to Bangladesh in 1978 as refugees. Further Rohingya massacres were repeated in 1991 through the State Law and Order Restoration Council, which was also checking the status of the Rohingya in the border regions. Consequently, another wave of 250,000 Rohingya refugees fled to Bangladesh between 1991 and 1992 (Wade 2017). In both instances, the Bangladeshi government sent most of the fleeing Rohingya back to Myanmar. Other institutional processes that targeted Rohingya Muslims during military rule were measures which severely limited social mobility.

By 1997, restrictions on movement were implemented in Sittwe and eventually made their way to other parts of Rakhine State, including Maungdaw and Buthidaung, all of which were regions with significant Rohingya populations and communities. The restrictions on movement involved checkpoints along the borders of the townships. For Rohingya to cross over from one township to another required a costly permit fee. However, whether one held a permit or not, authorities had the right to turn away people seeking to enter a township as they pleased. This led to the proliferation of a built-in bribery system, referred to as 'tea money', that accompanied the permit (Wade 2017). The institution of 'tea money' placed an economic burden on the Rohingya that de facto served to limit their freedom of movement between townships in Rakhine. Consequently, the Rohingya were restricted to living in ghettos. Not only did these policies limit cultural and social integration and exchange with the Burman majority, but they also limited access to higher education, employment opportunities, and healthcare.

Healthcare access was strategically limited by the state to regions of Rakhine where Rohingya were a majority. A report by Human Rights Watch found that in the 2000s in the townships of Maungdaw and Buthidaung, where Rohingya Muslims were the majority of the residents, there were only two doctors for a population of 158,000. This was a stark contrast to Sittwe, with 681 doctors, where Buddhists outnumber Rohingya Muslims (Myint 2013). Subsequently, in Buthidaung, 224 out of 1,000 children were dying before they reached the age of five (Myint 2013). In addition to the state's neglect of healthcare access, there were also active measures to limit the natural growth of the Rohingya. In 2005, state authorities instituted reproductive restrictions in the northern townships of Maungdaw and Buthidaung (Human Rights Watch 2020). Rohingya Muslims were subject to a two-child policy, which curtailed natural growth. The restrictions on reproductive rights along with the wilful neglect of healthcare access to Rohingya dominated regions, which directly contributed to the deaths of nearly one in every four Rohingya children under the age of five in Buthidaung, were examples of how the state took concrete steps to curb the population growth of the Rohingya. These policies and practices were justified and sanitised through unwarranted fears of the impending Islamisation of the Burman Buddhist-majority nation. Furthermore, these measures were reaffirmed by the state after military rule in 2013. Government officials justified the two-child law, claiming that it was aimed at addressing the rapid population growth among 'Bengali' communities in Myanmar (Myint 2013). The purposeful use of the term 'Bengali' to describe the Rohingya has been a consistent manoeuvre used by the state to reinforce a national mythology of the Rohingya being a foreign contaminant. The Rohingya have been perpetually viewed as 'Other' within this state imaginary, which aimed to exclusively link national belonging to Burman Buddhist identity (Bakali and Wasty 2020). Similar tactics have been employed by private actors, namely Buddhist monks and organisations, that have contributed to the flourishing of interpersonal forms of Islamophobia in Myanmar.

Interpersonal Islamophobia in Myanmar after military rule

Buddhist monks have traditionally played an important role in populist mobilisation in Myanmar. Much of this mobilisation was aimed at challenging and resisting the corruption of military rule. Therefore, the religious elite were instrumental in the transition from military dictatorship to a democratic government (Ibrahim 2018). It is important here to note that despite the military regime's promotion of Burman Buddhist nationalism, Buddhist groups and monks in Myanmar were distinct from the government and did not act at their behest. Buddhist groups regularly opposed military rule in Myanmar on grounds of corruption. Theravada Buddhist groups and the military regime had a common hatred towards the Rohingya. As such, the government often overlooked their targeting of the Rohingya. However, these groups were independent of the government and have been classified as private actors in this analysis. In addition to organising and mobilising against the military regime, Buddhist monks also made Buddhist supremacy a main tenet of their activism. Similar to baseless fears over cultural erosion that have become endemic in North American and European Islamophobic street protest movements (Bakali 2019b), interpersonal Islamophobia in Myanmar was formulated and articulated through a discourse of cultural preservation.

The Buddhist tradition most common in Myanmar is the Theravada tradition. This tradition differs significantly from Tibetan Buddhism with regard to pacifism and non-violence (Strathern 2013). The Theravada tradition in Myanmar is characterised by ultra-nationalism and the linking of religion with state power (Strathern 2013). As such, from this perspective, the state's acceptance of other religions is viewed as an existential threat to both the state and faith. Some strands of the Theravada tradition view non-Buddhists as lesser or sub-humans. Consequently, violence against other religious and ethnic communities is acceptable in the name of preserving Buddhism as a dominant state ideology (Bischoff 1996). The backdrop of interpersonal Islamophobia in Myanmar was framed around this type of religious zealotry, as a number of Muslim social structures and institutions were targeted by Buddhist extremist groups. The 969 Movement and the MaBaTha (Organisation for the Protection of Race and Religion) have been central in stirring up religious rivalry and violence, as well as providing an ideological foundation for interpersonal Islamophobia in Myanmar.

The 969 Movement was an outgrowth of a 1988 Buddhist nationalist movement that sought to preserve Buddhist purity in Burma (Coclanis 2013). One of the prominent leaders of this movement was Ashin U Wirathu, who openly called for economic boycotts of Muslim-owned shops and advocated for violence against Muslims of all ethnicities in Myanmar (Ibrahim 2018). The 969 Movement has denounced the Union Solidarity and Development Party, the remnant of the military dictatorship, which retains a quarter of the parliamentary seats in the governmental structure of Myanmar, and the National League for Democracy, the current democratically elected government of Myanmar, as being insufficiently anti-Muslim to preserve Burman Buddhist purity in the nation (Preston 2015). Ironically, both of these political parties have done very little, if anything, to protect the Rohingya minority in Rakhine State. Through these state entities, numerous laws have been implemented which have aggressively stripped away the rights, freedoms, and protections of the Rohingya. Furthermore, under the leadership of these groups, state-controlled and private media have been given carte blanche to target, vilify, and abuse the Rohingya in Rakhine State (Wade 2017). The 969 Movement claims that it does not directly command its followers to commit acts of violence against Muslims in Myanmar. According to them, if their speech leads to violence, it is an unintended consequence. However, such violence, in their view, is acceptable if it preserves and promotes Burman Buddhist supremacy (Walton and Hayward 2014). This twisted logic has resonance with prominent Western Islamophobes like Pamela Geller and Robert Spencer, who absolved themselves when their works were quoted at length and served as an inspiration for Anders Breivik, the Norwegian far-right terrorist who murdered seventy-seven people in a bombing and shooting spree in Oslo and on Utøya Island in protest at the supposed Islamisation of Europe (Lean 2012). In both instances, Islamophobic rhetoric stirred up and precipitated private actors into violent actions. The resulting violence was an unintended consequence; however, there was an inability to condemn the hate speech or the acts of violence, as the goal of such violence aligned with the essence of the messages.

Buddhist groups like the 969 Movement have had a strong populist appeal in Myanmar because they have been a source of resistance to the greed and corruption of the government under military dictatorship (Ware and Laoutides 2018). Furthermore, in the face of a crumbling infrastructure and economic crisis under the military regime, a number of these Theravada Buddhist groups became important providers of basic education for Myanmar's poor (Walton 2014). The MaBaTha has also had a substantial influence on the education system in Myanmar.

The core focus of the teachings of MaBaTha is one of preservation of the Buddhist faith from outside threats. MaBaTha has produced textbooks used in Sunday schools across Myanmar, which supplement state schooling. The key message of their textbooks is not of religious tolerance and the acceptance of other religious traditions; rather, these texts assert that Islam threatens the preservation of Buddhism in the nation (Walton 2014). In addition to spreading Islamophobic messages through supplementary education in Myanmar, the MaBaTha have also been at the forefront of campaigns that hinder the local Muslim economy. In conjunction with the 969 Movement, the MaBaTha have run a number of 'buy Buddhist' campaigns, effectively creating economic boycotts of Muslim-owned businesses. This has included movements to close Muslim-run slaughterhouses under the absurd pretence that Muslims will consume all of the cows and harm the nation's agriculture industry (Walton 2013). Actions such as these by private actors in Myanmar have crippled Muslim-owned businesses and created obstacles for the Rohingya to observe religious ritual practices and consume religiously authorised meat. Furthermore, the hatred, paranoia, and misinformation disseminated by these groups have not only created economic and social obstacles but have also prompted private actors to engage in religious violence, attack religious structures, and use sexual violence against the Rohingya (Bari 2018).

Through institutional and interpersonal processes, various spheres of life have been made insurmountable for the Rohingya. At the hands of the government, the Rohingya have been made stateless and have been confined to ghettos, limiting their access to healthcare, education, housing, economic opportunities, and social mobility. Furthermore, the state has actively taken measures to curtail the population growth of this community. These difficulties have been compounded by the Burman Buddhist religious elite, who have propagated Islamophobic messages to incite and stir private actors into violent actions against the Rohingya. Additionally, interpersonal discrimination has manifested through economic boycotts that have caused financial devastation and created barriers to ritual practices. The chapter turns now to explore the symbiotic relationship between institutional and interpersonal Islamophobia in Myanmar, which precipitated the Rohingya genocide in August 2017. This violence enacted against the Rohingya was sanitised through discourses relating the 'dangerous Muslim man', underscored by a posturing of exaltation, which formed the basis for War on Terror logic.

The co-dependence of institutional and interpersonal Islamophobia in Myanmar

In order to understand dialectic Islamophobia as a co-dependence between Islamophobia by the state and private actors, namely Buddhist extremist groups, it is necessary to understand Myanmar's government structure after military rule.

Myanmar's transition to democracy

There were a number of unsuccessful attempts to democratise Burma during military rule. The transition to a democratic government slowly took hold after Cyclone Nargis in 2008. Cyclone Nargis was a devastating natural disaster that destroyed 65 per cent of the country's rice fields, 95 per cent of buildings in the delta region, and left an estimated 138,000 dead (Seekins 2008). The military government grossly mismanaged the disaster response, which led to further protests in the nation. To quell this unrest the military regime was forced to allow elections in 2010. Through a continual process of political parties boycotting rigged elections, and growing public discontent, a democratic government was finally able to emerge in 2015. The National League for Democracy's (NLD) victory in the 2015 election, led by Nobel Peace Prize laureate Aung San Suu Kyi, signalled democratic progress and the potential for self-governance in the nation.

A key factor enabling Aung San Suu Kyi to win the election was her ability to gain support from various Buddhist groups. The utility of this relationship was mutually beneficial, as these groups consistently opposed the corruption of the military regime, while this alliance bolstered the NLD's support from the masses (Ibrahim 2018). However, despite the appearance of a democratically elected government, the military had placed checks and balances to ensure significant control and dominance over the civilian administration of the nation (Ibrahim 2018). The former military regime allowed for Myanmar to transition into a democracy by allotting 25 per cent of the parliamentary seats to the Union Solidarity and Development Party (USDP) (Bari 2018). As the military held key positions in the parliament, Aung San Suu Kyi and the NLD government were required to strike a balance between acquiescing to the demands of the military in administering the civilian population and pandering to the Buddhist extremist elites in order to maintain their base of popular support. In essence, the 'democratically' elected government was steeped in complex power dynamics, which required the NLD to submissively accept the brutality of the military and Buddhist extremists towards the Rohingya in order to maintain the semblance of a progressive democratically elected government. Through this multilayered political system, a clearer picture of dialectical Islamophobia and its co-dependent relationship between private and state actors emerges.

Despite tensions between the military dictatorship and Buddhist populist groups, both parties had a common disdain and hatred towards the Rohingya. Under military rule, the government legislated targeted laws, as well as wilfully ignored hate preaching, anti-Muslim campaigns, and religious-based violence incited by Buddhist extremists (Wade 2017). In this way, the military government was able to detract from popular discontent and deflate some of the tensions by finding common ground with these groups (Wade 2017). Ultimately, the corruption and mismanagement of the military government precipitated a necessary transition of governance, which brought the NLD to power. The NLD was an elitist party that gained populist appeal through alliances and support from Buddhist nationalist groups and figures. Hence, Islamophobic protest movements in Myanmar helped to bring about a democratic political system that was subservient to an ultra-Burman Buddhist nationalist agenda. This government functioned alongside a military faction that had complete control over civilian administration in parts of the country. Ironically, the persecution of Rohingya worsened under democratic rule because the NLD had to pander to both the USDP and the populist Buddhist extremist groups. In this fashion, dialectic Islamophobia in Myanmar was not solely a top-down process, where government policies and rhetoric emboldened private actors into action. Rather, elements of the government, namely the USDP, were able to become more aggressive and forceful in their repression of the Rohingya because their brutality towards the Rohingya aligned with the aims of Buddhist extremist groups that had brought the NLD to power. Their actions were purified through the pretence of acting in the name of a democratically elected regime and not a military dictatorship. As the NLD was a de facto mediator between the former military regime and extremist Buddhists, there was pressure to justify the actions of these groups, which ultimately precipitated the genocide.

War on Terror logic and the Rohingya genocide

Throughout the period of military rule, the state, along with Theravada Buddhist groups, perpetuated the national mythology of the Rohingya being foreigners and unwanted 'Others', exclusively referring to them as 'Bengalis' to reinforce this claim. The underlying rationale of this narrative was to support the notion of the Islamisation of Burma and the urgency to preserve and protect the purity of national identity along Burman Buddhist lines. This continued for many years and, in the context of the War on Terror, resistance to state and public persecution of the Rohingya became increasingly linked to the archetype of the dangerous Muslim man. For example, in June 2012 there was a spate of violence that lasted four days in Sittwe and other townships in Rakhine State between Burman Buddhists and Rohingya Muslims. In the aftermath of this violence, state officials along with Buddhist extremists spread unsubstantiated claims linking the Rohingya resistance in this conflict to terrorism. The then director of the President's Office,

Hmuu Zaw, circulated rumours that Rohingya terrorists from the RSO, who at this point were a defunct resistance movement, were crossing into Myanmar from other countries with weapons to terrorise Rakhine Buddhists (Allchin 2012). It is undeniable that Rohingya partook in violence against Burman Buddhist in this four-day conflict. However, in this instance and others, there was an explicit linking of violence committed by Rohingya within a discourse of terrorism and an inability to acknowledge equivalent acts of violence committed by Rakhine Buddhists in a similar fashion. In other words, terrorism was exclusively defined as violence committed by Rohingya, whereas Rakhine Buddhist were exalted above such labels. The lexicon used to describe Rohingya violence fell within a larger narrative of Muslims within the War on Terror. As Wade observes:

> [the] persistent framing of the violence as terrorism driven by religious zealotry took on a new force after June 2012 ... By raising the spectre of terrorism, opponents of the Rohingya could connect the events playing out on home soil to a broader conspiracy ... one fuelled by images that began to circulate on social media of the September 2001 attacks on New York and the destruction by the Taliban of the Buddhas of Bamiyan in Afghanistan the same year. (Wade 2017: 109–10)

This War on Terror logic also served as a useful tool to sanitise the state's role in the Rohingya genocide.

Aung San Suu Kyi had faced international criticism for her passive stance in the Rohingya genocide. A number of institutions stripped away honorary designations and fellowships bestowed on her, including Amnesty International's highest honour, the Ambassador of Conscience Award. Furthermore, Canadian institutions of higher learning withdrew their honorary Doctor of Philosophy designations, and the Canadian government revoked her honorary citizenship (BBC News 2018). Despite international rebuke, Suu Kyi staunchly defended her nation against claims of genocide. During the early stages of the genocide in September 2017, Suu Kyi and the state evoked War on Terror logic, claiming that the violence perpetrated against the Rohingya at this time was military 'clearance operations' to root out terrorists. She maintained these claims despite the emergence of satellite images of entire Rohingya villages being burned and destroyed (Safi 2017). In August 2018, when surmounting evidence of a genocide at the hands of the Myanmar military began to surface, Suu Kyi doubled down on her earlier allegations, asserting that 'the danger of terrorist activities, which was the initial cause of events leading to the humanitarian crisis in Rakhine remains real and present today' (Geddie and Ungku 2018). Suu Kyi's War on Terror logic not only aimed to sanitise and justify the military actions which led to the genocide, but also blamed the victims for the violence. This posturing persisted after formal charges of genocide were brought before the ICJ in November 2019.

Suu Kyi offered voluntary testimony defending her nation at the ICJ tribunals. In her statements she framed the August 2017 violence as a reaction to the dangerous Muslim, describing the genocide as an instance of 'intercommunal violence' where the military was taking actions against 'insurgents or terrorists' (Simmons and Beech 2019). Throughout Suu Kyi's testimony there was an inability to acknowledge the violence committed at the hands of the Myanmar military and Theravada Buddhist groups as terrorism, even though evidence presented at the tribunal detailed instances of brutal politically motivated violence, murder, and rape of civilians, as well as the destruction of Rohingya homes and villages (Simmons and Beech 2019). Despite the massive number of Rohingya casualties in the genocide, numbering in the tens of thousands, there was a rehashing of the notion that the Rohingya were connected to a broader narrative of Muslims and terrorism in the War on Terror. According to this logic, the Rohingya were not victims but the cause of the violence. As such, violence against the Rohingya was an unfortunate consequence, yet an inevitable byproduct of their own making. In this way, the destruction of Muslim homes and lives was sanitised by evoking War on Terror logic (Bakali 2021).

Conclusion

In this exploration, institutional Islamophobia has been described as processes, legislation, and laws sanctioned by the state to legalise and perpetuate anti-Muslim racism. Interpersonal Islamophobia was the fear, mistrust, and violence enacted by private actors and groups to oppress and vilify Islam and Muslims. The Rohingya genocide was the culmination of years of institutional and interpersonal Islamophobia in the absence of a unified and coherent resistance. Dialectic Islamophobia in Myanmar was a co-dependant relationship between institutional and interpersonal Islamophobia. This symbiotic relationship of institutional and interpersonal Islamophobia entailed state targeting of the Rohingya, which stirred and encouraged private actors into action. However, Buddhist extremist groups also empowered the state in post-democratic Myanmar, which led to mass atrocities. Despite the massive number of documented casualties and the fleeing of over 700,000 refugees to neighbouring Bangladesh, Aung San Suu Kyi and the state of Myanmar have denied allegations of genocide. In their defence, Suu Kyi invoked War on Terror logic to sanitise violence against the Rohingya. Understanding Islamophobia in Myanmar as a co-dependence of institutional and interpersonal Islamophobia provides nuanced understandings as to how the Rohingya genocide was able to take place in post-democratic Myanmar. The events in Rakhine State in August 2017 represented an Islamophobia 'breaking point', and illustrate the importance of resisting the various forms and manifestations of Islamophobia across global sites.

Manifestations of Islamophobia across global sites are formulated and influenced by localised economies, geopolitical realities, and relationships of power. In settler societies, Islamophobia is an extension of historically present racialised logics. In the War on Terror, Islamophobia manifested in institutional practices and policies, as well as interpersonal expressions of anti-Muslim bias in these states. In former imperial states, Islamophobia is organised around supremacist ideologies to combat Islamisation. This is accomplished through assimilationist politics. In these spaces, Islam and Muslims are presented as a threat through discourses on 'separatism' and 'political Islam', which are thinly veiled attempts to strip away Muslim agency. In formally colonised states of the global South, Islamophobia is manifested through the securitisation of the Muslim subject. This is done to serve imperial and Western interests. An Islamophobia breaking point represents the most severe manifestations of Islamophobia, as discussed in this chapter and others. This is an end point of interpersonal and institutional forms of Islamophobia, which bring about state violence, ethnic cleansing, and, in the case of Myanmar, genocide.

Ultimately, insights from this exploration provide valuable contributions to the emerging field of Islamophobia Studies by examining Islamophobia as a global phenomenon. Through this informed understanding of how institutional, interpersonal, and dialectic Islamophobia transcend global North and South barriers in the War on Terror, a more coherent narrative of resistance and activism to challenge variant forms and manifestations of Islamophobia emerges.

Note

1 Some of the insights and analyses in this chapter are drawn from my article Bakali (2021).

Bibliography

Alexander, M. (2012). *The new Jim Crow: mass incarceration in the age of colorblindness*, New York: The New Press.

Allchin, J. (2012). The Rohingya, myths and misinformation, *Democratic Voice of Burma*, 22 June.

Alsultany, E. (2012). *Arabs and Muslims in the media: race and representation after 9/11*, New York, NY: New York University Press.

Asat, R. and Diamond, Y. (2020). *Foreign Policy*, https://foreignpolicy.com/2020/07/15/uighur-genocide-xinjiang-china-surveillance-sterilization/ (accessed 1 August 2020).

Bakali, N. (2016). *Islamophobia: understanding anti-Muslim racism through the lived experiences of Muslim youth*, Rotterdam: Sense Publishers.

Bakali, N. (2019a). Challenging terrorism as a form of 'Otherness': exploring the parallels between far-right and Muslim religious extremism, *Islamophobia Studies Journal*, 5(1): 99–115.

Bakali, N. (2019b). The redefining of far-right extremist activism along Islamophobic lines, *Islamophobia Studies Yearbook*, 10(1): 82–98.

Bakali, N. (2021). Islamophobia in Myanmar: the Rohingya genocide and the 'war on terror', *Race & Class*, 62(4): 53–71.

Bakali, N. and Wasty, S. (2020). Identity, social mobility, and trauma: post-conflict educational realities for survivors of the Rohingya genocide, *Religions*, 11(5): 241–55.

Bari, M.A. (2018). *The Rohingya crisis: a people facing extinction*, Leicestershire: Kube Publishing.

BBC News (2018). Aung San Suu Kyi: Amnesty strips Myanmar leader of top prize, *BBC News*, 12 November, www.bbc.com/news/world-asia-46179292 (accessed 22 May 22).

BBC News (2020). Myanmar Rohingya: world court orders prevention of genocide, *BBC News*, world, 23 January www.bbc.com/news/world-asia-51221029 (accessed 28 June 28).

Beydoun, K. (2018). *American Islamophobia: understanding the roots and rise of fear*, Oakland, CA: University of California Press.

Bischoff, R. (1996). *Buddhism in Myanmar: a short history*, Kandy: Buddhist Publication Society.

Changoiwala, P. (2020). *Foreign Policy*, https://foreignpolicy.com/2020/02/21/india-muslims-deported-terrified-citizenship-amendment-act-caa/ (accessed 1 August 2020).

Coclanis, P. (2013). Terror in Burma: Buddhist vs. Muslims, *World Affairs*, 176(4): 25+.

Crouch, M. (2016). *Islam and the state of Myanmar: Muslim–Buddhist relations and the politics of belonging*, New Delhi: Oxford University Press.

Geddie, J. and Ungku, F. (2018). Myanmar's Suu Kyi says relations with military 'not that bad', *Reuters*, 21 August, www.reuters.com/article/us-singapore-myanmar-suukyi/myanmar-leader-suu-kyi-says-terrorism-in-rakhine-state-a-threat-to-region-idUSKCN1L60OP (accessed 5 December 2021).

Grosfoguel, R. (2012). The multiple faces of Islamophobia, *Islamophobia Studies Journal*, 1(1): 9–33.

Habib, M., Jubb, C., Salahuddin, A., Rahman, M., and Pallard, H. (2018). *Forced migration of Rohingya: the untold experience*, Ottawa: Ontario International Development Agency.

Harris, K. (2018). *CBC*, Rohingya refugee thanks Canada 'from the bottom ofour hearts' after genocide motion, www.cbc.ca/news/politics/rohingya-camp-canada-motion-1.4836078 (accessed 5 July 2020).

Human Rights Watch (1996). *Burma: the Rohingya Muslims; ending a cycle of exodus*, New York: Human Rights Watch.

Human Rights Watch (2013). Burma: revoke 'two-child policy' for Rohingya, *Human Rights Watch*, 28 May, www.hrw.org/news/2013/05/28/burma-revoke-two-child-policy-rohingya (accessed 10 June 2020).

Human Rights Watch (2020). *'Shoot the traitors': discrimination against Muslims under India's new citizenship policy.*

Ibrahim, A. (2018). *The Rohingyas: inside Myanmar's genocide*, London: Oxford University Press.

Kumar, D. (2012). *Islamophobia and the politics of empire*, Chicago, IL: Haymarket Books.

Kundnani, A. (2014). *The Muslims are coming: Islamophobia, extremism, and the domestic war on terror*, New York, NY: Verso.

Lean, N. (2012). *The Islamophobia industry: how the right manufactures fear of Muslims*, London: PlutoPress.

Lewis, P. (1997, October 24). Islamophobia: A challenge to us all, *Church Times*, 24 October.

Liogier, R. (2012). *Le mythe de l'islamisation: Essai du rune obsession collective*, Paris: Seuil.

McPherson, P. (2017). 'The villages are burning down.' Fear and fire send Rohingya fleeing to Bangladesh, *Time*, 31 August, https://time.com/4922715/myanmar-rohingya-violence-rakhine (accessed 3 August 2020).

Médecins Sans Frontières (2018). *'No one was left behind': death and violence against the Rohingya in Rakhine State, Myanmar*, Geneva: Médecins Sans Frontières.

Moro Christian People's Alliance (2012). *The human rights situation of the Moro people in the Philippines*, Quezon City: MCPA.

Myint, M. (2013). *The final report of Inquiry Commission on Sectarian Violence in Rakhine State*, Sitwe: Rakhine Inquiry Commission.

Preston, A. (2015). Safron terror: an audience with Burma's 'Buddhist Bin Laden' Ashin Wirathu, *GQ Magazine*, 15 February.

Razack, S. (2008). *Casting out: the eviction of Muslims from western law and politics*, Toronto, ON: University of Toronto Press.

Roberts, S. (2018). The biopolitics of China's 'war on terror' and the exclusion of the Uyghurs, *Critical Asian Studies*, 50(2): 232–58.

Runnymede Trust (1997). *Islamophobia a challenge for us all*, London: Runnymede Trust.

Safi, M. (2017). Aung San Suu Kyi says 'terrorists' are misinforming the world about Myanmar violence, *The Guardian*, 6 September, www.theguardian.com/world/2017/sep/06/aung-san-suu-kyi-blames-terrorists-for-misinformation-about-myanmar-violence (accessed 5 November 2021).

Sageman, M. (2004). *Understanding terror networks*, Philadelphia: University of Pennsylvania Press.

Seekins, D. (2008). The social, political and humanitarian impact of Burma's cyclone Nargis, *Asia-Pacific Journal*, 6: 1–13.

Sheehi, S. (2011). *Islamophobia: the ideological campaign against Muslims*, Atlanta, GA: Clarity Press.

Simmons, M. (2019). Myanmar genocide lawsuite is filed at United Nations court, *New York Times*, 11 November, www.nytimes.com/2019/11/11/world/asia/myanmar-rohingya-genocide.html (accessed 27 June 2020)

Simmons, M. and Beech, H. (2019). Aung San Suu Kyi defends Myanmar against Rohingya genocide accusations, *New York Times*, 11 December, www.nytimes.com/2019/12/11/world/asia/aung-san-suu-kyi-rohingya-myanmar-genocide-hague.html (accessed 3 July 2020).

Strathern, A. (2013). Why are Buddhist monks attacking Muslims? *BBC News*, 2 May, www.bbc.com/news/magazine-22356306 (accessed 1 June 2020).

Taub, A. and Fisher, M. (2017). Did the world get Aung San Suu Kyi wrong? *New York Times*, 31 October, www.nytimes.com/2017/10/31/world/asia/aung-san-suu-kyi-myanmar.html (accessed 5 June 2020).

Thobani, S. (2007). *Exalted subjects: studies in the making of race and nation in Canada*, Toronto: University of Toronto Press.

UN News (2018). 'No other conclusion', ethnic cleansing of Rohingyas continues – senior UN rights official, *UN News*, 6 March, news.un.org/en/story/2018/03/1004232 (accessed 3 July 2020).

Wade, F. (2017). *Myanmar's enemy within*, London: Zed Books.

Walton, M. (2013). A primer on the roots of Buddhist/Muslim conflict in Myanmar and a way forward, *Islamic Commentary*, 23 July, 4.

Walton, M. (2014). What are Myanmar's Buddhist Sunday schools teaching? *East Asia Forum*, 16 December, www.eastasiaforum.org/2014/12/16/what-are-myanmars-buddhist-sunday-schools-teaching/ (accessed 1 August 2020).

Walton, M. and Hayward, S. (2014). *Contesting Buddhist narratives: democratization, nationalism, and communal violence in Myanmar*, Honolulu: East-West Center.

Ware, A. and Laoutides, C. (2018). *Myanmar's 'Rohingya' conflict*, Oxford: Oxford University Press.

Younis, T. (2019). Counter-radicalization: a critical look into a racist new industry, *Yaqeen Institute for Islamic Research*, 21 March, https://yaqeeninstitute.org/tarekyounis/counter-radicalization-a-critical-look-into-a-racist-new-industry/ (accessed 2 August 2020).

Zenz, A. (2020). China's own documents show potentially genocidal sterilization plans in Xinjiang, *Foreign Policy*, 1 July, https://foreignpolicy.com/2020/07/01/china-documents-uighur-genocidal-sterilization-xinjiang/ (accessed 1 August 2020).

Index

CPSIA information can be obtained
at www.ICGtesting.com
Printed in the USA
LVHW080057030123
736274LV00006B/459